The year [illegible]:
Morecambe FC 2006-07

Compiled by: Steven Hewitt and Glen Cooper

Foreword by: Morecambe FC chairman, Peter McGuigan

Match reports: Derek Quinn, Steven Hewitt, Glen Cooper and Sean O'Connor

Photographers: Darren Andrews, Garth Hamer, Steve Pendrill, Jason Bellinger and Nigel Slater

Appendix statistics: Neil Marsdin

The Visitor
thevisitor.co.uk

at heart publications

First Published in 2007 by:
At Heart Ltd, 32 Stamford Street, Altrincham,
Cheshire, WA14 1EY
in conjunction with
The Visitor
Victoria Street, Morecambe, LA4 4AG

ISBN: 978-1-84547-175-0
Printed and bound by Bell & Bain Ltd, Glasgow

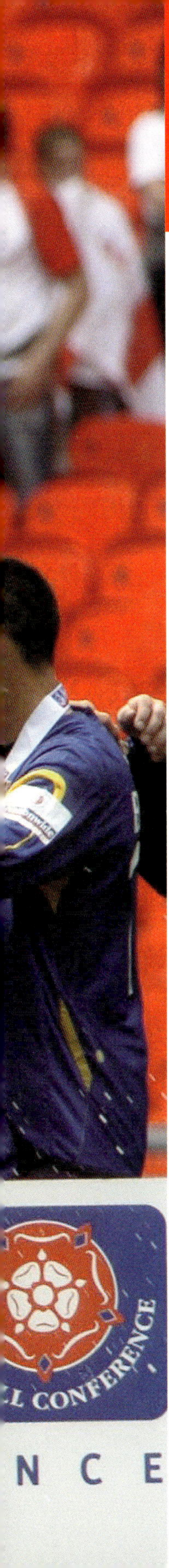

Contents

Foreword

A FEW SEASONS ago the Board of Morecambe Football Club issued a statement saying that the objective of Morecambe Football Club was to gain promotion to the Football League. There were those, however, who either didn't believe the ambitions of the football club or indeed, who just didn't think it possible that an unfashionable club such as Morecambe would ever play in the Football League.

The promotion winning season, for me, actually started immediately after the final whistle against Hereford in the play-off semi-final at the end of the previous season. Defeat that night was hard to accept and the mood was one of utter disbelief and disappointment. My mood changed, however, when I heard the incredible noise being made by our magnificent supporters who continued to cheer the team long after the game had finished. I remember thinking to myself that we had to double our efforts the following season and deliver Football League status, not just for the players, management and, indeed, the town of Morecambe but mainly for our fantastic supporters. From then on, I couldn't wait for the new season to begin.

Sammy McIlroy and Mark Lillis were appointed as our new management team and then went about the task of strengthening the squad in order to progress our dreams of Football League status. However, there was a nervous start to the new campaign and at one stage quite a number of people doubted that we would make the play-offs. However, the defining point for me was our 3-2 victory at York where I noticed a confidence and a belief in the way the team was playing. After that game I was absolutely convinced we would reach the play-offs and subsequently gain promotion to the Football League. The journey through the rest of the season is well-documented later in this book and I am sure that most people had their own memories during the course of the season as we marched towards Wembley.

The second leg play-off semi-final against York at Christie Park was a tense affair, far more so than the first leg. As the game reached its conclusion, the crowd were screaming for the referee to blow his whistle. My thoughts immediately at the end of the game – Morecambe at Wembley!! Who would believe it?

During the period leading up to Wembley there was an incredible buzz, both at the football ground and all around the town. As soon as match tickets went on sale, the excitement was almost fever pitch. How many supporters would we take to Wembley? Would we manage to take 10,000? Throughout all of this period, the one thing I remember most of all was the way in which Sammy and Mark managed to keep the players focused on the game. Morecambe Football Club was playing for a place in the Football League. The fact that the final was being played at the new Wembley Stadium was not a priority. We were going there to win – absolutely no doubt about that. You could see that feeling etched on the faces of every player. Sammy and Mark did a brilliant job. I have never seen a team as focused as ours and thereafter I was very confident that we would win the game.

The day of the match finally arrived and as kick-off approached I still felt very confident that we would win, even if our supporters were outnumbered 3 to 1 by the Exeter fans. However, we were definitely not out-shouted. Enough has been said and written about the game itself and I am sure that

everyone who was there will remember the experience for the rest of his/her life. It really was a truly unforgettable experience.

At the final whistle, as the reality of our achievement started to sink in, I felt so delighted for Sammy and Mark, the players, the backroom staff, my fellow directors and other club staff. However, the two groups for whom my heart went out to were, firstly, those volunteers who give up so much of their time with no cost to the club and without whom this club would not function. Secondly, to our magnificent supporters who made the long journey to Wembley and helped so much in the support of their team to get the result we deserved. Many of our supporters at Wembley were also at Hereford twelve months previously and perhaps they didn't realise it but indirectly they contributed so much to get their team to the Football League.

On behalf of the board, I would like to take this opportunity to thank everyone connected with Morecambe Football Club either directly or indirectly in taking their club to the Football League.

Where do we go from here? Our experience to date shows that there is a large gap between the Conference and the Football League. It is therefore our immediate objective to do all we can to stay in the Football League. We recently announced details of a proposed new stadium which should be ready for the 2009/10 season. When completed, this should give the club the financial stability to operate in the Football League and hopefully, at the same time, help us to achieve our medium-term objective, which is to gain promotion to League 1. Maybe we are about to embark upon a new chapter in the history of Morecambe Football Club but that may be a story at a later date. In the meantime, enjoy the book and many, many thanks for your support.

Peter McGuigan
Chairman
Morecambe Football Club

12th August 2006

Morecambe 0 Burton Albion 1

Webster 77 (pen)

'NOT the start we wanted' was Sammy McIlroy's verdict on Morecambe's defeat to Burton Albion at Christie Park – the first game since McIlroy took over as permanent manager.

Burton full-back Aaron Webster scored from the spot in the 77th minute to secure victory for Nigel Clough's side. This was the first time they had beaten the Shrimps in the Conference in five seasons, bringing to an end a run of eight successive Morecambe wins. The home side had started the game well with new signing Craig Stanley showing some good touches on his debut. It was he who provided the pass for Michael Howard for the Shrimps full-back to shoot in the sixth minute. Unfortunately his effort from 30 yards was straight at Burton debutant, 43-year-old goalkeeper, Kevin Poole. Poole's opposite number, Steven Drench, was called on three minutes later when Burton's right-back Gary Rowett tried his luck from way out. His shot looked to be dipping in until Drench tipped it over. Drench was not unduly worried for the rest of the half, comfortably saving a Webster free-kick and a Darren Tinson header.

The only other danger came when Howard raced back to deny former Conference Golden Boot winner, Daryl Clare, on 19 minutes just as he was about to shoot.

Clare also had two goals disallowed on an afternoon where he showed that he still had the predatory instincts that have given Conference defences nightmares in the past.

For the home side, their best efforts of the first half were headers from set-pieces, Stanley's effort being cleared by Ryan Austin and Jim Bentley nodding wide.

After the break, Morecambe upped the tempo and looked more likely to score but again clear-cut opportunities were rare. Michael Twiss' cross shot was well held by Poole. Ged Brannan's cross caused problems in the 56th minute but Burton were able to clear for a corner. Their best chance was in the 58th minute. Danny Carlton created a shooting opportunity as he brought the ball down, only for Tinson to slide in and take the ball away. Thompson's 25-yard free-kick got a deflection soon after. However Poole was able to scramble across and push the ball clear before Burton got the breakthrough two minutes later. Andy Ducros had a good game on the left wing and he cut inside, taking Rowett's cross and flicking the ball up where Brannan handled the ball, the referee having no option but to give the penalty.

Webster sent Drench the wrong way, slotting the ball in the corner.

Morecambe's efforts to get back in the

David Perkins in action against Burton Albion.

game were in vain. Their best attempt came with the last move of the match when substitute David McNiven headed straight at Poole after coming off the bench in injury-time.

"We didn't play enough football and didn't do enough in the final third. A crowd of 1,900 is tremendous. I was so disappointed we didn't give them anything to go home with."
Sammy McIlroy

Morecambe: Drench 7, Brannan 5 (Yates 81), Howard 7, Bentley 6, Blackburn 8, Thompson 6 (McNiven 90), Hunter 7 (Rigoglioso 66), Stanley 7, Perkins 6, Twiss 7, Carlton 6. Unused subs: Meadowcroft, Davies.
Burton Albion: Poole, Rowett, Webster, Corbett, Tinson, Austin, Fowler, Clare (Shaw 90), Ducros, Harrad (Scoffham 85), Holmes. Unused subs: Stride, Henshaw, Brayford. Booked: Ducros.

Referee: P Varley
Attendance: 1,907
Man of the match: **Chris Blackburn.**

15th August 2006

Northwich Victoria (0) 0 Morecambe (1) 2

Twiss 27, 90

MORECAMBE picked up their first points of the season and their first Conference win in 10 years in Cheshire against Northwich Victoria.

Michael Twiss was the difference with two goals as the Shrimps dominated. Jim Bentley's Achilles injury meant a debut for Danny Meadowcroft, while full-back Adam Yates replaced Ged Brannan. Yates was outstanding from start to finish and, but for Twiss, would have taken the man of the match award.

The match didn't start well for the Shrimps when, on 14 minutes, Michael Howard was adjudged to have handled the ball from a cross. The linesman flagged the incident and the referee pointed to the spot for the second penalty against Morecambe this season. But this time Steven Drench stopped the poor effort from Vic's top striker, Jonny Allen. The Shrimps were the most likely to score, dominating possession and playing some great attacking football, and they took the lead on 27 minutes.

A delightful one-two with Garry Hunter set up Twiss, and he unleashed an unstoppable left-footed, 20-yard strike low into the corner of the net.

Northwich offered very little resistance throughout the match, save for shots from Chris Williams and Kevin Townson.

The Shrimps always looked to control the game and they too peppered shots from distance through Twiss, Danny Carlton and Craig Stanley. However they were unable to extend their lead until the closing moments of the game. Twiss added a second in injury-time with another fine strike after a run into the box to give the Shrimps their first three points of the new season.

McIlroy was particularly pleased with the Northwich game when he made transfer-listed Dave Perkins captain in the absence of Jim Bentley.
"The performance was first class and we want to get that every game. I thought Perks' reaction was superb."

Morecambe: Drench 7, Yates 8, Perkins 7 (McLachlan 63), Howard 7, Meadowcroft 7 (Brannan 68), Blackburn 7, Twiss 8, Stanley 8, Carlton 7, Hunter 7, Thompson 6. Unused subs: Rigoglioso, McNiven, Davies.

Northwich Victoria: Senior, Battersby, Griffiths, Charnock, Gallimore, Byrne (Roca 78), Elliott (McCarthy 16), Carr, Williams, Allan (Brayson 66), Townson. Unused subs: Connett, Payne.

Attendance: 1,346.
Man of the match: **Michael Twiss.**

Jim Bentley

by Glen Cooper

AS WELL AS the influences of Sammy McIlroy, Mark Lillis, the Morecambe board and previous manager, Jim Harvey in getting The Shrimps into the Football League, there's been another major driving force.

Skipper Jim Bentley joined Morecambe in 2002 after a successful stint as Telford United's popular leader and the hard-tackling Scouse motivator soon became a favourite of the Christie Park regulars.

His on-field presence has been mirrored off the park with players and officials alike paying tribute to his qualities in helping generate a vibrant and cohesive dressing room spirit.

One experienced pro – Ged Brannan – who retired from playing after the Wembley win, described him as the best captain he had ever worked under.

Newcomers to the Morecambe squad have been initiated into the 'family' by Bentley carting them into the dressing room in a wheelie-bin from which they are required to emerge with a song.

No place for inflated egos at Bentley's Christie Park!

His personal performances are hugely efficient but often so understated that it has been said he is noticed most when he is NOT playing.

Evidence of that came in the 2006/7 season when an injury kept him out for much of the campaign's start.

Without him Morecambe suffered a stuttering couple of months during which they hovered around mid-table.

His reintroduction in mid-October coincided with a run of form that saw The Shrimps progress quickly up the league and, from the start of December, they were never out of the top six.

'Jimbo' was an ever present for the last couple of months in which the team consolidated in third position, for once cruising into the play-offs and on to the biggest day in the club's history.

It was noticeable that the SKY TV cameras that followed the team up the Wembley steps captured Bentley receiving the biggest and most emotional congratulations from the Morecambe officials, most poignantly a generous embrace from chairman, Peter McGuigan.

It was unfortunate that Bentley's inspiration and mentor, dad Jack (himself a Telford playing legend), couldn't attend the game in person, prevented by illness that was sadly to claim his life just a week after the final.

In the 2007 close-season some had the temerity to suggest that the step up to Football League level might

find the skipper wanting, speculating that he may be undone by pacier forwards.

But Jack would be pleased to know that, true to form, his lad has rammed those views firmly back down the doubters' throats as emphatically as he has been dispatching the attacking intentions of those pacy forwards in a start to Football League life in which he's been as reliable as ever.

One fan recently posted on the 'shrimpsvoices' internet message board that, because of his general presence and influence on the whole club, Jim Bentley is Morecambe's greatest ever player.

People may disagree but most, would, we'd suggest, start their 'All Time Shrimps XI' with 'Bentley (captain).'

19th August 2006

Woking 1 Morecambe 1

(Sole 90) (D McNiven 90)

SUPER-SUB David McNiven was a happy man after picking the perfect time to score his first Morecambe goal on Saturday.

The former Leigh and Scarborough striker earned the Shrimps a point with a goal deep into injury-time. He pounced onto a loose pass by Woking left-back Danny Bunce. There was little danger as Bunce received the ball on the edge of his own area with literally seconds to go. But the former Cambridge defender struck the ball into the path of McNiven who remained amazingly cool as he curled the ball into the empty net with keeper Shwan Jalal stranded. It was a goal that delighted McNiven – and his team-mates. He said: "It's always nice to get your first goal for a new club and it couldn't really have come at a better time I suppose. It was a bit of a surprise when the ball came to me but I just had a look up and thankfully hit the target. I was glad for myself but also for the lads because they certainly didn't deserve to lose the game. They had created all the best chances and it would have been a real shame to have left here empty-handed."

McNiven's analysis was spot-on as the Shrimps, although far from their best, did forge the better openings. The fact that Woking keeper, Jalal, was man of the match spoke volumes about the passage of play as he was called upon to make several fine stops. But the truth, too, is that Woking was really there for the taking. They were a side clearly lacking confidence and direction, with just one point from their opening three games. Craig McAllister was willing up front but he was left with little support and the Morecambe defence, still missing the injured Jim Bentley, had few problems.

Jalal was in action after just four minutes to gather a Garry Thompson volley. Later, on 13 minutes, he raced from his goal to put off Danny Carlton who latched on to Garry Hunter's superb throughball but volleyed wide. Woking finally threatened on 37 minutes with a Gary MacDonald free-kick that curled wide of the right-hand post. Morecambe then regained dominance with Michael Twiss sending Jalal sprawling again with a left-foot shot.

"After the Burton game, we had to respond and to be fair to the boys they have responded. Four out of six points from difficult places like Northwich and Woking is a step in the right direction but we know we can still improve."

Sammy McIlroy

A SPECIAL memorial match will take place for Gary Dullaghan at Christie Park on Sunday, September 3, kick-off 2pm. Around 40 former players have expressed an interest in playing to raise money for the family of Gary, who died suddenly in July, aged 41. John Coleman, Paul Burns and Ben Lavelle are expected to play while Michael Knowles and Bryan Griffiths hope to travel from Amercia and Spain respectively to be at the game. Morecambe physio, Dave Edge, has helped organise the game. He said: "This is going to be a fun day in memory of an extremely popular character. We have had a massive response from the players we have contacted and everyone has said they would love to play. The game will be a fitting tribute to Gary," he added.

The first half saw a real lack of quality but both sides stepped up a gear after the break. Craig Stanley should have given the Shrimps the lead on 48 minutes, but rushed a shot from six yards out when he had time and space. He was almost made to pay as the home side enjoyed their best spell of the game. Steve Ferguson took advantage of a mistake by Adam Yates to run on goal and take the ball round Steven Drench. He then saw his effort scrambled off the line by the covering Danny Meadowcroft. Moments later, Meadowcroft was outmuscled by McAllister but thankfully saw the Cards' striker shoot wide. The Shrimps then regained the upper hand with Stanley twice denied by Jalal. The impressive keeper then made the save of the day with a double block, saving from Twiss and then recovering to block McNiven's desperate attempt to poke the ball home.

With that the game looked set to teeter out goalless until suddenly, and somewhat surprisingly, Woking took a shock lead on 90 minutes. Twiss looked to shield the ball out of play for a goal kick but was outfoxed by McAllister who played the ball into the danger zone for Giuseppe Sole to sidefoot past Scott Davies, on for the injured Drench.

Just as the Shrimps thought they were going to face a long journey home pointless, up stepped McNiven to produce a lethal, and timely, finish.

Morecambe: Drench 7 (Davies 71), Yates 7, Howard 7, Meadowcroft 7, Blackburn 8, Thompson 7, Hunter 7, Stanley 7, Perkins 7 (Brannan 84), Twiss 7, Carlton 7 (D McNiven 75). Unused subs: McLachlan, S McNiven.
Woking: Jalal, Jackson, El-Salahi, MacDonald, Bunce, Oyedele, Murray, Smith (Sole 72), Berquez, Ferguson (Lambu 79), McAllister. Unused subs: Evans, Howe, Ruby. Booked: MacDonald.

Referee: P Gibbs.
Attendance: 1,222
Man of the Match: **Chris Blackburn.**

26th August 2006

Morecambe 3 Stevenage Borough 3

(Twiss 23, 47, Carlton 49) (Morison 1, 26, 59)

MORECAMBE began the Bank Holiday weekend with a draw in this six-goal thriller. It was a game that delighted the neutrals but frustrated the managers, as both defences did their best to turn this match into the highest scoring of the season so far.

Both sides looked sharp on the attack and exploited the gaps made available to them, creating a seemingly endless array of chances.

On the bright side for the Shrimps, Michael Twiss continued his fine start to the season with another two goals, taking his tally to four. Danny Carlton read the script and delivered his lines with a goal just a day after announcing he wanted to stay at Christie Park.

Unfortunately Stevenage's Steve Morison had failed to read that script fully and spoiled Carlton's day by scoring a high quality hat-trick. This was just his second game for Boro since a five-figure move from Bishops Stortford.

The day could not have started worse for the Shrimps as they went a goal down on 44

Michael Twiss header after 23 minutes.

Julian can't stop Twiss' equaliser.

seconds. Morison was on hand at the far post to stab home Luke Oliver's knockdown.

Twiss replied for the first time on 23 minutes when he headed home an excellent Adam Yates cross. Morison restored Boro's advantage three minutes later when he was left alone in the box to head home a cross from veteran Steve Guppy.

The Shrimps then enjoyed their best spell of the game with Garry Hunter and Garry Thompson both drilling shots inches wide and Wayne Curtis forcing Alan Julian into a save before the break.

It was Curtis who would inspire the Shrimps in the second half with some powerful runs and crosses from the left-hand side in his first game of the season.

On 47 minutes he crossed for Twiss to score his second, making it 2-2. Two minutes later, he repeated the feat with another fine ball into the area for Carlton to slide home and give the Shrimps the lead. Boro hit back almost immediately with Adam Miller hitting a post before Morison curled in a superb equaliser after Morecambe's fatal attempts to play offside.

Celebration time.

Both sides could have taken the full points with Morison blotting his day by heading wide from close range at one end and Craig Stanley coming close at the other from a screaming effort. Hunter forced Julian into the best save of the afternoon and Thompson should have done better than volley high and wide as the game came to a frantic end.

Morecambe: Robinson 7, Yates 7, Howard 7, Meadowcroft 7, Blackburn 7, Thompson 7, Hunter 7, Stanley 7, Curtis 8, Twiss 9, Carlton 7. Unused subs: McLachlan, D McNiven, Rigoglioso, Brannan, S Davies.
Stevenage: Julian, Fuller, Nutter, Oliver, Goodliffe, Miller, Boyd, Hicks (Henry 66), Morison, Guppy, Dobson (Thorpe 73). Unused subs: Wright, Gaia, Stamp. Booked: Hicks, Oliver.

Referee: A Haines.
Attendance: 1,524.
Man of the match: **Michael Twiss.**

28th August 2006

Halifax Town 1 Morecambe 1

(Torpey 45) (Twiss 61)

MORECAMBE boss Sammy McIlroy was full of praise for star-striker Michael Twiss after he earned the Shrimps a share of the spoils at the Shay on Monday.

Twiss scored his fifth goal in five games with a superb free-kick to earn his side a deserved point. Much of the game was played with 10 men after the 22nd-minute sending-off of Michael Howard. Twiss' quality was there to see all afternoon in a game that Morecambe dominated for long periods, despite being a man short.

McIlroy said: "Michael Twiss is on fire at the minute and long may it continue.

"He was excellent all the way through again and once we were awarded a free-kick on the edge of the box I screamed at him to take it and hit the target. That is exactly what he did and I was delighted for him and the lads because they gave it their all after being reduced to 10 men. They didn't feel sorry for themselves and they rolled their sleeves up and attacked to the end and probably deserved to win the game on the balance of play."

The sending off of Howard on 22 minutes for a second yellow card after a push on Ryan Sugden and a foul on Danny Forrest certainly changed the pattern of the game. Until that moment Morecambe had laid siege to the Halifax goal.

Danny Carlton had a golden chance after just 45 seconds but saw his attempted lob saved by former Shrimps keeper Craig Mawson. Mawson was quickly in action again to turn a Twiss drive onto the woodwork and block an excellent Wayne Curtis shot.

Garry Hunter pulled a right-foot shot just wide after a clever Carlton lay-off. Craig Stanley was denied his first Morecambe goal by Matt Doughty's goal-line clearance from a Twiss corner. Halifax's best period came just before the break with Lewis Killeen seeing a shot well blocked by the excellent Chris Blackburn and Ryan Robinson forced into a save from Steve Torpey. The home side was rewarded for its pressure two minutes into injury-time with a neat goal on the break as they used the extra space well. Sugden laid the ball to the left and Torpey made no mistake with a cool, curling finish.

The Shrimps to their credit came out fighting at the second half bell.

On 47 minutes, Twiss just lost his footing at the vital moment after weaving an opening for himself before Carlton headed a corner into the side netting. Twiss was not to be denied, however, and he gave the Shrimps a deserved equaliser with a low free-kick from the right-hand side of the area that whistled past the stranded Mawson.

Halifax looked to step up the pace but were constantly thwarted by a solid Morecambe defence, Blackburn and Danny Meadowcroft linking well together.

When Halifax did threaten in the final minute Adam Yates produced a superb covering tackle after Andy Campbell had come within an inch of connecting with Matt Doughty's dangerous cross. There was still time for one more moment of controversy. David McNiven looked to have been tripped in the area only for the referee to wave play on – much to McIlroy's annoyance. In the end the point was well won and well deserved, leaving the Shrimps unbeaten away from home so far this season.

"You could see all that ambition and determination on Monday after we went down to 10 men. We didn't let our heads go down, we rolled up our sleeves, kept at it and I don't think you would have known which team had the 10 men for much of the time. We have two big home games coming up now and I hope the fans come out in force to watch us."

Sammy McIlroy

MORECAMBE boss Sammy McIlroy was expecting Thursday night's transfer window to pass off quietly at Christie Park. Striker Danny Carlton told McIlroy last week that he wanted to stay at Christie Park, despite the ongoing interest from Blackpool, which has persisted again this week. Carlton said:

"The speculation over the past few weeks is now behind us. I want to play football and I want to play for Morecambe."

Morecambe: Robinson 7, Yates 8, Howard 6, Meadowcroft 8, Blackburn 8, Thompson 7 (Brannan 33), Hunter 7, Stanley 7, Curtis 7 (McNiven 73), Twiss 9, Carlton 7. Unused subs: McLachlan, Rigoglioso, S Davies. Booked: Howard, Thompson, Carlton. Sent off: Howard.
Halifax Town: Mawson, Doughty, Quinn, Forrest, Foster, Killeen, Sugden (Campbell 67), Roberts, Thompson (Fry 19), Torpey (Smeltz 74), Uhlenbeek. Unused subs: Matthews, Young. Booked: Uhlenbeek, Quinn.

Referee: M Matadar.
Attendance: 1,909.
Man of the match: **Michael Twiss.**

2nd September 2006

Morecambe 2 Weymouth 0

(Meadowcroft 30, Curtis 61)

MORECAMBE recorded their first home win of the season and showed signs that things were beginning to click into place for Sammy McIlroy's side.

The Shrimps produced a solid performance in monsoon conditions to pick up the three points and see Weymouth suffer their first defeat of the season.

In doing so they extended their unbeaten run to five games since the opening day defeat against Burton Albion. There were plus points all over the field for McIlroy in the way the Shrimps adapted to the awful conditions. Michael Twiss may not have scored but was influential in both goals while in defence Danny Meadowcroft produced another excellent performance, capped by his first goal for the club. The young centre-half carried on his mature display against Halifax with another fine effort in tandem with Chris Blackburn.

Weymouth produced only one real clear chance, which was superbly saved by Ryan Robinson. At the other end, Weymouth's Aaran Lee-Barrett was always the busier keeper and had to pick the ball out of the net twice, both as a result of deadly Twiss corners. The first was on the half hour when Twiss' inswinger was headed on by Blackburn. Meadowcroft was on hand to slide the ball into the net from six yards out.

Meadowcroft opens the scoring.

The second had a similar ring to it. Twiss delivered to the near post again and Wayne Curtis stole a march on his marker to flick the ball into the top right-hand corner of the Terras' goal. Two set-pieces, two goals and a very happy McIlroy and backroom staff. Apart from those moments the sides tried their best to entertain, although the conditions made it almost impossible to piece attacking moves together.

Weymouth themselves looked a solid and experienced team who will do well this year. But on this occasion things didn't really gel. They were frustrated to see one goal disallowed for a push when Rafael Nade headed an Abdul El Kholti cross into the net on 20 minutes. Simon Weatherstone threatened twice with shots from distance.

Their best chance, which perhaps proved to be the turning point of the game, came minutes before the Shrimps went 2-0 up. A long clearance from the Weymouth keeper Lee-Barrett eluded Adam Yates and Nade got the blindside of him.

McIlroy said: "The balls from Michael Twiss were magnificent and they were two good goals. We knew it was going to be a tough game in the conditions. But it was the same for both sides and I thought we adapted better and deserved to win the game."

The striker did well to cut inside and shoot but saw Robinson pull off a fine save.

When Ben Smith mis-cued the rebound well wide from a good position, Weymouth looked to forge a reply but the defence remained on top and a welcome three points were gathered.

Three points for Morecambe.

Morecambe: Robinson 7, Yates 7, Perkins 7, Meadowcroft 8, Blackburn 7, Thompson 7, Hunter 7, Stanley 7, Curtis 7, Twiss 8, Carlton 7 (McNiven 86). Unused subs: McLachlan, Rigoglioso, Brannan, Davies.

Weymouth: Barrett, Tully, Vickers (James 78), Downer, El Kholti (Logan 64), Crittenden, Smith, Weatherstone, Elam (Howell 46), Nade, Eribenne. Unused subs: Mathews, Tindall. Booked: Elam Vickers.

Referee: C Pawson.
Attendance: 1,333.
Man of the match: **Danny Meadowcroft**

9th September 2006

Morecambe 0 Oxford United 3

(Basham 22, Gilchrist 32, Burgess 90)

BOSS Sammy McIlroy made his feelings clear after the Shrimps suffered their second home defeat of the season on Saturday. "You can't defend as poorly as we did and expect to get results against teams like Oxford," was his forthright summation of the afternoon. And he was right.

The Shrimps matched Jim Smith's unbeaten side for much of the game and as the experienced visitors' boss said after the game "caused us more problems than any other team we have come across this season." But the brutal truth was they gifted Oxford one goal and played a major part in their own downfall for the second, something you just can't afford to do against a side as good as Oxford.

A third goal deep into injury time added to McIlroy's misery. At the other end of the field, Morecambe failed to find the target for the second time this season at home. They were denied on several occasions by some fine saves from visiting keeper Billy Turley. There were some good chances too. The best fell to Michael Twiss on the stroke of half-time. Played through by Garry Hunter, he only had the keeper to beat but Turley reacted sharply to stick out a leg and clear the danger. Danny Meadowcroft also had a golden chance a minute into the second half when Danny Carlton's corner flashed across the goal. However he failed to get a strong enough touch and presented Turley with a chance to grab the ball.

When Carlton's header hit the crossbar from another excellent Adam Yates cross, you could sense that this wasn't going to be Morecambe's day. The game changed from the moment the Shrimps handed Oxford an opening goal on 22 minutes. A long ball into the Morecambe penalty area should have been dealt with easily but Meadowcroft's attempted header back to Ryan Robinson fell woefully short and Steve Basham nodded home the loose ball. The defence was left wanting again 10 minutes later as Oxford scored a soft second. Robinson could only palm away Chris Willmott's header from Carl Peteffer's corner and defender Phil Gilchrist was on hand to head home the loose ball from six yards out.

The visitors had a chance to make it 3-0 on 49 minutes from the penalty spot after Robinson was held in the box by David Perkins but Ryan Robinson made a fine save to keep his side in the game. Unfortunately, despite plenty of possession, Oxford's five-man defence, which included former

Morecambe on the attack.

Premiership player Rufus Brevett, showed all its experience to remain solid. The Shrimps pushed to the end but their defences were breached for a third time on 93 minutes with the goal of the game. Andy Burgess showed his quality with a fine strike three minutes into injury time.

Burgess collected the ball on the right-hand side and curled a lovely effort past Robinson's right hand.

The Shrimps certainly started well. Turley was called into action in only the sixth minute when he produced an excellent flying save to tip away a 30-yard drive from Garry Thompson. Moments later the Oxford keeper was relieved to see a Twiss long-range volley fly just wide. Carlton then flashed a shot over the bar after a storming run took him to the edge of the box before the Shrimps' slick start came to a crushing end.

Garry Thompson wins a header.

"We are not firing on all cylinders yet, 70 per cent of our play is very good and we can go to another level. I was very disappointed with the scoreline, it was never a 3-0 game. When you analyse it afterwards, I think with the ball we were as good as them."

Sammy McIlroy

Morecambe: Robinson 7, Yates 7, Perkins 7, Meadowcroft 6, Blackburn 7, Thompson 6 (McNiven 68), Hunter 6, Stanley 7, Curtis 6, Twiss 7, Carlton 6. Unused subs: McLachlan, Howard, Brannan, Drench.
Oxford United: Turley, Anaclet (Day 46), Brevett, Quinn, Willmott, Gilchrist, Hutchinson, (Dempster 71), Pettefer, Burgess, Robinson, Basham, (Obudabe 64). Unused subs: Tardiff, Kennet. Booked: Anaclet, Robinson, Hutchinson, Quinn, Day, Turley.

Referee: C Oliver
Attendance: 2,314
Man of the match: **Craig Stanley.**

12th September 2006

York City 2 Morecambe 3

(Woolford 48, Donaldson 75 pen) (Twiss 20, 76, Thompson 40)

TWO more goals from Michael Twiss, who took his tally for the season to seven, gave the Shrimps the points in this exciting game.

Twiss took advantage of some woeful York defending for both his goals and had the Shrimps been more clinical in front of goal, they could have won by a greater margin. In the end, they had to overcome the disappointment of seeing York pull back a two-goal deficit before Twiss showed his quality in front of goal just when it mattered most. Twiss opened his account on 20 minutes after some shocking defending. Garry Thompson's cross from the right fell for James Dudgeon but his clearance was woeful and Twiss nipped in to drill the ball through the legs of young keeper Arron Reid.

Although York enjoyed long periods of possession, the Shrimps always looked the more threatening going forward. Their pressure paid off with a second goal five minutes from the break with a clever free-kick that came straight off the training ground. As York expected a cross into the box from the right, Craig Stanley laid the ball off sideways and Thompson met it perfectly with a sidefoot past Reid.

The game should have been settled before half-time when Wayne Curtis had a golden chance to make it 3-0 from James Craddock's mistake. His lob over the advancing Reid was too strong, though, and the ball went out of play. It was a miss that could have left him with nightmares as York came back strongly in the second half with a much more powerful display. With just three minutes of the second half played they were back in the game with a well-taken goal from Martyn Woolford. The young winger volleyed home Mark Convery's deep cross from an acute angle.

York maintained the pressure with Woolford just failing to control the ball as he looked set to break free and Craig Farrell unfortunate to be pulled back by the referee for an earlier foul.

As York pressed there were gaps for Morecambe to exploit. They wasted another golden chance to extend their advantage when Danny Carlton was put free on goal but drilled a shot into the side netting when he should have scored.

It was another miss that could have been costly as the game changed dramatically 15 minutes from time. York were awarded a hugely controversial penalty when David Perkins was adjudged by a linesman to have

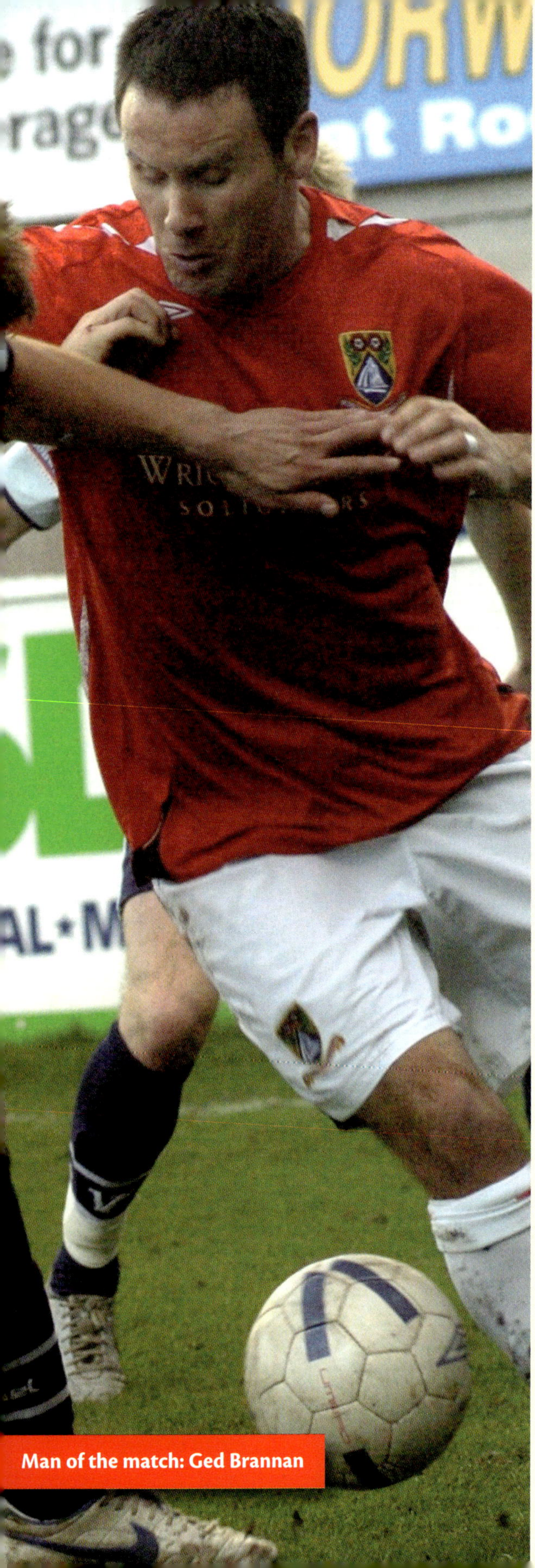

brought down Convery when he clearly took the ball. Clayton Donaldson took advantage of the spot-kick by firing past Steven Drench and the home side were on top. Then up stepped Twiss who made his class tell again with a fine winner. The York defence played their part once again as Dudgeon failed to clear a long ball and Twiss picked up the pieces to shoot past Reid from 12 yards out. Twiss came close to sealing his hat-trick when he shot over three minutes from time. In the dying moments of injury time Drench produced a fine save to deny centre-half David McGurk who stabbed a shot forward from six yards out.

Morecambe: Drench 7, Yates 7, Perkins 7, Brannan 9, Blackburn 7, Thompson 7, Hunter 7, Stanley 7, Curtis 7 (Howard 78), Twiss 8, Carlton 7 (McLachlan 86). Unused subs: Meadowcroft, McNiven, Davies. Booked: Yates, Perkins, Brannan, Stanley.
York City: Reid, Craddock, Peat (Lloyd 46), Bishop, McGurk, Dudgeon (Parslow 78), Convery, Panther (McMahon 53), Donaldson, Farrell, Woolford. Unused subs: Webster, Rhodes. Booked: Panther, Peat.

Referee: K Evans.
Attendance: 2,233
Man of the match: **Ged Brannan.**

16th September 2006

Dagenham and Redbridge 2 Morecambe 1

(Rainford 18, 51) (Carlton 43)

MORECAMBE boss Sammy McIlroy found it hard to hide his frustration after seeing his side undone once again by set-pieces.

Not for the first time the Shrimps failed to defend deadball situations and were made to pay dearly by a Dagenham side who had surprised everyone by the start they had made to the season. "It just isn't good enough," fumed McIlroy at the end as the Shrimps suffered their first away defeat of the campaign. It was all the more disappointing for the boss and the Morecambe spectators as they had hoped to see their side build on the success of their excellent midweek victory at York. Many would argue that York were a far better footballing team than Dagenham but the Daggers' route one approach caused the Morecambe defensive line problems all afternoon.

Individually the defenders all had decent games under the pressure of Dagenham's aerial bombardment, but collectively there was a lack of someone to take charge at times of need and the loss of injured skipper Jim Bentley was all too evident.

Both Dagenham goals came from corners and both were due to sloppy defending, which ultimately gifted the home side the points.

The first came on 18 minutes when keeper Steven Drench failed to collect Sam Saunders' corner. Midfielder Dave Rainford took advantage to direct a downward header into the empty goal. Dagenham's second came via a similar route six minutes into the second half. Sam Sloma's corner wasn't cleared and Rainford was there again to fire the ball past Drench.

In between, Morecambe showed they too could be dangerous at corners with a goal of their own. In a move that has paid dividends on several occasions, Michael Twiss curled the ball into the near post and Danny Carlton nipped in sharply ahead of his marker to head home. That was a rare highlight on a disappointing afternoon for the Shrimps who found it difficult to get through a stout home defence. Wayne Curtis did have a great chance to hit back after Rainford's opener when put through by Garry Thompson but he shot straight at Tony Roberts. Two minutes later Carlton was denied a close range tap-in from an excellent Curtis cross by a fine covering tackle from Scott Griffiths. Unfortunately, clear-cut chances were then at a premium as the

Dagenham defence stood firm. Thompson was shackled well by the excellent Griffiths and the Shrimps were left relying on shots from distance, which failed to trouble Roberts. At the other end, Dagenham should have extended their advantage.

Craig Mackail-Smith placed a shot wide of the left-hand post after beating the offside trap. Paul Benson was denied his sixth goal of the season by an acrobatic goal-line clearance by Chris Blackburn when he latched onto another piece of hesitant defending. It was such hesitant moments that were costing the Shrimps dear this season.

ONE of the men responsible for Morecambe FC's biggest-ever shirt sponsorship deal has joined the board. Solicitor Stephen Wright who, with business partner Simon Lord, has invested thousands of pounds in the club, was announced as a new director on Tuesday. He said: "I feel greatly honoured and privileged. This is a highly responsible position because the directors are really the trustees of the club, charged with the duties of handling the affairs of the club to ensure not only that the club is successful now, but so it also successfully carries on for future generations.

"I was very flattered to be asked by the current members of the board. I am looking forward to the challenges and future successes which no doubt lie ahead."

Stephen, 40, lives in Morecambe and has supported the club since the age of six.

Morecambe: Drench 6, Yates 6, Perkins 7, Brannan 8, Blackburn 7, Thompson 6, Hunter 6, Stanley 6, Curtis 6 (McNiven 77), Twiss 7, Carlton 6. Unused subs: Meadowcroft, McLachlan, Howard, Davies. Booked: Stanley.
Dagenham and Redbridge: Roberts, Foster, Uddin, Leberl, Griffiths, Sloma, Rainford, Akurang, Saunders, Mackail-Smith, Benson. Unused subs: Hogan, Batt, Lettajellow, Weatherstone, Bruce. Booked: Leberl.

Referee: D Sheldrake.
Attendance: 1,237.
Man of the match: **Ged Brannan.**

"The lads know that it is not good enough. I thought we coped quite well with the long ball against Dagenham, it was just the set-plays. It is mistakes that are costing us and it's not just defenders, it is the whole group, we're not doing the ugly side of the game. I was very, very disappointed on Saturday. Even though Dagenham were flying high, we know we could have got a result."

Sammy McIlroy

19th September 2006

Morecambe 0 Tamworth 0

MORECAMBE failed to overcome a drab Tamworth team in this awful goalless draw at Christie Park on Tuesday night.

The Shrimps were allowed to dominate possession but they had to settle for a point after failing to get through a packed Tamworth defence. Mark Cooper's side came for the draw and that is just what they got on a frustrating evening for everyone.

The result meant that the Shrimps were going into this weekend's game with Kidderminster with only one win from five home games. A win against Mark Yates' strugglers was important if they were to move away from the middle of the table.

Perhaps the most disappointing statistic from the evening was that despite all the possession Morecambe produced just one shot on target when, 20 minutes from the end, midfielder Craig Stanley forced Sean Bowles into a neat save with a 20-yard volley.

An uneventful first half saw no clear chances with the only effort of note being a 25-yarder from Michael Twiss that flew well wide of the right-hand post. The second period at least gave the Morecambe fans something to shout about. Carlton came close to opening the scoring with a header from a dangerous Adam Yates cross that whistled just wide of the left-hand upright on 52 minutes. As Morecambe enjoyed their best period of the game, they came close again three minutes later with a Twiss header from a good Carlton cross. The Shrimps continued to push forward with Thompson finally beginning to threaten down the right and Matty Shaw making some good runs down the left on his debut for the club.

A David Perkins cross was again just too high for Carlton who found a rare bit of space in the area before the Shrimps came close to stealing a late winner.

A Twiss corner rifled across the Tamworth goal line and former Blackpool player Shaw looked set to mark his first start with a dream goal but somehow he failed to get the decisive touch at the far post as the chance and the points went begging.

Morecambe: Drench 6, Yates 7, Perkins 7, Brannan 6, Blackburn 6, Thompson 6, Hunter 6 (McLachlan 68), Stanley 6, Howard 6 (Shaw 60), Twiss 6, Carlton 6. Unused subs: Meadowcroft, McNiven, Davies.
Tamworth: Bowles, Smith, Storer, Weaver, Kemp, Stevenson, Deakin, Kendrick (Friars 61), Bradley, Atieno (Devlin 78), Burton (Williams 68). Unused subs: Touhy, Law. Booked: Smith, Bradley, Kendrick, Stevenson.

Referee: S Cummins.
Attendance: 1,248.
Man of the match: **Adam Yates.**

23rd September 2006

Morecambe 0 Kidderminster Harriers 1

(Christie 72)

MORECAMBE assistant boss Mark Lillis gave a brutally honest view of his side's fortunes after they slumped to their third home defeat of the season against Kidderminster.

Speaking after the 1-0 defeat, he said: "There comes a time when players have to take a good, hard look at themselves in the mirror to make sure they are happy with what they see. We've told them a few home truths today and if we are to get our season going they need to consider their own performances."

Fraser McLachlan surges forward.

Lillis said he wanted the side to reflect on their displays this season ahead of the forthcoming trip to Grays. He was hopeful they would produce the type of performance that would give the season the boost it badly needed.

A total of 13 points from 11 games was not the sort of start many expected but Lillis was sure the Shrimps would turn things round. "We are a family and like all families we will fall out every now and again but we need to get a few things out in the open and get back to working together to produce the type of form that took us into the play-offs last season," he said.

The Kidderminster game was another frustrating one for Morecambe fans.

It was certainly better than the drab clash with a dire Tamworth in midweek but once again there were few clear chances created. It might have been a different story if Garry Thompson hadn't produced the miss of the season on 25 minutes. He somehow missed an open goal from three yards out when he blasted David McNiven's fine cross over the bar. Thompson forced Scott Bevan into a neat save earlier with a cross that would have gone in at the near post. The keeper also had to be alert to save superbly from McNiven's diving header at the start of the second half.

After that, Chris Blackburn volleyed inches wide from 12 yards out before Danny Carlton wasted another excellent chance by heading weakly at Bevan.

Unlike Tamworth, however, Kidderminster had an attacking edge and missed some good chances of their own. On 39 minutes midfielder Simon Russell dragged a shot wide of the right-hand post from 12 yards out after a good lay-off by Iyseden Christie.

Five minutes later, Russell burst through from midfield once again. He ran onto Gavin Hurren's superb ball but was foiled by an excellent save from Steven Drench.

After a bright start to the second half, the Shrimps were forced on the back foot by a period of Kidderminster pressure with substitute Michael Blackwood in the thick of the action. His hard work up front led to a Gavin Hurren shot that was comfortably saved by Drench before heading just past the post after a dangerous cross from John Harkness. Then came the deciding moment of the game. A free-kick from Jake Sedgemore was flicked on by Andrew White. Christie reacted sharper than the Morecambe defence to beat Drench to the ball and score from close range.

"There is a long way to go, a lot of points to play for, it is not a crisis but we are very unhappy with the way things are going at the moment. We had an hour after the game on Saturday and a lot of home truths were said and a lot of words spoken. A lot of players said their points and the staff said their points and there were lots of positives to come from it. It's good when you clear the air. It's no used me ranting and raving all the time, you've got to give the players the chance to speak their mind. For an hour after the game, it was not a happy dressing room and rightly so because we lost a game we shouldn't have lost. It has been the worst week that I have had since I have been at Morecambe but I can assure people that I will turn it around."

Sammy McIlroy

Morecambe: Robinson 6, Yates 7, Perkins 7, Brannan 6, Blackburn 6 (Meadowcroft 88), Thompson 6 (Shaw 72), Hunter 6, McLachlan 7, Twiss 7, McNiven 7, Carlton 6. Unused subs: Davies, Smith, Howard. Booked: Perkins, McLachlan, Carlton.
Kidderminster Harriers: Bevan, Sedgemore, Harkness, Creighton, Whitehead, Russell (Smikle 79), Penn, Hurren, McGrath (Blackwood 55), White (Reynolds 84), Christie. Unused subs: Taylor, McClen. Booked: Hurren, Penn, Harkness.

Referee: J Collin.
Attendance: 1,496.
Man of the match: **Adam Yates.**

30th September 2006

Grays Athletic 0 Morecambe 1

(McNiven 57)

IT wasn't pretty – but it was just what the doctor ordered.

After a week which Sammy McIlroy described as the "worst since joining Morecambe" the Shrimps boss oversaw a battling victory over a Grays team who had enjoyed a good start to the season. Without the injured Wayne Curtis and Garry Thompson, McIlroy was forced to reshuffle his pack and although the lack of width was noticeable at times, the Shrimps did more than enough to win the game with a display full of effort and determination.

The midfield was asked to work overtime to protect their defence and they did just that. Fraser McLachlan in particular did his utmost to break down any threatening Grays' move and prevent the ball from reaching the Conference's top-scorer Aaron McLean. It worked well as McLean was given no service and midfield threats Michael Kightly and Dennis Oli were closed down at every opportunity. Chances were rare as a result but the Shrimps always looked the more likely to break the deadlock. And that is what they did just before the hour. Adam Yates, who got forward whenever he could, produced a lovely cross from the right and David McNiven nipped in front of his marker to divert the ball into the bottom right-hand corner of the goal.

After showing little threat Grays came back immediately and almost scored a quick equaliser. Former Canvey striker Lee Boylan found some rare space and crossed superbly from the left. Home skipper Jamie Stuart rose well but headed against the foot of the right-hand post when he perhaps should have scored. From there nine-goal McLean headed

THE smile that spread across Sammy McIlroy's face as his players celebrated the great 1-0 win at Grays conveyed more than mere satisfaction at three hard-earned points. The preceding week had, by the Morecambe manager's own admission, been his worst since arriving at Morecambe.

"We need to start getting it right at home and I'm confident we will. Fans are getting annoyed and maybe that's to be expected but I know what's going on behind the scenes and I know the determination of everyone at the club to put things right. I believe we have the squad to do that with good quality all round and competition for places. I know that when we start picking up those home wins we can motor up this league. And when we get into the top few places I believe we'll stay there."

Sammy McIlroy

inches wide 10 minutes from time and Glenn Poole forced Drench into a block at the second attempt from a 25-yard free-kick. It was the Shrimps who came the closest to adding to the scoreline, however. McNiven, who came close with a first-half header from another Yates cross, came within a whisker of giving Morecambe a 49th-minute lead. With a clever, curling effort from the edge of the box after a neat Danny Carlton lay-off he just evaded the left-hand post. Craig Stanley then came close to scoring his first goal for the Shrimps on 66 minutes. He clipped a delightful effort just past the left-hand post with Bayes well beaten. With six minutes to go, Brannan failed to hit the target as he sneaked in at the far post to get his head onto a Michael Twiss corner. Five minutes of injury time did little to calm the nerves of the Shrimps' supporters but they held on without any real worries for a fine three points. It was hoped to be a win that would spur the side on to bigger and better things.

Morecambe: Drench 6, Yates 7, Perkins 7, Brannan 6, Blackburn 6, Howard 6, Stanley 6, McLachlan 7, Twiss 7, McNiven 7 (Hunter 80), Carlton 6. Unused subs: Davies, Meadowcroft, Thompson, Yates. Booked: Perkins, Brannan, McNiven.
Grays Athletic: Bayes, Sangare, Stuart, Sambrook, Green (Slabber), Kightly, Nicholls, Poole (Martin), McLean, Oli, Boylan. Unused subs: Knowles, Smith, Williamson. Booked: Stuart.

Referee: D Ford
Attendance: 1,056.
Man of the match: **Fraser McLachlan.**

3rd October 2006

Morecambe 1 Rushden and Diamonds 0

(Carlton 53)

A SOLID Morecambe performance earned a second successive win against Rushden and Diamonds.

The Shrimps secured only their second home win of the season with a second half goal from Danny Carlton enough to brush aside a dogged, but limited, Rushden and Diamonds. It was the first time in the season that the Shrimps had claimed back-to-back wins.

It was more solid than scintillating but with flair players such as Garry Thompson and Wayne Curtis still out injured, McIlroy has been forced into a change of tactics.

With Fraser McLachlan once again dominant in midfield, these tactics seemed to be paying off. The Shrimps produced the best moments of the game in the opening hour with Paul Hart's Diamonds showing little threat until they went behind.

Goal hero Carlton volleyed over on three minutes. Michael Twiss then went close from 30 yards with a sweetly-struck shot flying inches past the post. Carlton then failed to take advantage of a slip from Diamonds defender Paul Watson with a weak shot that failed to worry Eyre. David Perkins flashed a left-foot shot just wide and the Shrimps were almost handed the lead by Rushden defender Jon Ashton who headed Adam Yates' cross against his own woodwork.

The visitors threatened briefly when Marcus Kelly forced a smart save from Drench on 22 minutes. Jackson went on to waste the game's first clear opening.

Andrew Rigby crossed perfectly for the unmarked Jackson six yards from goal but the chance went begging. Morecambe soon regained the initiative and came close again. Wayne Hatswell attempted a clearance from inside his own box, the ball rebounded off the covering Yates and almost sneaked into the bottom left-hand corner of Eyre's goal.

The Shrimps' pressure continued in the second period with Michael Howard forcing Eyres into a neat block after a neat overlap. Carlton then produced the decisive moment of the game with a good downward header from Twiss' deep cross. Diamonds hit back with David Savage seeing a shot deflected for a corner and Ashton heading a corner wide from close in.

Morecambe: Drench 7, Yates 7, Howard 7, Brannan 7, Blackburn 8, Perkins 7, Stanley 7, McLachlan 7, Twiss 7, McNiven 7 (Hunter 85), Carlton 7 (Shaw 75). Unused subs: Thompson, Davies, Meadowcroft. Booked: Perkins.

Rushden and Diamonds: Eyre, Wilson, Watson, Ashton, Hope, Hatswell, Savage, Rankine, Kelly, Jackson (Pearson 80), Rigby (Berry 60). Unused subs: Crane, Tomlin, Shaw. Booked: Ashton.

Referee: R Fletcher.
Attendance: 1,252.
Man of the match: **Chris Blackburn.**

7th October 2006

Crawley Town 4 Morecambe 0

(Rendell 13, 44, 51 pen, Scully 90)

MORECAMBE suffered their heaviest defeat of the season and their second on the road at Crawley. Schoolboy errors crept back in after an excellent disciplined result against Rushden and Diamonds.

It was the experienced pair of Ged Brannan and Chris Blackburn in the heart of the Morecambe defence who were the offenders with two woeful defensive howlers. Blackburn got his marching orders five minutes into the second half and by then the result was a foregone conclusion. Yet the Shrimps started brightly for the first 10 minutes of the half. Shrimps right-back Adam Yates made an excellent run into the 18-yard box. A precision cross was delivered to striker David McNiven who perhaps should have done better with his two attempts.

His first shot on the turn from 12 yards out was blocked. He was then given another opportunity to find the net but Crawley centre-half Dave Woozley made an excellent headed clearance off the line.

But it was the home team who took advantage of the first gift of the afternoon.

A long throw on the left flank from Jamie Lovegrove was headed clear by Ged Brannan at the second attempt straight at the feet of Scott Rendell. Unmarked Rendell had time to fire underneath the body of Steven Drench. Michael Twiss then gifted possession to Ben Strevens at the edge of the 18-yard box after failing to link up a one-two with Blackburn. He was, however, able to scramble back to block Strevens' shot. This goal gave Crawley renewed confidence after only scoring five goals in their previous six home matches. Danni Bulman's 25-yard drive was saved at the second attempt by Drench on 22 minutes. The situation was worsened with the injury to striker Danny Carlton. He left the field with a knee injury on 24 minutes after a collision with Lee Blackburn. That brought Matthew Shaw into the action alongside David McNiven. The Shrimps were restricted to long-range attempts from Shaw, Craig Stanley and McNiven without testing the keeper. At the other end the shots were unleashed with accuracy and Bostwick forced Drench into making a fine save after good work by Strevens. On 44 minutes, Crawley were gifted their second goal. Blackburn fluffed his lines and presented the ball for Rendell to fire home with precision past Drench from 18 yards.

Whatever was said at half-time hadn't been digested before Crawley came out and started to tear the Shrimps' defence apart. Rendell turned provider with an excellent cross from the right wing and Strevens should have opened his account with a header.

On 51 minutes, a slip-up by Michael Howard allowed Gary Mills to run through the defence into the 18-yard box. Here he was clearly fouled by Blackburn and the referee had no choice but to red card Blackburn and add to his misery.

Rendell stepped up and fired straight with Drench well beaten.

Bulman should have scored with his acrobatic volley on 64 minutes and Danny Meadowcroft had to head clear to deny an advancing Strevens.

There were only two significant moments for the Shrimps in the second half, both involving Craig Stanley. On 67 minutes he hit the post after linking up well with Twiss on the left flank. Then on 73 minutes Shaw provided an excellent cross from the right and Stanley had the best chance of the game to score a goal but couldn't take it.

Tony Scully deservedly added a fourth on 90 minutes nodding in at the far post from Lee Blackburn's cross from the right. That capped an awful day for Sammy McIlroy's men and the small travelling support. Many wondered how a team who finished so well the previous year could be making so many mistakes.

Morecambe: Drench 5, Yates 7, Howard 5, Brannan 5, Blackburn 5, Perkins 5, Stanley 7, McLachlan 5 (Hunter 80), Twiss 6, McNiven 5 (Meadowcroft 54), Carlton 5 (Shaw 24). Unused subs: Thompson, Davies. Booked: Stanley. Sent off: Blackburn.
Crawley Town: Hamer, Hiley, Judge, Woozley, Lovegrove (Brown 81), Bulman, Mills, Bostwick (Scully 52), Blackburn, Strevens (Edwards 76), Rendell. Unused subs: Tolfrey, Macleod. Booked: Blackburn.

Referee: N Kinseley.
Attendance: 890.
Man of the match: **Craig Stanley.**

"I'm not just picking on the goalkeeper and the defenders, it is a team effort. The group of 11 players didn't do the business on Saturday. We've got to instill into the lads when to defend and when to play – it's the ugly side of the game we are not doing. We were beaten by a very average side. But we are five points off the play-offs, we know what we have got to do and are capable of doing it."

Sammy McIlroy

10th October 2006

Altrincham 0 Morecambe 2

McLachlan 23, Carlton 81

MORECAMBE picked up a deserved third win in four games after a thoroughly professional performance to see off Altrincham.

Sammy McIlroy's side outclassed their opponents and even when Garry Thompson was sent off and they were a man short for 35 minutes, the Shrimps were still in charge.

The Morecambe boss decided to play all his cards after the 4-0 defeat to Crawley with both Jim Bentley and Thompson coming back after injury.

Consigning that crushing at Crawley to history was clearly the motivation, particularly for the Shrimps defence, who, led by Bentley, never shirked a challenge.

It only took a couple of minutes for the Shrimps' skipper to powerfully head clear an Altrincham long ball, showing his authority from the off.

There were positive early touches down the right from Thompson too as the Shrimps started well. Fraser McLachlan clipped the bar with a deflected cross in the ninth minute.

The Shrimps stayed on top and should have had a penalty on 20 minutes when Thompson beat his man but unfortunately Steven Rose seemed to bring him down.

It looked an odds-on spot-kick but referee Smedley gave a corner instead. Three minutes later, though, the Shrimps were in front. Michael Howard swung over a cross from the left to Danny Carlton, who was in acres of space as the Alty defence stopped, expecting offside. Carlton turned and shot but Richard Acton pulled off the first of several great stops, parrying the ball up in the air. McLachlan was first to react and nod the ball into the roof of the net. It wasn't all plain sailing for the Morecambe backline. Home midfielder Val Owen was twice able to get in shots from the edge of the box after crosses weren't cleared. However, that was that for Altrincham in the first period with the Shrimps finishing on top. They stayed on the front foot after the break too and only 42 seconds had elapsed before Twiss showed his undoubted class.

He picked the ball up about 35 yards out, moved forward a few steps and unleashed a left-foot rocket that flew past Acton and came back off the post. The rebound went straight to Carlton who was brought down on the edge of the box. Thompson again forced Acton into action from the free-kick, the goalkeeper getting down well to turn away the shot. Thompson's game was to end a few minutes later, the referee showing him a red card after clashing with Karl Munroe. Thompson actually won the free-kick but Munroe's reaction, which earned him a yellow, prompted what the referee later termed a headbutt from Thompson.

That decision only affirmed the Morecambe players' resolve. All four defenders kept things tight and Steven Drench was not called into action. The midfield kept the ball superbly with Carlton also working hard in attack. For the last half hour, the visitors had the better chances. McLachlan broke from midfield to get onto Adam Yates' cross and should have scored but again Acton saved well. Yates was again full of energy as the Shrimps took the game to Alty instead of hanging on to their lead.

An amazing run from the right-back brought the crucial second goal in the 81st minute. He was brought into the game by some clever play by Stanley and Yates. Getting to the corner flag, he cut inside his man and slid the ball across to where Carlton tapped in from four yards. Altrincham sub Steve Bushell had to go off injured with five minutes remaining as the match finished 10 v 10. The home side never looked like scoring as the Shrimps erased the memory of Crawley with a clean sheet.

Morecambe: Drench 7, Yates 9, Howard 7, Brannan 7, Bentley 8, Perkins 7, Stanley 8, McLachlan 7 (Hunter 78), Thompson 6, Twiss 8, Carlton 7. Unused subs: McNiven, Shaw, Davies, Meadowcroft. Sent off: Thompson.
Altrincham: Acton, Aspinall, Munroe, Rose, Peyton, Band, Chalmers (Bushell 69), Potts (Bowler 59), Lawton, Owen, O'Neil (McFadden 53). Unused subs: Scott, Hussin. Booked: Aspinall, Munroe.

Referee: I Smedley.
Attendance: 1,085.
Man of the match: **Adam Yates.**

WAYNE Curtis will be another three weeks as he recovers from what has now been diagnosed as a broken metatarsal in his foot. The injury has become prevalent in football in recent seasons with England stars such as David Beckham, Wayne Rooney and Gary Neville all suffering. However, Curtis' break is in one of the smaller bones and is not as serious as some of the more high-profile injuries.

14th October 2006

Morecambe 2 Exeter City 2

(Carlton 38, Stanley 75) (Mackie 1, Stansfield 57)

CRAIG Stanley's first Morecambe goal may have taken him longer than he would have liked – but he certainly couldn't have picked a better moment.

The former Hereford man was wearing the captain's armband after both Jim Bentley and Ged Brannan had gone off. He produced a superb 25-yard volley that flew into the bottom right-hand corner of Martin Rice's goal to give the Shrimps a deserved point.

The warnings given by boss Sammy McIlroy after the 4-0 self-inflicted defeat at Crawley a week earlier obviously went unheeded as the visitors scored the simplest of goals. Rice's long punt was flicked on and, as the defence dithered, in nipped the ever-dangerous Jamie Mackie to take the ball round Steven Drench and score from a tight angle.

To their credit Morecambe came back well and dominated the game for long periods with some neat possession football. This play led Exeter boss Paul Tisdale to say the Shrimps were the best 'passing side he had seen all season'. Fraser McLachlan was

Danny Carlton scores.

Craig Stanley taking the captain's armband.

Exeter go one-up early on.

close to providing an early equaliser with a seventh-minute header from a Michael Twiss corner that was cleared off the line by Paul Buckle. The Shrimps continued to press with Ged Brannan just failing to meet a dangerous Michael Howard free-kick. Adam Yates missed the target from close range after Rice could only parry a deflected long-range Stanley effort. When skipper Jim Bentley was forced to leave the field on the half hour, things looked bleak. However with Danny Meadowcroft impressing the Shrimps stayed firm and managed to get the break-through the home fans were crying out for. On 38 minutes, Brannan floated the ball into the area. Although Chris Blackburn's header was blocked, the ball fell neatly for Danny Carlton who drilled home from 10 yards.

Morecambe were the first to threaten in the second period with Meadowcroft directing a header over the bar from a Carlton corner before the visitors took the lead for a second time. Exeter had always looked dangerous on the break with Mackie a constant threat. The young striker, who has caught the eye at St James's Park since moving from MK Dons, again proved too sharp for the Morecambe defence as he inspired Exeter's second. After collecting the ball on the left, he brushed past several weak challenges before creating space to shoot. Drench did well to parry the effort but Adam Stansfield was on hand to bundle the ball home from six yards out. The Morecambe keeper was then forced to make a fine save low to his right from Lee Phillips. That proved to be a turning point as Morecambe stormed back into the game with Stanley's superb strike which beat an unsighted Rice low to his left.

Craig Stanley equalises in the 75th minute.

The Shrimps then went in search of the winner with Rice in tandem with defender Dan Woodards, making a fine double save from Carlton and then David Perkins. Phillips wasted a glorious late opportunity at the other end to stab the ball wide of the left-hand post with only Drench to beat. It was a thrilling end to an excellent game, but once again the Shrimps were left thinking what could have been if it were not for those defensive errors.

"The home form has been up and down but it is still only October. We will put that right,"
Assistant Manager, Mark Lillis

Morecambe: Drench 7, Brannan 7 (Lloyd 59), Howard 7, Bentley 7 (McLachlan 29), Blackburn 7, Yates 8, Stanley 9, McLachlan 7 (McNiven 69), Perkins 7, Twiss 7, Carlton 7. Unused subs: Smith, Davies.
Exeter City: Rice, Woodards, Jones, Edwards, Richardson, Taylor, Moxey (Challinor 55), Buckle, Gill, Mackie (Clay 85), Stansfield (Phillips 66). Unused subs: Jones, Ada. Booked: Moxey.

Referee: P Quinn.
Attendance: 1,582.
Man of the match: **Craig Stanley.**

21st October 2006

Aldershot Town 0 Morecambe 1

(Osano 45 og)

MORECAMBE secured their fifth away win of the season with a fine, dogged display at the Rec.

Boss Sammy McIlroy praised his side for a 'brave' display against a good, home team who put them under intense pressure for long periods. The Shrimps, still without regulars such as skipper Jim Bentley, Garry Thompson, Garry Hunter and Wayne Curtis, gave perhaps their most resolute performance of the season clinching a win that took them to within two points of the play-off zone. The individual errors that had proved so costly this season were nowhere to be seen as the Shrimps threw themselves into challenges and produced some superb last-gasp blocks to deny the Shots.

When the home side did threaten they come up against an in-form Steven Drench who made a string of fine saves. The win was all the more creditable considering that Morecambe lost their main striker Danny Carlton early in the game to a knee injury that could see him out of action for three months. The Shrimps were rewarded for their bravery with a bizarre own goal from Shots' full-back Curtis Osano giving them victory. Adriano Rigoglioso, making his first appearance of the season after being recalled from his loan spell at Forest Green, dinked in a cross from the right, which should have caused the Shots defence no problems. But the youngster somehow managed to direct a looping header over his own keeper Nikki Bull and could only look on in horror as the ball ended up in the back of the net. The goal, two minutes into first half injury-time, came at a perfect moment for the Shrimps who had been put under some intense pressure towards the end of the half. Central midfielders Mark Moseley and Ben Harding were not afraid to try their luck from distance and came close on several occasions. On 32 minutes, Harding forced Steven Drench into a fine save with a 25-yard drive that was heading for the right-hand corner. Four minutes later he tested the Shrimps' keeper again with a shot that took a wicked deflection.

The Shrimps travel to Solihull for the final qualifying round tie and McIlroy has warned his players not to take the Nationwide North side for granted. He said: "We will be going down there and everyone will be expecting us to beat them but they are going to be up for it. Forget the League situation, we have got to be professional and do the job right. If we do that, I am sure we will come away with a result. It's great for the club if you can get a little bit of a run. Our main ambition is to get to the play-offs but a good cup run keeps the players ticking over and is great for the supporters."

Moseley had aimed his sights on goal with several efforts that flew wide from long range before drilling a 43rd-minute drive into the side netting after cutting inside from the left wing.

Morecambe began the second half brightly. Substitute David McNiven, a replacement for Carlton, forced Bull into a great save on the hour after being put through by a wonderful ball from Michael Twiss and then firing wide on the turn from eight yards out. The final 20 minutes, however, saw the Shrimps really roll up their sleeves and graft for the points as Aldershot laid siege to the Morecambe goal.

John Grant headed a Darren Barnard cross narrowly wide of the left-hand post before Drench saved well from Barnard's long-range effort. The Morecambe keeper then produced a fine double block to turn away a Joel Grant effort and then Dave Lee's follow up. John Grant then fired wide again from the edge of the area. With five minutes to go, central defender Andy Edwards saw a header from Lee's corner scrambled off the line by Michael Howard and David Perkins when he perhaps should have scored. Two minutes from time Adam Yates diverted a goalbound Harding shot for a corner as the Shrimps held on for perhaps their best win of the Nationwide Conference campaign so far.

SAMMY McIlroy was delighted with how his side dealt with Aldershot on Saturday, especially with Danny Carlton's injury adding to the club's injury list.

He said: "At the end of the day, the squad really battled. They were the most physical side we have come up against and it worried me. But it was all hands to the pump and we did really well to come away with a goal. I said after the game that was the first bit of luck we have had, we were due a bit. Ged Brannan and Chris Blackburn were outstanding. Defensively we were very solid and Steven Drench made a couple of good saves when needed. Every clean sheet is good but when you think about it, take away the Crawley goals and we have not conceded that many – and the ones we are conceding are often from mistakes." The win keeps the Shrimps in touch with the sides who look to be among the potential play-off contenders. McIlroy said: "All of a sudden we are three points off fourth place – and we know we can still do better. It is a marathon not a sprint, we are just sitting in there with the pack, which I always said was where we wanted to be."

Morecambe: Drench 8, Yates 8, Howard 9, Brannan 8, Blackburn 8, Rigoglioso 8 (Meadowcroft 90), Stanley 8, McLachlan 8, Perkins 8, Twiss 8, Carlton 7 (McNiven 23). Unused subs: Shaw, Smith, Davies. Booked: Perkins.

Aldershot Town: Bull, Edwards, Osano, Winfield, Barnard, Lee, Harding, Molesley (Smith 63), Williams (Joel Grant 57), John Grant, Gayle. Unused subs: Wells, Ridgway. Booked: Osano, Winfield.

Referee: S P Beck.
Attendance: 2,394.
Man of the match: **Michael Howard.**

28th October 2007

Moor Green 1 Morecambe 2

(English 60) (McNiven 48, Stanley 90)

MORECAMBE have been involved in some dramatic FA Cup ties over the years and this one was no different as a last-gasp winner earned the Shrimps a place in the first round proper of this year's competition.

Craig Stanley was the hero with a well taken goal three minutes into injury time. The drama was even more intense as Moor Green had a great opportunity to win the tie themselves in the final minute of normal time.

As if to emphasise the thin line between success and failure in football, Stanley was almost the Shrimps' villain as he gave away a soft free-kick on the left. From Darren Middleton's deadball Andrew Penny headed over from close range when he should have scored. With the clock ticking down, play moved to the other end of the park. Penny then failed to clear the danger, giving Adriano Rigoglioso the chance to cross for Stanley who finished superbly at the far post much to the delight of the Shrimps' travelling support.

Although a classic cup finish the game will hardly linger long in the memory.

Morecambe enjoyed the greater share of the possession for the vast majority of the game but a stoic defence gave them few clear chances. The first half saw little goalmouth action with the Shrimps being forced to shoot from distance. Stanley was the first to threaten with a well-struck shot from the edge of the area on 18 minutes which was well blocked by home keeper Daniel Lewis. Lewis was then largely a spectator until Adam Yates tried a speculative effort five minutes from the break. Steven Drench was similarly untroubled with his only threat when Middleton volleyed into the side netting on eight minutes. The keeper was grateful though to see David Morrison loft a long-range effort over the bar after a poor clearance from the stopper. The game came to life in the second half as the Shrimps opened the scoring three minutes after the break. Michael Twiss produced the first moment of true quality in the game with a storming run from just inside the Moor Green half. After brushing off several would-be challengers, he delivered the perfect low cross from the byline which was met at the back post by David McNiven.

When Rigoglioso forced Lewis into a neat save a few minutes later the Shrimps looked well on top. But then the home side raised their game and were rewarded with a shock

> *"At the moment we are getting better results away than we are at home. We are going to have to try and put that to bed – it is down to us."*
>
> ***Sammy McIlroy***

equaliser. A Middleton cross from the left skimmed off the head of Chris Blackburn and Junior English dived in at the far post to head past Drench from close range. Buoyed by this the home side went on to enjoy the greater share of the possession without really threatening until that telling final-minute Penny miss.

In the end it was Stanley who had the final word as the Shrimps secured a first round home tie with Kidderminster Harriers.

Morecambe: Drench 7, Yates 7, Howard 7, Brannan 7, Blackburn 7, Rigoglioso 7, Stanley 7, McLachlan 7 (Smith 39), Hunter 7 (Curtis 71), Twiss 8, McNiven 7 (Shaw 76). Unused subs: Davies, Meadowcroft. Booked: Blackburn, Stanley.
Moor Green: Lewis, Midworth, Follett, Saunders, Penny, Fleming (Anderson 83), Morrison, Middleton, Davidson (Moore 76), English (Faulds 76), Trianer. Unused subs: Bridgwater, Scott. Booked: Fleming.

Referee: R Fletcher.
Attendance: 2,394
Man of the match: **Michael Twiss.**

Garry Hunter.

4th November 2006

Morecambe 1 Gravesend and Northfleet 0

(R Smith 42 og)

FOR the second Conference game in succession, Morecambe picked up a valuable three points thanks to a bizarre own goal.

A fortnight previously Curtis Osanu had given the Shrimps victory at Aldershot with a header past his own keeper. Gravesend defender Ross Smith followed suit with a similarly strange effort. Both goals came just before the break and both proved to be the vital moments of tight games. There were few present who could understand Smith's actions as he headed a bouncing ball past Lance Cronin after the Fleet keeper had fumbled an Adriano Rigoglioso corner. There was even a small silence before the Shrimps' fans in the North Stand had realised what had happened and were able to cheer. Boss Sammy McIlroy was the first to admit the goal was a stroke of luck and 'long may it continue' was his opinion.

Overall this was a pre-Bonfire night game that produced few fireworks.

With the Morecambe defence looking as strong as it has all season, led superbly by the returning Jim Bentley, the Conference's top scorer Charlie MacDonald was rarely given a sniff of goal. In the end, he managed to work himself two openings but both shots from the edge of the area failed to trouble Steven Drench.

Gravesend's best moments came after the introduction of tricky substitute Jon Keeling. The former Canvey Island man attacked the full-backs and produced some dangerous crosses which fortunately came to nothing. At the other end, Cronin made up for his earlier error with the goal with a smart second-half save at his near post from Wayne Curtis before another good block in injury time from newcomer Conal Platt. The former Liverpool trainee, who has been given the opportunity to show what he can do, came on for the last few minutes. He showed a superb turn of pace to beat his marker and forge the opening and should have earned a penalty after being fouled in the area by James Smith.

Morecambe's best moments came from dead-ball situations, particularly corners.

Michael Twiss' right-wing inswingers caused mayhem in the Gravesend defence on several occasions and the Fleet were fortunate not to concede more own goals.

Left-back Sacha Opinel volleyed one corner inches over his own crossbar and James Smith came close to diverting a Garry Thompson cross into the top right corner of his own net. Morecambe's main threat came from Curtis in the second half after he was moved up front. As well as forcing Cronin into a neat save, he drilled a fierce shot inches past the left-hand post after breaking free of a flat-looking defence.

In the end, the Shrimps took the three points. No-one would deny they had some luck along the way and all were hoping for similar in the forthcoming FA Cup clash with Kidderminster.

"The league is the priority but it's nice to have a bit of glory in the cup for the fans, players and directors. The cup brings the fans out. We got a result on Saturday which we needed at home. Our away form has been superb but at the end of the day we want Christie Park to be a fortress like it was last year."

Sammy McIlroy

Morecambe: Drench 7, Yates 7, Howard 7, Bentley 8, Blackburn 7, Thompson 7 (Platt 89), Stanley 7, Perkins 7, Curtis 7, Rigoglioso 7 (McLachlan 82), Twiss 7. Unused subs: Davies, Brannan, McNiven. Booked: Bentley, Stanley.

Gravesend and Northfleet: Cronin, Hawkins, Opinel (Keeling 75), Long (Coleman 87), J Smith, Slatter, Quinn, Sodje, Ricketts (Ekoku 89), MacDonald, R Smith. Unused subs: Moore, Mott.

Referee: M Oliver.
Attendance: 1,429.
Man of the match: **Jim Bentley.**

Wayne Curtis and Jim Bentley celebrate the only goal.

11th November 2006

Morecambe 2 Kidderminster Harriers 1

(Curtis 42pen, Twiss 74) (Hurren 88)

MORECAMBE moved one step closer to another taste of FA Cup glory with this excellent victory over their Conference rivals at a windswept Christie Park.

The Shrimps secured a second round tie at Paul Sturrock's Swindon Town with an excellent display in atrocious conditions. In driving rain and swirling winds Morecambe ironically played some of their best football for some time. Adriano Rigoglioso was at the hub of most of the attacking moves and seemed to be finding the type of form that led to his move to Doncaster a few years ago. The midfield of David Perkins and Fraser McLachlan seemed to be everywhere. With Garry Thompson and the forever-improving Adam Yates linking up superbly on the right, the Shrimps certainly looked a more dangerous attacking force.

But, as with most cup ties, they certainly didn't have it all their own way.

Their hearts were very much in their mouths when Harriers striker Andy White went down after a challenge from Steven Drench on 19 minutes and when Gavin Hurren pulled a goal back a minute from time.

Although Harriers will argue that case for the penalty strongly, overall few could argue against the result. Rigoglioso made his presence felt as early as the third minute when he played in Wayne Curtis with a delightful throughball. It forced a neat block from Harriers keeper Scott Bevan who raced out of his area to save with his chest.

Bevan did well again to superbly tip away a well-struck Rigoglioso free-kick on 25 minutes before defenders Stuart Whitehead and Jeff Kenna made vital clearances as the Shrimps threatened to make the breakthrough.

Morecambe were finally rewarded for their efforts three minutes from the break when Bevan brought down Garry Thompson as he raced on to a long ball.

After a lengthy delay while the referee dealt with the visitors' complaints, Curtis made no mistake with a well-struck spot-kick. The visitors never really recovered their composure as Morecambe dominated the second half. On 49 minutes, Bevan was forced to tip away a viciously curling cross from Michael Twiss that was heading for the top corner. He then went on to make equally good stops from Thompson and McLachlan as Morecambe played some fine flowing football. Rigoglioso then fired inches wide before Morecambe were rewarded for their efforts by a second goal 16 minutes from time. Twiss latched onto a Thompson cross to fire past Bevan's right hand with a sweetly-hit strike that gave the keeper no chance.

To their credit, Kidderminster hit back strongly with Russell Penn volleying over from close range after a right-wing corner. Later Hurren connected with Kenna's free-kick at the far post to give them scent of a comeback.

David McNiven

Morecambe: Drench 7, Yates 7, Howard 7, Bentley 7, Blackburn 7, Thompson 7, McLachlan 7, Perkins 7, Twiss 7, Rigoglioso 8, Curtis 7. Unused subs: Davies, Platt, Hunter, Brannan, McNiven.
Kidderminster Harriers: Bevan, Kenna, Blackwood, Whitehead, Creighton, Hurren, Penn, Smikle (Reynolds 77), Nelthorpe (McGrath 64), White (Taylor 81), Christie. Unused subs: Taylor, Howarth. Booked: Bevan, Blackwood.

Referee: D Richardson.
Attendance: 1,673.
Man of the match: **Adriano Rigoglioso.**

TWO of Morecambe's summer signings are in the England U23 National Game squad to face Holland in the European Challenge Trophy on November 29. Adam Yates and Craig Stanley were selected as was Danny Carlton, who is injured.

Sammy McIlroy said: "They thoroughly deserve it. When you bring in a player, sometimes you pull out a plum or you get egg on your face – when I saw Adam Yates, I knew there was a player there while Craig Stanley has been fantastic."

Four minutes of added time only served to add to the nerves of the Morecambe faithful but the Shrimps held on to keep the dream alive.

18th November 2006

Cambridge United 1 Morecambe 3

(Carey-Bertram 90 pen) (Twiss 13, 65, Curtis 58)

MORECAMBE boss Sammy McIlroy could pay goal ace Michael Twiss no higher compliment than to compare him to the late Ferenc Puskas.

After seeing Twiss score two stunning goals to help the Shrimps to their fourth league victory in the last five games, a delighted McIlroy was quick to pile on the praise. He said: "In a week where the man with the great left foot died it was perhaps apt to see Twissy scoring two goals of such quality. They were unbelievable strikes and helped us to another important victory."

It is a run of form that has convinced skipper Jim Bentley that the Shrimps can challenge for honours this season. He said: "Things are going really well at the minute and we are playing some great stuff. The spirit now is probably the best I have known it in my time here and I think that is showing now on the pitch. Everybody is fighting for everybody else, the football is really coming together and when you have someone who can score goals like Twissy, you must feel as though you have a chance of success."

The Cambridge radio phone-in at the end of the game was full of home fans praising Morecambe for their performance and it was clear to see why. Although there were excellent performances all over the park, it was Twiss' goals that would have been the talking point for the travelling Morecambe fans. He put the Shrimps ahead in the 13th minute with his eighth league goal of the season. After sharing a neat one-two with Adriano Rigoglioso on the edge of the box, he drilled a shot past Paul Crichton into the roof of the net from eight yards out. But if that was good, his second was even better. After collecting the ball 30 yards out, he let fly with a stunning strike that whistled into the top left-hand corner of the stranded Crichton's goal. Twiss was a constant threat and came close on two further occasions after superb runs.

One ended with a curling shot, which landed on top of the crossbar, and the other a strike, which curled inches wide of the left-hand post.

In between his efforts, Wayne Curtis added to his tally for the season with a glancing header from Rigoglioso's cross that dipped under the crossbar. Rigoglioso was only denied a goal himself by a fine Crichton save from a well-struck free-kick.

The Shrimps always looked in charge and Cambridge were only able to produce rare moments of threat. Former Crawley midfielder Danny Brown volleyed wide from the edge of the area in the second minute. Richie Hanlon and Michael Gash both forced

> *"Those two goals, if you saw them in the Premiership we would still be talking about them. Gary Lineker and Alan Hansen would be going on about them for ages. They were unreal and they were the icing on the cake. When he hits them, they stay hit. Let's just hope he keeps going. Him and the team are on a roll, it is not just individual performances."*
>
> ***Sammy McIlroy***

Drench into neat saves with similar efforts. The only blip on the afternoon came when the home side were awarded a penalty three minutes into injury time. Michael Morrison went over in the box after a Blackburn challenge and former Hereford striker Danny Carey-Bartram sent Drench the wrong way.

Morecambe: Drench 7, Yates 7, Howard 7 (Brannan 88), Bentley 7, Blackburn 7, Thompson 7, Stanley 7 (McLachlan 83), Perkins 7, Twiss 9, Rigoglioso 8, Curtis 7. Unused subs: Davies, McNiven.
Cambridge United: Crichton, Bloomer, Duncan, Morrison, Jaszczun, Bridges (Wooleaston 68), Brown, Hanlon, Pitt, Richardson, (Carey-Bertram 68), Gash. Unused subs: Peters, Marum. Booked: Morrison, Duncan, Brown, Jaszczun, Gash.

Referee: S Tomlinson.
Attendance: 3,142.
Man of the match: **Michael Twiss.**

Adriano Rigoglioso.

25th November 2006

Morecambe 1 Forest Green Rovers 1

(Thompson 13) (Robinson 28)

IT was almost inevitable that one day Jim Harvey would return to Christie Park and in some way foil his former side's ambitions.

The former Shrimps boss was back on his old stomping ground for the first time since his summer sacking. He made his point in more ways than one as he was clearly overjoyed to see his new Forest Green side come away with a draw. At the final whistle, he punched the air with delight and hugged the majority of his players. The customary handshake with new boss Sammy McIlroy was forgotten however, leaving a slightly and unnecessary sour taste to the afternoon.

Craig Stanley breaks into the box.

Since taking over from Gary Owers a month into the new season, Harvey has turned Forest Green into a very solid outfit and in truth they were worthy of their point. Morecambe were far from their recent best and lacked the cutting edge they have possessed in recent weeks. The Shrimps did however start well and were on the attack immediately. Adriano Rigoglioso forced Steve Williams into a save with less than 30 seconds on the clock and Garry Thompson shot wide of the left-hand post from distance.

The early pressure soon paid dividends as the Shrimps took the lead after just 13 minutes. The Forest Green defence, which included another former Morecambe favourite in John Hardiker, failed to clear their lines and Thompson took full advantage with a well-taken goal from an acute angle. Five minutes later, Jim Bentley had a golden opportunity to make it 2-0 but headed a Michael Twiss corner over from close range. At this stage there looked to be only one team in the game. Then Forest Green began to create a few problems. With battling midfielder Simon Clist and right winger Les Afful looking sharp, Harvey's team grew in stature. Matt Robinson drilled a shot wide of the left-hand post after a storming run took him to the edge of the Morecambe box. Later former Barnet man Clist fired a similar effort high and wide before the visitors pulled a soft goal back.

One of Morecambe's major failings this season had been their poor defending of set-pieces and it proved costly again in this game. Hardiker delivered a long throw to the near post, Darren Jones flicked on and Robinson was on hand to volley past Steven Drench from 12 yards out. The goal gave Forest Green a clear lift and they ended the half the stronger as Drench was forced to save well from Clist again and Allan Russell. Despite plenty of possession, Morecambe found it difficult to threaten although they did come close to adding a second goal four minutes after the restart.

A Rigoglioso corner was flicked on by Chris Blackburn and Bentley looked set to bundle the ball home from close range. Somehow, however, he managed to divert it over the crossbar from about three yards out. From there, both defences remained firmly on top forcing both sides to try their luck from distance, with no real success.

Craig Stanley saw two shots drift wide of the target in the closing stages and the ever busy Clist forced Drench into two further saves low down after storming runs down the centre. Afful dragged a left-foot shot wide of the left-hand post and Rigoglioso forced Williams into a neat save from a well-struck volley. New loan signing Jamie Burns looked to

Jim Harvey and Jim Bentley before kick-off.

provide an extra attacking edge and produced some neat touches. The Shrimps could still not break the visitors' defences, though, and had to settle for a draw to extend their unbeaten run to eight games.

> ***"Saturday was frustrating but, even though we didn't play particularly well we didn't lose, we were the better team and had the chances to have won comfortably."***
>
> ***Sammy McIlroy***

Morecambe: Drench 7, Yates 7, Howard 7, Bentley 7, Blackburn 8, Thompson 7 (Burns 70), Stanley 7, Perkins 7, Twiss 7, Rigoglioso 7 (Platt 70), Curtis 7. Unused subs: Davies, Brannan, McLachlan. Booked: Blackburn.
Forest Green: Williams, Lawless, Nicholson, Jones, Clist, Russell (Griffin 72), Hardiker, Preece, Afful (Meechan), Giles, Robinson. Unused subs: Beesley, Stonehouse, Harrison. Booked: Clist.

Referee: S Proctor Green.
Attendance: 1,561.
Man of the match: **Chris Blackburn.**

Sammy McIlroy and Jim Harvey on the touchline.

Harvey and McIlroy

by Glen Cooper

WHEN Forest Green Rovers travelled to play Morecambe on November 25, 2006 there was more at stake than a mere Conference three points.

Sammy McIlroy was almost half way through his first full season as The Shrimps' manager and in charge of that Saturday's opponents was his one time friend and colleague Jim Harvey.

The same Harvey, of course, who had been the architect of the modern day Morecambe Football Club set-up and who had been replaced in the close-season by McIlroy in what turned out to be pretty acrimonious circumstances.

The pair had served together as a management team at the Northern Ireland national side whose shirt they had both worn with pride and distinction in their playing days.

When Harvey suffered a heart attack during the build-up to a match the previous season it was McIlroy who was brought in to guide the team to an eventually unsuccessful Conference play-off semi-final.

The duo joined hands that night to take the applause of commiserating Morecambe fans at Hereford's Edgar Street.

Morecambe's board, steered by chairman and principle financial backer Peter McGuigan, obviously saw something in McIlroy – and assistant Mark Lillis – that they liked.

For the past couple of seasons they had expressed frustration that their ambition of League football had not been achieved. But outwardly they were still putting their faith in Harvey as the man to realise the dream.

But McIlroy's brief, temporary tenure must have shone a new light on the way forward for Morecambe and, after 12 years at the helm, Jim Harvey was summoned to the club to be told that his services were no longer required.

Morecambe didn't make an immediate announcement about his successor but few doubted that McIlroy would, at least, be offered the opportunity to make his temporary role a permanent one.

When that offer eventually materialised – and was accepted – Harvey felt betrayed and the friendship ended there and then.

McIlroy insisted he had no prior knowledge of the board's decision to sack Harvey.

But he said that his time at the club had rekindled a desire for football that had been soured during his last post when he found himself at odds with officials at Stockport County.

Evidence of the rift between the two men, who can (with McGuigan and benefactor Mr J.B. Christie) justifiably claim to have had the most significant impact on Morecambe FC in its entire history, was evident in that November fixture (and again at Forest Green at the end of February).

Harvey's clenched fist salute to the visiting directors after a hard-fought draw at Christie Park was mirrored by McIlroy's air-punching celebration following a comfortable 3-1 win at The New Lawn.

Contact between the two during both games was 'cool' to say the least.

In what turned out to be the most important season in The Shrimps' history the 'Harvey factor' was perhaps the one sad memory.

Here was a manager who had taken a grip of the club from its very roots, bringing a completely new regime from the moment he stepped into the top job in 1994, succeeding Leighton James, whom he had worked under as assistant.

Harvey imposed a holistic approach at Morecambe, bringing youth teams – including products of a revolutionary new academy system – into the Morecambe family.

All the age-group sides were coached in the image of the first team making the progression from one to the other as smooth and successful as possible.

Performances were attractive and flowing as Harvey took Morecambe into the upper echelon of non-league football and, particularly at home, many games were just a joy to watch.

This included those played by a young Reserves side which itself went on to unprecedented levels of achievement in its own circles.

He hadn't quite been able to take the first team into the League in a quick enough timescale for the club's ambitious board but his legacy is, to this day, still evident throughout the club.

Fans – of whatever prior opinion about Harvey's tenure – wanted to honour their former boss at the FGR game, while at the same time showing loyalty to the new man in charge. It was a slightly awkward atmosphere.

Throughout the season which finally saw Morecambe promoted to the Promised Land there was a noticeable change of style and attitude.

The team, with experienced additions like Neil Sorvel and Danny Adams, became more resolute – clawing back deficits in games that previously would have been beyond redemption and maintaining a record of never losing games in which they scored the first goal.

The away form improved significantly with McIlroy adopting a more offensive attitude on the team's travels.

The flipside of that was that 'Fortress Christie' as it had become known under Harvey, was less impenetrable and the football at home was less flamboyant, all of which even had some fans bemoaning the managerial switch early in this most momentous of seasons.

But, as witnessed by what transpired to be the biggest milestone event in the club's history to date, it all came out right in the end.

Interesting, though, that the two Wembley goalscoring heroes (Thompson and Carlton) were both Harvey protégés – both products of the academy which was at the very heart of Morecambe's modern day success.

What Harvey started, McIlroy finished and the fans of Morecambe Football Club are forever grateful to them both.

2nd December 2006

Swindon Town 1 Morecambe 0

(Roberts 89 pen)

MORECAMBE boss Sammy McIlroy said he was full of praise for his players after they were cruelly knocked out of the FA Cup at Swindon.

McIlroy said he was 'devastated for his players' to see his side crash out to a last-minute Christian Roberts penalty. They had been dominating the game against a side currently sitting second in League Two. Said the Shrimps' boss: "My lads were heroes, every one of them and I can't believe they lost the game. They put on a magnificent display and I'm devastated for each and every one of them. They have made me and the Morecambe fans proud and we simply didn't get what we deserved. The fact their goalkeeper was man of the match said it all for me."

Last season the Shrimps were knocked out of the LDV Vans Trophy in injury time by Bradford City after being by far the better team and who can forget those late hammer blows at Oxford United and Emley? In the end, the game was decided by a penalty after Michael Howard caught Lukas Jutkiewicz in the box right at the death. When Roberts, who wasn't given an inch all afternoon by the superb Jim Bentley and Ged Brannan, sent Steven Drench the wrong way from the spot there was a collective huge sigh of relief from the home fans. The only downside to the day was the fact that the Shrimps could not turn pressure into goals.

"You have to score when you are on top and we didn't do that at the end of the day," said McIlroy. "Their goalkeeper made some great saves and we came close on numerous occasions but we just couldn't get the goal our play deserved."

Morecambe's football was excellent throughout and they used the space superbly, dominating in midfield and shackling what was supposedly the best front pairing in Division 2. The Shrimps may have

Dear Mr McIlroy,
I just wanted to put pen to paper to say what a credit you and your team were to yourselves and the Conference.

After watching you give us the hardest 90 minutes we've had this season, the sooner you are promoted to the Football league the better. Secondly, your supporters were fantastic outsinging us for 90 minutes. I went home on Saturday with my 14-year-old son knowing you deserved something out of that game.

Good luck for the rest of the season, and we hope to see you at the County Ground next season.

Andy Titcombe
Swindon.

been the underdogs but they were never overawed. Had it not been for Swindon's former Crawley keeper Phil Smith, the Shrimps would have at least been in the hat for the third round draw. Smith was forced to make a string of fine saves in the first half, the best being a full-length dive to tip away a superb Adriano Rigoglioso free-kick.

Moments later, he broke the Shrimps' hearts again with a stunning reflex save to punch away a wicked deflection from Curtis Weston that was heading for the goal.

The always-dangerous Rigoglioso came close again on 37 minutes with a well-executed lob from 25 yards. Although it beat Smith it unfortunately floated inches wide of the left-hand post. Moments later, the Shrimps were on the attack again as Craig Stanley burst through from midfield. However he could only lob the ball into Smith's grateful hands instead of finding the unmarked Michael Twiss in the six-yard box.

"We've seen what this side is capable of – if we'd got the goals we should have done it would have been just about the perfect performance." As well as praising the players, McIlroy paid tribute to the backing his men received from the hundreds of travelling Morecambe fans. "That support was absolutely magnificent and, with the team giving them everything they could in return I was hugely proud to be Morecambe manager. It certainly should give my players a real boost for the rest of the season."

Sammy McIlroy

Morecambe: Drench 8, Yates 8, Howard 8 (Platt 90), Bentley 8, Brannan 8, Thompson 8 (Burns 88), Stanley 8, Perkins 8, Twiss 8, Rigoglioso 9, McLachlan 8. Unused subs: Davies, Smith, McNiven. Booked: Howard, Bentley, Brannan.
Swindon Town: P Smith, J Smith, Nicholas, Williams, Ifill, Whalley (Pook 48), Brown (Zaaboub 73), Shakes (Lutkiewicz 76), Weston, Roberts, Peacock. Unused subs: Stewart, Brownlie. Booked: Ifill, Roberts, Weston.

Referee: P Taylor.
Attendance: 5,942.
Man of the match: **Adriano Rigoglioso.**

After being second best for the first half Swindon upped the tempo at the start of the second period. They finally tested Steven Drench with a shot from distance on 52 minutes. Shakes threatened again with a well-struck drive that forced the Morecambe keeper into an excellent save on the hour. From there the Morecambe defence dealt admirably with everything Swindon could throw at them. McIlroy's side continued to look the more dangerous going forward with Rigoglioso coming desperately close again. With a free-kick he clipped the outside of the left-hand post and Garry Thompson fired just wide after a great run. The best effort of the second period, however, fell to Michael Twiss who set off on one of his mazy runs at the heart of the defence before drilling a left-foot shot just off target. With time running out and Swindon looking relieved at the draw, they went on to snatch the tie in the most dramatic fashion. It was a heart-breaking moment for everyone involved with Morecambe – and one they simply didn't deserve.

9th December 2006

Morecambe 1 Stafford Rangers 0

(Thompson 40)

MORECAMBE moved closer to the play-off zone with a hard-earned victory over a stubborn Stafford Rangers at Christie Park.

The Shrimps extended their unbeaten run to seven Conference games thanks to a superb strike from Garry Thompson and climbed to sixth in the table. It is a position boss Sammy McIlroy says he is delighted with going into the busy, vital Christmas period. He said: "This is a good place to be at this time of the season. We are very much in there and I know we can get better and although there is a long way to go there is no reason why we can't maintain our push all the way now."

Adriano Rigoglioso challenges for the ball.

GED Brannan was weighing up an offer to leave Morecambe and move to Southport as assistant manager. Haig Avenue boss Paul Cook has approached Brannan about a move, but Sammy McIlroy is hoping he will stay at Christie Park.
McIlroy said: "I have told Ged how I feel and it is going to be his decision. He has been a great pro for me and is a fantastic lad to work with."

The win was Morecambe's fifth 1-0 victory this season, the sign of a solid, focused team and although some fans would like to see teams killed off, past history shows the team who concedes the fewest goals often wins the Conference. Thompson's winner was undoubtedly the highlight of the game. After an excellent performance up front at Swindon, he started in the striker's role again. He caused the Stafford defence all sorts of problems, culminating in his sweet left-foot strike past Danny Alcock on 40 minutes. There had been other chances to take the lead before that with Thompson himself wasting a good opportunity after just nine minutes, when he headed Michael Howard's excellent left wing cross straight at the grateful Alcock from close range.

At the start of the second half, he raced onto a cross from Craig Stanley which drifted just over the bar. Later, after a storming run which started from inside his own half, he was only denied a second goal by a great covering tackle from Stafford full-back Nathan Talbott. Jim Bentley was also guilty of wasting a gilt-edged opening when he somehow missed the target from three yards at the far post after Alcock had failed to collect an inswinging Rigoglioso corner. Rigoglioso himself then came close with a volley on the turn.

Stafford came into the game on the back of a good run themselves and Phil Robinson's well-organised side certainly felt a little aggrieved at not having taken something from the game. They had the ball in the back of the net in the ninth minute when Chris Basham was adjudged offside as he slotted home the rebound after Steven Drench had saved sharply from Guy Madjo's deflected header. Madjo came close again when he weaved his way into the box and drilled a shot past Drench but against the foot of the right-hand post. The Shrimps then enjoyed a long spell on top but Stafford finished the game strongly. With 20 minutes to go, Craig Lovatt forced Drench into a smart save with a shot from distance before the Morecambe keeper did well again to race from his goal and block at the feet of Basham.

Then came two incidents which infuriated Rangers' boss Robinson. Firstly a cross from Basham seemed to connect with Bentley's arm. Secondly Madjo went down in the box in injury time after a mix-up between Chris Blackburn and Drench almost allowed him a free run on goal. The visitors then wasted a clear opening themselves on 83 minutes. Basham's cross was met by

Adam Yates crosses from the right.

substitute Danny Edwards at the far post but he headed wide of the target when he looked sure to score. It proved to be an important let-off for the Shrimps who were happy to collect the points taking them into the Christmas period in a healthy position.

"We are on a great run of form, the performances are getting better and the squad is getting stronger."

Sammy McIlroy

Morecambe: Drench 7, Yates 7, Howard 7, Bentley 7, Blackburn 7, Stanley 7, Perkins 7, McLachlan 7, Twiss 7, Rigoglioso 7 (Burns 76), Thompson 8. Unused subs: Davies, Brannan, Curtis, McNiven.
Stafford Rangers: Alcock, Sutton, Talbott, Daniel, Murray, Basham, Lovatt, Olaoye, Murphy, Madjo, Grayson (Edwards 73). Unused subs: Street, Gibson, Quailey, Barlow. Booked: Murphy.

Referee: C Harwood.
Attendance: 1,373.
Man of the match: **Garry Thompson.**

16th December 2006

Morecambe 2 York City 1

(Twiss 56, Curtis 60) (Donaldson 79)

MICHAEL Twiss once again proved just how vital he is to Morecambe's promotion hopes with another starring role in this FA Trophy victory.

Twiss scored one and played a major part in the second as the Shrimps overcame the York side. It was the sort of display that has led clubs such as Accrington Stanley to openly state their desire to sign the former Manchester United man in the January transfer window.

His first goal came straight from a corner as his wicked inswinging effort beat the York keeper and defenders on the line. But the second came from nowhere after a typical trademark Twiss run. Michael Howard broke up a York attack and the winger took control. He ran at the York defence with pace and after dipping his shoulder one way and going

MORECAMBE FC directors gave the club's fans the Christmas present they'd been longing for when they announced a new contract had been agreed with star-striker, Michael Twiss. Twiss met with officials yesterday, Tuesday, to put pen to paper on a three-year extension to his current contract which would have expired at the end of this season. The deal puts an end to speculation linking the club's top-scorer – and one of the top players in non-league football – with several Football League sides.

It will keep him at Christie Park until 2010, by which time he will be 32.

Manager Sammy McIlroy said: "I am delighted to have re-signed such an influential player. Michael is a quality act and proven goal-scorer and I am sure this signing will send out the right message to the other members of the squad that we are negotiating with at present and to all Morecambe supporters.

"It sends out a very positive message that a player of Michael's quality wants to commit his long-term future to Morecambe."

Twiss said: "I am more than happy to sign and commit my future to Morecambe Football Club. I love it here, the players, the officials, staff, management and fans, everything about the club.

"I am enjoying my football and want to be a part of the progress of this football club."

the other he let fly with a stinging shot. It beat Tom Evans but came back off the post before being bundled home by the onrushing Wayne Curtis.

It was the ability of Twiss to do something out of the ordinary that proved the difference on the day and that is why the Shrimps were so keen to extend his contract as soon as possible.

Twiss brought a drab game to life 10 minutes into the second half when his vicious corner somehow made its way past a crowd of bodies and over the line. Four minutes later he came to the fore again as he played a major role in the Shrimps' second, his shot hitting a post before Curtis tapped in. Ironically the Shrimps' goal surge came just moments after York had spurned a golden opportunity. Craig Farrell lobbed the ball over Steven Drench and the crossbar after being put through by Clayton Donaldson on 52 minutes.

York did pull one back with 11 minutes to go when Donaldson curled a fine effort past Drench's right hand to set up a nervous finale for the Shrimps. Manny Panther and Steve Bowey both sent shots wide in the closing stages and Bowey, a long-time Morecambe target in years gone by, thought he should have had a penalty after a dramatic last-minute tumble in the box. The Shrimps held their nerve though to earn a second round tie at home to Mangotsfield United on January 13. For the first 45 minutes, it was hard to believe that both these sides were promotion candidates.

Both were taking the generous Christmas spirit a bit too far as they gave the ball to their opponents all too easily. Both sides had stressed that the Conference was their priority this season and it seemed to show as the first period seemed to drag on for eternity.

Morecambe had the majority of the possession but it was York who had the better chances with Panther forcing Drench into a fine save low to his right and former Carlisle striker Farrell curling a right-foot effort inches past the left-hand post.

The Shrimps began sharply with Howard testing Evans in the fourth minute before Garry Thompson and Twiss both ballooned well-struck volleys well over the bar.

Twiss was to find the target in the second half, however, to see the Shrimps through to the next stage and give them a confidence boost ahead of the Conference meeting between the two sides on New Year's Day.

Morecambe: Drench 8, Yates 7, Howard 7, Bentley 7, Blackburn 7, Stanley 7, Perkins 7, McLachlan 7 (Platt 54), Twiss 9, Rigoglioso 7 (Burns 74), Thompson 7 (Curtis 73). Unused subs: Davies, Brannan.
York City: Evans, Lloyd, Peat, McGurk, Goodliffe, Bowey, Panther, McMahon (Craddock 69), Woolford (Greenwood 74), Donaldson (Webster 82), Farrell. Unused subs: Dudgeon, Reid. Booked: Bowey.

Referee: C Harwood.
Attendance: 1,070.
Man of the match: **Michael Twiss.**

26th December 2006

Southport 1 Morecambe 2

(Baker 36) (Blackburn 77, Yates 80)

TEN-MAN Morecambe came back from the dead to steal three points in this Conference Christmas cracker. Two late goals from defenders Chris Blackburn and Adam Yates, his first for the club, gave the Shrimps the victory few would have thought possible at half-time.

When the teams changed ends the Shrimps were a goal down and also reduced to 10 men after David Perkins had lunged clumsily at goal-scorer Carl Baker. His sending off looked set to further weaken a Shrimps side that were well below par and second best to a Southport team that played far better than their lowly league position suggested.

Apart from a brief early spell of dominance the Shrimps looked a shadow of the team that had risen to the verges of a play-off sport in recent weeks. It was the Sandgrounders, second to bottom at the start of play, who looked the more fluent side.

Southport had come close to opening the scoring on several occasions in the first half hour with Dino Maamria hitting the foot of the right hand post with a neat shot on the turn and Baker, the best player on the pitch at this stage, twice forcing Steven Drench into neat blocks. On-loan Blackpool midfielder Ciaran Donnelly also had a goal disallowed for offside. Drench proved the Shrimps' saviour again with a superb save to tip away a close range Maamria header before the home side took a deserved lead. The goal came from a rare Jim Bentley mistake. He lost possession to Baker 30 yards out and the Southport midfielder ran on goal and produced the calmest of finishes to loft the ball over the advancing Morecambe keeper.

After losing Perkins, the Shrimps fared little better at the start of the second half as Southport piled on the pressure. They had two more goals disallowed for offside with Maamria and Michael Powell both having efforts ruled out. They also managed to hit the woodwork again as Powell slammed a volley against the crossbar from close range with Drench well beaten. The Morecambe keeper had earlier made a stunning save to deny Powell from a similar situation and also saved well again from Baker as Southport pushed for a second goal.

Perhaps buoyed by Southport's inability to kill off the game Morecambe finally began to raise their game after an hour. Adriano Rigoglioso forced Francois Dubourdeau into a flying save with a right wing cross and Craig Stanley drilled a rasping shot from the edge of the area just over the bar. Michael Twiss then forced Dubourdeau into a flying save from a looping header which was destined for the top left hand corner.

The Shrimps could have been given a boost with 15 minutes to go. There was another case for a red card when Southport's Kevin Lee brought down Wayne Curtis. This time though referee Cummins only showed a yellow.

The Shrimps' pressure then paid dividends with two goals in quick succession to stun the home side. With 11 minutes to go Chris Blackburn hammered home Bentley's knock down from the edge of the area, bringing his side back into the game.

The celebrations had barely died down when the Shrimps then added a swift second. Adam Yates collected the ball on the right-hand side and delivered a cross into the area which somehow flew past everyone and into the bottom right hand corner of the Southport goal sparking wild celebrations. There was still time for Southport to waste another glorious chance as substitute Joe Fowler headed wide from six yards on 85 minutes. He looked sure to score. In the end the Shrimps held on for what was one of their most memorable victories for some time.

Morecambe: Drench 9, Yates 7, Howard 7, Bentley 7, Blackburn 7, Stanley 7, Perkins 6, Platt 6 (Burns 70), Twiss 7, Rigoglioso 6 (McNiven 78), Curtis 6. Unused subs: Robinson, Brannan, McLachlan.
Southport: Dubourdeau, Lane, Lee, Kirkup, Rowland (Gray 86), Powell (Boyd 80), Donnelly, Hollickin (Fowler 72), Doherty, Baker, Maamria. Unused subs: Bagnall, Tait.
Booked: Lee, Maamria.
Referee: S Cummins.
Attendance: 1,804.

Man of the match: **Steven Drench.**

Carl Baker, became Morecambe's record signing when he moved from Southport.

30th December 2006

Tamworth 0 Morecambe 1

(Curtis 64)

A COOL finish from Wayne Curtis fired Morecambe into a play-off spot at the Lamb.

Curtis, taking over the striker's role due to injuries to Danny Carlton and Garry Thompson, scored the only goal of the game on 64 minutes, securing another valuable three points to help the Shrimps' promotion push.

Sammy McIlroy's side certainly deserved their victory although once again a stubborn Tamworth made things difficult. In September Tamworth piled bodies behind the ball to record the most boring of 0-0 draws at Christie Park.

In many ways it came as something of a relief when the Shrimps took the lead through the simplest of goals. Shrimps keeper Steven Drench cleared long, Michael Twiss flicked on and Curtis kept his cool to stroke the ball past the onrushing Cameron Belford.

Despite dominating the possession and playing some neat football in wet and windy conditions the Shrimps found clear cut chances hard to come by. Garry Hunter, back in the side after a two month injury lay-off, fired wide in the second minute before skewing a far post volley well wide.

Jamie Burns, making his first start for the Shrimps, shot wide of the right hand post on 18 minutes, and busy midfielder Craig Stanley dragged a right foot effort wide from the edge of the box. As Morecambe pushed forward, Tamworth failed to test Drench in the first period but started the second sharply. The Morecambe keeper reacted sharply to dive on to a loose ball in the six yard box after a goalmouth scramble and Chris Blackburn made a vital clearance from a dangerous Darryl Taylor cross. The Shrimps soon took control again with Hunter seeing an attempted lob blocked by Belford before Curtis struck the winning goal.

Tamworth fought back with John McGrath shooting straight at Drench and Steve Burton firing wide from the edge of the area. In the final minute Drench produced his best save of the afternoon to hold onto a well struck shot from Matt Williams that skimmed across the greasy surface helping the Shrimps hold onto another welcome three points.

Morecambe: Drench 7, Yates 7, Howard 7, Bentley 7, Blackburn 7, Stanley 8, Hunter 7 (Brannan 89), McLachlan 7, Burns 7 (Rigoglioso 69), Twiss 7, Curtis 7. Unused subs: Robinson, McNiven, Walmsley. **Tamworth:** C Belford, Smith, Burton, Taylor (Stevenson 89), Kemp, Weaver, McGrath, Kendrick (Storer 24), Laight, Atieno (Williams 81), Heslop. Unused subs: Law, L Belford. Booked: Storer.

Referee: J Waugh.
Attendance: 1,029.
Man of the match: **Craig Stanley.**

1st January 2007

Morecambe 1 York City 3

(Blackburn 75) (Donaldson 44, Farrell 47, Bowey 60)

MORECAMBE'S recent impressive run of form came to an end with this New Year's Day defeat.

The Shrimps produced a poor performance to suffer their first Conference defeat since October 7 last year and in doing so slipped back out of the Conference play-off spots. Sammy McIlroy's side were never at their best against a York team who played some neat football throughout, bossed the midfield and seemed to be a yard quicker in body and mind throughout.

Apart from a bright start when Fraser McLachlan came close to opening the scoring in the first minute with a volley that drifted just wide of the right hand post the Shrimps only started to test the visitors after they had gone 3-0 down. Chris Blackburn pulled one goal back 15 minutes from time when he headed home a Michael Twiss corner but it proved to be a mere consolation.

Substitute David McNiven, given a rare chance to show what he can do, looked lively and twice forced York keeper Tom Evans into saves from neat volleys. Wayne Curtis also tested the visitors' stopper but it was all too little too late. It was York who had the better chances in the first half. With Neal Bishop and Steve Bowie dominant in midfield they began to force a number of openings. Jim Bentley had to make a vital tackle to deny Craig Farrell from latching on to Bishop's neat through ball. Darryn Stamp missed a golden opportunity when he headed wide from close range. Steven Drench then had to save well to his left from a neat Bowie curler. The Morecambe keeper thwarted Stamp again when he raced from his line to claim another testing through ball.

Drench was finally beaten a minute before the break as the Conference's top scorer Clayton Donaldson raced in to bundle the ball home from close range. The Morecambe keeper could only parry a Bowie strike that took a wicked kick off the surface. The Shrimps then conceded a sloppy second two minutes after the break when York countered quickly and Farrell curled home

York get on the scoresheet.

Chris Blackburn nods home but it was only a consolation.

MORECAMBE boss Sammy McIlroy will have a new face in his squad for Saturday's trip to Oxford United. Jason Walker, who has played in the Scottish League with Morton, has been training with the Shrimps squad and with the opening of the transfer window on New Year's Day, can now play. McIlroy said: "He will be a good addition to the squad and I am looking forward to getting him on board."

Manny Panther's lay-off from the edge of the area with a right-foot shot that beat Drench to his left.

Morecambe tried to come back with Craig Stanley shooting wide from 25 yards and Wayne Curtis forcing Tom Evans into a neat save with his trailing leg.

Morecambe: Drench 6, Yates 7, Howard 6, Bentley 6, Blackburn 7, Stanley 7, Hunter 6 (Walmsley 66), McLachlan 6 (Brannan 66), Twiss 7, Rigoglioso 6 (McNiven 48), Curtis 6. Unused subs: Robinson, Lloyd.

York City: Evans, Craddock, Goodliffe, Parslow, Lloyd, Bishop, Bowie (McMahon 83), Panther, Donaldson, Farrell, Stamp (Woolford 90). Unused subs: Greenwood, Webster, Reid.

Referee: D Richardson

Attendance: 2,029.

Man of the match: **Adam Yates.**

But as Morecambe pushed forward York scored again. Man of the match Bowie, a long time target for the Shrimps several seasons ago, stabbed home the loose ball from 12 yards out after another right wing attack led by Farrell and Panther.

Blackburn set up a platform for a comeback but time ran out as Morecambe slipped to their first defeat in 10 Conference games.

6th January 2007

Oxford United 0 Morecambe 0

THE Shrimps secured a good point against the Conference title favourites with an excellent performance at the Kassam Stadium. Sammy McIlroy's side showed great spirit to bounce back from their New Year's Day defeat against York with a display that showed they have the resolve needed to launch a concerted play-off push this season.

The Shrimps controlled the game for long periods and often gave their opponents a lesson in possession football earning them praise from wily U's boss Jim Smith after the game.

After calling off a proposed move to Southport earlier in the week, Ged Brannan was brought into the midfield and his experience and style was evident from the off. He dictated things from the heart of the midfield along with the excellent Craig Stanley and Garry Hunter, who had his best game since returning from injury. The home side, without a win since November 25 last year, were forced to work extremely hard to maintain their unbeaten home record. They only showed their class in patches at the beginning and the end of the game.

Oxford missed a great chance to open the scoring at only seven minutes when Andy Burgess' cross was headed against the crossbar by Rob Duffy and Yemi Obudade flashed the rebound over the bar. At the other end of the game, the Shrimps had skipper Jim Bentley to thank for blocking a goal bound shot from Obudabe in injury time after Steven Drench had spilled a throughball after Duffy shot straight at the Morecambe keeper when he was given some rare space in the box.

In between those efforts, Morecambe created the better chances. David McNiven, who impressed up front, tested Turley from distance and was then inches away from converting a dangerous Adam Yates cross. The Oxford keeper then had to react sharply to stop an audacious lob from Hunter which would have crept under the crossbar. Stanley then went close with a long-range drive that flew just wide of the left-hand post before. The Shrimps then wasted a glorious chance themselves when Wayne Curtis fired over from close range when he should have done better.

The second half followed a similar pattern with Oxford starting well. Drench did

Ged Brannan will be staying at the club. He had agreed to join Paul Cook at Southport as assistant manager but that fell through when Cook was sacked.

McIlroy said: "I didn't want him to go anyway but it was Ged's decision and assistant manager's jobs don't often come up. But he is a great player to have, he is experienced and never lets you down." He added: "I want 18 players fighting for 11 places and we are getting close to that."

well to hold on to a bouncing ball in the box after Obudabe managed to make a rare break into the area. He later did well to hold on to a free-kick from the on-loan Manchester United midfielder Danny Rose. From there the Shrimps began to hold the upper hand again. Michael Twiss forced Turley into the best save of the game on 64 minutes after cutting in from the left wing and producing a stinging shot that the former Rushden and Diamonds keeper did well to punch clear. Five minutes later, Michael Howard came close to scoring a rare goal with a blistering 25-yarder that sizzled just wide.

In the closing stages, Bentley then saw a well-struck volley unfortunately strike Oxford defender Barry Quinn as it looked set for the top corner and saw the rebound tipped over by the busy Turley.

Morecambe: Drench 7, Yates 9, Howard 7, Bentley 7, Blackburn 7, Stanley 8, Hunter 7, Brannan 8, Twiss 7, Curtis 7, McNiven 7 (Rigoglioso 87). Unused subs: Davies, Meadowcroft, Walmsley, McLachlan.
Oxford United: Turley, Anaclet, Santos, Quinn, Gilchrist (Day 54), Johnson, Pettefer, Rose, Burgess, Duffy, Odudabe. Unused subs: Tardif, Dempster, Hargreaves, Brevett.

Referee: I Smedley.
Attendance: 5,489.
Man of the match: **Adam Yates.**

The day was almost spoiled at the death by Oxford's late flurry. However few would deny that the Shrimps deserved their points and showed just how much they had improved since their 3-0 defeat by the U's at Christie Park earlier in the campaign.

"I was delighted with the response after the York game and the performance at Oxford was excellent. We are right in amongst it and that is where we want to be. If we can get the majority of points out of those games, we will be in there. We have got a big month and we need everyone fighting for the cause and the fans to get behind the side. There are going to be twists and turns right to the end of the season and we have just got to take every game as it comes."

Sammy McIlroy

13th January 2007

Morecambe 5 Mangotsfield United 0

(Twiss 9, 54, Hunter 61, Howard 70, Walker 90)

ANOTHER wonder goal from Michael Twiss helped Morecambe ease into the last 16 of this year's FA Trophy.

Twiss sparked a second half goal blitz with a sensational second to finally kill off the Shrimps' Southern League opponents. Taking the ball 25 yards out on the left Twiss took a quick look up, saw keeper Steve Book off his line, and then produced a superb volley over the keeper and into the empty net. It was the latest in a string of superb goals for the Shrimps' top-scorer who took his tally for the season to 13 in all competitions.

As well as Twiss' strike the game was noticeable for Michael Howard's first Morecambe goal. The popular left-back, who is close to making 80 first team appearances for the Shrimps found the net for the first time in two seasons with a well-taken goal 20 minutes from time. Sharing a neat one-two with new signing Jason Walker he ran on goal and produced a cool finish. To cap off a professional performance from the Shrimps, former Morton striker Walker made his mark quickly with a well-taken goal in the final minute to add further gloss to the score line.

It was Twiss who gave the Shrimps a perfect start with a ninth-minute goal as he took advantage of some slack marking to drill the ball past Steve Book with his right foot.

It would have been no surprise if Morecambe supporters heard new striker Jason Walker sigh with relief when he finally made his Shrimps debut on Saturday.

The 22-year-old striker has actually been at Christie Park since July but injury and red tape have meant he couldn't pull on a shirt. Already he has started to make up for lost time, scoring after 25 minutes of his debut to round off the Shrimps' comfortable 5-0 win over Mangotsfield in the FA Trophy.

Walker said: "It was a relief to finally make my debut; I've been waiting long enough. I wanted to show the fans what I can do. Hopefully I can add something to the squad and we can get promotion which is long overdue – we should have gone up by now."

Walker turned down a new deal with Morton and brought the curtain down on six years in Scottish football having been signed by Dundee aged 16. He has played at both Ibrox and Parkhead, as well as at Hampden Park. "I got offered a new contract at Morton but I had been up there for six years and didn't want to stay any longer. I wanted to give English football a shot and see what I can do down here."

Chris Blackburn.

Morecambe: Drench 7, Yates 7, Howard 7, Brannan 7, Blackburn 7, Stanley 7 (McLachlan 65), Hunter 7 (Walker 65), Perkins 7, Curtis 7, Twiss 8, McNiven 7 (Rigoglioso 65). Unused subs: Davies, Meadowcroft.
Mangotsfield United: Book, Arndale, Allward, Warren, Price, Wilmot (Sylvester 46), Hawkins, French, Claridge, Morrisey (Cornwall 46), Lane (Cain 72). Unused subs: Shatford, Howells.

Referee: J Collin.
Attendance: 859.
Man of the match: **Michael Twiss.**

Mangotsfield then enjoyed a good period and caused the Morecambe defence problems. Dave Morrisey beat Steven Drench to an Eliot Wilmott free-kick but saw his header loop over the crossbar. The big striker was in the thick of the action again 10 minutes from the break when he was found in space at the back post but lashed a shot wide when he should have done better. A goal then could have changed the course of the game but after some strong words at half-time, the Shrimps took control in the second period.

The second half started with Morecambe upping the tempo considerably. Wayne Curtis fired a shot over the bar from close range when he looked set to score before Twiss put the Shrimps 2-0 ahead with his superb lob over Book. There was no looking back from that moment and the Shrimps added three more goals. Garry Hunter latched on to David McNiven's flick to stroke the ball home before Howard's rare gem. Walker then introduced himself to the Shrimps' supporters with a well-taken strike from Howard's lay off, helped by a neat dummy from Adriano Rigoglioso.

16th January 2007

Morecambe 5 Lancaster City 0

(Walmsley 16, 51, Walker 46, Jarvis 49, Taylor 90)

Lancashire United Co-operatives Challenge Cup quarter-final

THREE goals in the space of six second half minutes killed off Lancaster's hopes of producing a cup shock in this United Co-operative Challenge Cup quarter-final tie. Barrie Stimpson's side turned round a single goal down and showed some promising signs after a good end to the first half. Then it all went drastically wrong as the Shrimps struck three times in quick succession to kill the game off. A further goal at the death gave the game a somewhat false score line in a game watched by a good crowd.

In the end the Shrimps' quality in front of goal proved decisive. Lancaster enjoyed a good start with Leon Gierke forcing Scott Davies into a scrambling save low down to his left after trying his luck from 30 yards. Gierke then forced Davies into action again with a header from the resulting corner that the Shrimps keeper did well to hold on to. But against the run of play Morecambe took the lead and never really looked back. In their first real attack, the Shrimps went ahead when Kieran Walmsley let fly with a superb 30-yard effort that flew into the left-hand corner of Guy Roberts' net.

The Shrimps then largely controlled possession without troubling Roberts again and looked in full control until the closing minutes of the half. Neil Uberschar was unfortunate to see a goal bound shot deflected clear by a Morecambe defender's trailing leg before Neil Marshall flashed a header over from the resulting corner.

At this stage, the game was tight but within a few minutes of the restart the Shrimps had raced into a 4-0 lead. Jason Walker added a second when he raced onto a loose ball, rounded Roberts and slid the ball home. Impressive youngster Paul Jarvis went on to score a third with a header from Adriano Rigoglioso's curling cross.

When Walmsley slotted home Michael West's right-wing cross on 51 minutes the contest was over. Lancaster fought back looking for a consolation with Aaron Helliwell shooting wide. Gierke, too, came close to a consolation when he headed a dangerous Marshall cross again the post nine minutes from time. With time running out, youngster Aaron Taylor finished the scoring with a sweet finish from the edge of the box.

Morecambe: Davies 7, Leigh 8, Wisdom 8, Langford 7, Meadowcroft 7, Walmsley 7, West 7 (Baker 83), McLachlan 7, Walker 7 (Taylor 75), Rigoglioso 7 (Pickersgill 85), Jarvis 8. Subs not used: Bell, Anderson.
Lancaster City: Roberts 6, Rigby 7, Marshall 7, Love 7, Cudworth 6, Henry 6 (Connerton 75), Galley 7. Helliwell 7, Gierke 7, Uberschar 7 (Durnan 55), Williams 7 (Mulholland 17). Sub not used: Makin.

Referee: G Johnson.
Attendance: 772.

20th January 2007

Morecambe 1 Dagenham and Redbridge 1

(Thompson 27) (Benson 72)

A GOAL from Dagenham top-scorer Paul Benson robbed Morecambe of three points at a windswept Christie Park.

The Daggers' top-scorer struck 18 minutes from time to earn a share of the spoils after Garry Thompson scored a neat first-half goal on his return after a hamstring injury. On a day where flowing football was almost impossible because of the wild gusts circling Christie Park, a draw was perhaps the fair result. But on reflection the Shrimps will be hugely disappointed with the scrappy goal they conceded. The defence had several chances to clear the danger from a corner and Benson took full advantage to fire past Steven Drench who could only manage to grasp the ball after it had crossed the line.

Sammy McIlroy left out Rochdale-bound David Perkins and moved Ged Brannan to midfield with Thompson replacing new dad David McNiven up front. The changes seemed set to pay early dividends as Morecambe started brightly. Wayne Curtis was put through in the first minute by Craig Stanley but was denied by a good tackle before Adam Yates fired the loose ball wide. Curtis was then denied another run on goal by Scott Griffiths' excellent tackle and Anwar Uddin showed the visitors' defensive steel once again foiling Thompson. Brannan headed a Michael Twiss cross wide and Jim Bentley came close with a similar effort before the Shrimps took the lead with a fine goal. Thompson ran onto Michael Howard's pass and curled a delightful effort past Tony Roberts from the edge of the box.

The Shrimps pushed forward looking to extend their lead against a Dagenham side struggling to cope with the conditions. Brannan's cross from Craig Stanley's short corner was perfect. Although Bentley found the right direction with his header it didn't have the power to beat the excellent Sam Sloma on the line. The visitors only began to show their mettle after the break. Craig Mackail-Smith, who is set to join Peterborough at the end of the month, began to get more involved in the game. He played in Glen Southam, forcing Howard to produce a fine tackle, and then set up the same player again, forcing a neat block from Drench.

As the game entered its final stages, Thompson forced experienced Daggers' keeper Roberts into a fine save before the visitors hit top gear.

Howard once again produced a vital tackle to deny Benson a clear shot on goal. The striker then added to his tally for the season by deflecting a cross which crept over the line. The Shrimps produced a late flurry with substitute Jason Walker close to connecting with a Michael Twiss cross. Thompson was left pleading for a penalty but in the end they had to settle for a point.

Garry Thompson fires in Morecambe's goal.

Neil Sorvel was expected to go straight into the Morecambe squad for Saturday's trip to Stafford Rangers as manager Sammy McIlroy strengthened his options for the run-in. He said: "He is an experienced player, a good passer and a typical Morecambe player who can spot a pass. When we won the Conference twice he was a big part of the side. He will have a big presence. Sorvel's arrival fills a gap left in the midfield by the departure of Dave Perkins, who has linked up with former Morecambe player Keith Hill at League Two club Rochdale, moving for an undisclosed fee.

Morecambe: Drench 7, Yates 7, Howard 7, Bentley 7, Blackburn 7, Stanley 7, Hunter 7 (Walker 86), Brannan 8, Curtis 7, Twiss 7, Thompson 7. Unused subs: Davies, McLachlan, Rigoglioso, McNiven.
Dagenham and Redbridge: Roberts, Foster, Uddin, Blackett, Griffiths, Saunders, Leberl, Southam, Sloma (Akurang 75), Benson, Mackail-Smith. Unused subs: Cole, Lette Jallow, Strevens, Hogan.

Referee: A Halliday.
Attendance: 1,711.
Man of the match: **Ged Brannan.**

23rd January 2007

Morecambe 0 Southport 0

MORECAMBE boss Sammy McIlroy was left frustrated again after his side failed to get the better of struggling Southport.

For the second year in succession, the Sandgrounders held the Shrimps to a 0-0 Christie Park draw with a dogged, resolute performance. Morecambe once again had the majority of the possession and played some neat approach play but their lack of clout up front once again proved costly and vital points were dropped as a result.

It was the second home draw of the week for McIlroy's side and another frustrating night for home fans who had seen their side win only four of their 14 League games at Christie Park that season, one of the worst home records in the Conference. For all their pressure and pretty football clear chances were rare. Southport keeper Paul Harrison only had one real save to make when he reacted sharply to tip away an effort from Michael Twiss on 69 minutes.

Harrison was forced into action early in the game with a scrambling block from Garry Thompson's low drive. It was the speedy winger who always looked the Shrimps' biggest threat in the first half. Looking sharp after his recent absence, Thompson volleyed into the side netting and flashed a cross come shot across the goal after sharing a neat one-two with Adam Yates down the right-hand side. Clear chances were at a premium, though, and Southport always looked lively on the counter themselves. Tony Gray and Carl Baker linked well up front until Gray was forced to leave the field with a hamstring injury after just 23 minutes. Baker, who impressed against the Shrimps in the reverse fixture on Boxing Day, again showed touches of class to bring other players into the game. Despite his threat, Southport failed to test Steven Drench and the game became something of a midfield battle until the hour mark when gaps began to appear for the Shrimps.

Substitute David McNiven went close to opening the scoring with a curler from the edge of the box that flew just wide of the left-hand post. Later skipper Jim Bentley was thwarted as his goalbound header span wickedly off the surface and missed the target. When a penalty appeal for a tackle on Thompson by Mark Boyd was waved away by the referee, the Shrimps looked intent on making the pressure count.

Twiss then forced Harrison into the save of the match. Despite frantic pressure with the likes of Jason Walker, McNiven, Twiss and Thompson all eager to get forward, Southport hung on rather more comfortably than many Morecambe fans would have liked.

It was a result that once again left McIlroy

Garry Hunter sums up a frustrating night for Morecambe

frustrated at seeing two important promotion points dropped. He said: "That was a game we should have won. Some of our football, especially in the second half was terrific but we just couldn't put the ball away again."

Morecambe: Drench 6, Yates 7, Bentley 7, Blackburn 7, Howard 7, Stanley 6, Brannan 6 (McNiven 60), Hunter 7, Twiss 6, Curtis 6 (Walker 60), Thompson 7. Unused subs: Davies, Meadowcroft, McLachlan.
Southport: Harrison, Birch, Lee, Dugdale, Rowland, Lane (Fowler 85), Boyd, Powell, Donnelly (Olsen 90), Baker, Gray (Paterson 24). Unused subs: Bagnall, Clancy. Booked: Lane.

Referee: C Pawson.
Att: 1,484.
Man of the match: **Garry Thompson.**

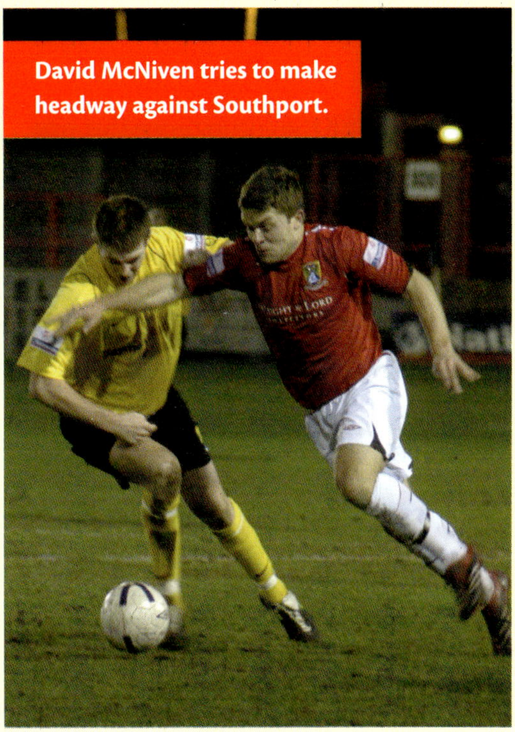

David McNiven tries to make headway against Southport.

27th January 2007

Stafford Rangers 1 Morecambe 3

(Madjo 53) (Twiss 10, Yates 32, Thompson 40)

MORECAMBE maintained their superb run of form away from Christie Park with this convincing victory over struggling Stafford. After two home draws, the Shrimps secured their ninth away win of the campaign, and their first league success of 2007, and in doing so moved back into the play-off zone.

Sammy McIlroy's side, which included new signing Neil Sorvel and the on-loan Northampton front man Jerome Watt, managed to find the cutting edge that had been sorely missing in recent weeks and took the chances that came their way. It was a performance that left Stafford stunned. They didn't play badly but every time Morecambe attacked they looked like scoring in the first 45 minutes. It helped that the Shrimps were gifted the opening goal on 10 minutes. In a goal similar to the one he scored against York recently, Twiss swung in a vicious corner from the right, the near-post defender failed to clear and the ball ended up in the back of the net much to everyone's surprise.

Energised by the early boost, the Shrimps continued to push forward with Garry Thompson, playing up front again, put through by Garry Hunter. His shot was then beaten down by an excellent covering tackle from Stafford skipper Wayne Daniel. Thompson was a constant threat going forward and he turned provider just after the half hour with the killer pass for Adam Yates to put the Shrimps 2-0 up. Yates, who had a superb game in both defence and attack, made a determined overlap down the right, to meet the ball and drive a sweet right-foot shot that flew into the right-hand corner.

The Shrimps, playing with real confidence, added to their lead five minutes before the break with another well-taken goal. Credit once again went to Hunter who hounded Stafford midfielder David Oldfield and forced him into a mistake in the middle of the boggy pitch. As he lost possession, Hunter swooped and played in Garry Thompson who ran on goal and curled an effort past the helpless Alcock.

Such was Morecambe's dominance in the first half that Stafford, despite the willing Guy Madjo and Dolapo Olaoye up front, only threatened briefly.

Midfielder Craig Lovatt should have done

"People have commented about losing two youngish players in Perkins and Rigoglioso while bringing in an older one in Neil Sorvel. What we have in Sorvel is just a bit of experience which may be crucial as we get to the business end of the season. He has tasted promotion before and comes with a lot of knowledge. We saw on Saturday how he can influence this team. He was very effective and his positional sense allowed Craig Stanley to push forward more and have possibly his best game for us – that's a new dimension for us."
Sammy McIlroy

better than shoot well over the bar from the edge of the box after a neat lay-off from Madjo. The big striker later shot straight at Steven Drench after a neat turn on the edge of the box. Madjo was rewarded for his efforts early in the second half with perhaps the goal of the game. The stocky striker again turned sharply on the edge of the area and produced a wonderful left-foot shot that flew into the top right-hand corner of Drench's goal.

That gave the home side a clear lift and although they enjoyed much greater possession in the second period they struggled to threaten. Oldfield had a half chance after Drench parried away Neil Grayson's shot. However, it was Morecambe who came the closest to adding to the score line when Thompson volleyed into the side netting and Ged Brannan flashed a late free-kick high and wide. It was a win that delighted assistant boss Mark Lillis. He said: "We were disappointed to come away from the last two home games with draws so this was a very important three points and should give us a real confidence boost. I thought it was a very professional performance on a poor pitch. The main difference was that we took our chances when they came along."

Morecambe: Drench 7, Yates 8, Howard 7, Watt 6 (Brannan 70), Blackburn 7, Stanley 7, Hunter 7, Brannan 8, Sorvel 7, Twiss 7, Thompson 7 (Walker 84). Unused subs: Davies, McLachlan, Curtis.
Stafford Rangers: Alcock, Talbott, McAughtrie, Daniel, Lovatt, Grayson, Madjo, Olaoye (Edwards 68), Griffith, Sutton, Oldfield (Gibson 50). Unused subs: Hopkinson, Williams, Gibson.

Referee: G Stretton.
Attendance: 957.
Man of the match: **Adam Yates.**

3rd February 2007

Morecambe 1 Stevenage Borough 1

(Thompson 90 pen) (Morison 45)

MORECAMBE secured last night's FA Trophy replay thanks to an injury time penalty in this dramatic cup tie.

Garry Thompson was the Shrimps' hero as he kept his cool to score the spot-kick awarded four minutes into injury time. The game looked to be lost when Barry Fuller was adjudged to have handled a ball deep into the Stevenage box.

The game itself was another one where Morecambe found it hard to get going at home. Boss Sammy McIlroy called it a 'disjointed' performance and admitted he was desperate for the home fans to see the same type of commanding display that away supporters had seen week in, week out. But although they were far from their best, chances were spread out fairly evenly among the sides. Morecambe keeper Steven Drench had to be at his best on several occasions to foil Boro's hit man, Steve Morison. Drench saved well from Morison's first-half header and Boro's top-scorer should have done better than fire a shot into the side netting after being put through early in the second half. But Morison, who scored a superb hat-trick against the Shrimps in the 3-3 draw at Christie Park earlier in the season, was on target in first half injury time.

Chris Blackburn made a rare mistake, giving the ball away on the edge of his own area and Morison made no mistake as he steered the ball past Drench's left hand.

Drench kept his side in the game with a superb save from Adam Miller. As the game moved into the final stages, he tipped away a close-range effort after a strong run from the Borough midfielder. But although Morecambe failed to reach their peak they did cause the visitors' defence some problems.

Keeper Julian had to be alert to tip over a looping volley from Garry Hunter and palm away a Neil Sorvel drive. Jim Bentley was unlucky to see a header hit the crossbar before a late final surge with Danny Carlton brought on for his first action since October. Thompson came close with a sweet shot from the edge of the area that Julian saved at full stretch before the final dramatic moments.

Morecambe: Drench 8, Yates 7, Howard 7, Bentley 7, Blackburn 6, Stanley 7, Hunter 7, Watt 6 (Walker 67), Sorvel 7 (Carlton 86), Twiss 6, Thompson 8. Unused subs: Brannan, Meadowcroft, Davies.
Stevenage Borough: Julian, Fuller, Nutter, Gaia, Binns (Cole 63), Miller, Beard, McMahon, Henry, Morison (Oliver 80), Nurse. Unused subs: Slatter, Dobson, Potter. Booked: Fuller

Referee: A Haines.
Attendance: 1,131.
Man of the match: **Garry Thompson.**

6th February 2007

Stevenage Borough 3 Morecambe 0 (after extra-time)

(Morison 94, Nurse 102, Miller 115)

SAMMY McIlroy said this week that it was 'baffling' how the Shrimps have fared so differently at home and away. The Shrimps are currently top of the Conference away form table with 30 points out of 52 available. But at Christie Park, they come 17th out of 24 with just 18 points from 14 games. McIlroy said "We are going to have to get to the bottom of it because this is a crucial stage of the season. There are enough games left for us to get it right. If we can pick up our home form then I am nearly sure we will be there (in the play-offs)."

MORECAMBE'S run in the FA Trophy came to an end at Stevenage last Tuesday night. Three extra-time goals denied Sammy McIlroy's side a place in the last eight of this year's competition as Stevenage's extra firepower proved the difference between the two sides.

Steve Morison was once again the man to break Morecambe's hearts with the all-important first goal four minutes into extra-time. The highly-rated striker made it five goals from three games against the Shrimps this season with a quality strike. With his first real clear chance of the game, he turned neatly past Chris Blackburn and drilled Jon Nurse's lay-off past the helpless Steven Drench to put the home side in the driving seat. Provider Nurse then turned goal-scorer eight minutes later when he put the finishing touch to a move he began in his own half. After finding Adam Miller he carried on his run past a static Morecambe midfield and produced a neat finish. Miller then rubbed salt into the Shrimps' wounds when he added a late third. As Morecambe pushed Jim Bentley forward, gaps appeared at the back which Miller exploited, running on to Nurse's throughball to stoke the ball past Drench.

Ironically the Shrimps then created their best chances. Twiss headed an excellent Jerome Watt cross over from close range. Later Bentley saw Julian produce the best save of the game from a bullet header, moments before the final whistle which ended Morecambe's Wembley dream. Morecambe produced a far better performance than the one they gave in the first game but they still lacked the craft and guile to break down the Stevenage defence. Keeper Alan Julian was only forced into a save in the final minute of extra-time. The first half saw Morecambe in control for long periods with the recalled Ged Brannan controlling things in midfield. Some neat crisp play saw the Shrimps dictate for long periods without ever really threatening.

Stevenage came close to scoring a quick-fire opener on only six minutes. Miller side-footed an excellent cross from the always-dangerous Mitchell Cole against the foot of the left-hand post. The Shrimps came back almost immediately. Chris Blackburn headed past Alan Julian from close range after latching on to Michael Twiss' lay-off only to see his effort ruled out for offside. It was the Shrimps who continued to dictate the pace. Bentley had a good claim for a penalty turned down on 17 minutes after a little shove in the back blocked his jump and Garry Hunter tested Julian from long range. Craig Stanley and Garry Thompson both fired efforts wide from distance and Blackburn was inches away from connecting with Adam Yates' excellent cross on the stroke of half-time.

But the second half saw the home side move up a gear and Mark Stimson's side began to dominate. Daryl McMahon saw two left-footers curl the wrong side of the post before Morison gave a glimpse of his threat with a smart shot on the turn that deflected inches wide of the left-hand post.

In the end it was clear that the Shrimps would have to wait another year before looking to emulate the 1974 Trophy success with the play-offs now a clear priority. Sammy McIlroy said: "For the first 90 minutes we did brilliantly but a couple of mistakes cost us. We wanted a long run in the Trophy but the league is the priority and Stevenage is a hard place to go."

Morecambe: Drench 7, Yates 6, Howard 7, Bentley 7, Blackburn 6, Stanley 6, Hunter 6, Sorvel 8, Brannan 6 (Watt 102), Twiss 7, Thompson 6 (Walker 96). Unused subs: Carlton, Meadowcroft, Davies.
Stevenage Borough: Julian, Fuller, Nutter, Gaia, Cole, Miller, Beard, McMahon, Henry, Morison (Slabber 116), Nurse. Unused subs: Oliver, Dobson, Potter, Binns. Booked: Miller.

Referee: P Gibbs.
Attendance: 1,056.
Man of the match: **Neil Sorvel.**

Neil Sorvel.

10th February 2007

Gravesend and Northfleet 2 Morecambe 1

(MacDonald 9 pen, Ledgister 56) (Stanley 14)

SAMMY McIlroy is facing perhaps his most testing time yet as Shrimps manager after two away defeats in a week and a mounting injury list.

The Shrimps' boss could be facing something of a mini crisis ahead of the weekend game with Cambridge United after collecting more injuries to key players on Saturday. Already without hamstring victim Adam Yates and others including Fraser McLachlan, Wayne Curtis and Jamie Burns, the Shrimps saw the influential Michael Twiss and Chris Blackburn pick up injuries at Stonebridge Road that could leave them out of action.

It was a worrying end to a disappointing afternoon for the Shrimps who were the cruel victims of one poor penalty decision and robbed of another at the other end. The penalty decision was a galling one as it came so early and presented the Fleet's top scorer Charlie MacDonald with an early chance to take his goal tally to 19 for the season. MacDonald fell easily under Jim Bentley's challenge and it came as something of a shock when the referee pointed to the spot. MacDonald accepted the gift and sent Steven Drench the wrong way to give Gravesend a dream start.

The Shrimps were rocked but bounced back almost immediately with an equaliser five minutes later. Craig Stanley, the Shrimps' best player on the day, was the goal hero when he took advantage of a poor clearance to fire past Luke McShane low to his right at his near post. Stanley then tried his luck again with a shot from distance which was well held by McShane. Home midfielder Mark DeBolla then made a desperate last-gasp clearance to clear the danger as Garry Thompson's free-kick caused panic in the home side's defence. Jason Walker, given his chance to show McIlroy what he could do up front, was then denied a penalty after falling under McShane's challenge.

From there Gravesend raised their game. The always-dangerous MacDonald came close to extending the home side's lead in injury time when denied by a superb save from Drench. Gravesend maintained the tempo for the start of the second half and forced a string of corners before taking the lead for a second time on 56 minutes.

On-loan Southend midfielder Joel Ledgister took advantage of hesitation in the Morecambe six-yard box. Nipping in behind Michael Howard at the far post he volleyed home Stacy Long's deep cross.

Gravsend continued to push forward with MacDonald forcing the Morecambe defence into some last-gasp clearances. Long then drilled a shot just over the bar from the edge of the area, before the Shrimps staged a late flurry. Before picking up his late knock, Twiss was unlucky not to equalise with a shot that beat McShane but was cleared off the line by former Wycombe defender Paul McCarthy. McShane did well to spot the danger and foil Thompson as he threatened to latch on to Peter Hawkins' poor back header but when Garry Hunter's volley flew way off target, the Shrimps' hopes of another late equaliser were dashed. There was still time for more frustration on the Morecambe bench when Sacha Opinel's headbutt on Ged Brannan went unnoticed by a referee who made few fans among the Morecambe faithful that afternoon.

Morecambe: Drench 6, Brannan 7, Howard 7, Bentley 7, Blackburn 6 (Meadowcroft 41), Stanley 8, Hunter 7, Sorvel 6 (Lloyd 74), Twiss 6, Walker 6 (Watt 79), Thompson 7. Unused subs: Langford, Davies.
Gravesend and Northfleet: McShane, R Smith, Hawkins, McCarthy, Opinel, Moore (Sodje 88), Quinn, Ledgister (Coleman 88), DeBolla (Ricketts 77), Long, MacDonald. Unused subs: J Smith, Mott. Booked: Opinel.

Referee: G Lewis.
Attendance: 1,156.
Man of the match: **Craig Stanley.**

Twiss, who has scored 14 goals this season, has been relatively injury-free since moving to Christie Park and his loss could be key as the Conference promotion race hots up. Blackburn is due back in three weeks and Yates in two weeks. He pulled out of the England game but Craig Stanley was due to play. Neil Sorvel got out of his sickbed to play on Saturday after being on antibiotics since Tuesday. McIlroy also recalled Paul Lloyd from his loan spell at Bamber Bridge and brought young Reserve teamer Andy Langford in as sub.

McIlroy said: "We were down to the bare bones but I am not going to make any excuses. Things are against us at the moment but we have just got to do the best we can with what we have got."

MORECAMBE boss Sammy McIlroy was scouring the loan market this week after seeing his side hit by injuries with star striker Michael Twiss possibly out until the summer. Twiss picked up a suspected medial knee ligament injury at Gravesend on Saturday and he is expected to be out until at least mid-April.

And with Adam Yates, Chris Blackburn, Fraser McLachlan, Jamie Burns and Wayne Curtis all not fully fit, McIlroy has been searching for an emergency loan ahead of the weekend. "I am not one to dwell on injuries but it is beginning to take its toll," said McIlroy.

Pull out a plum

by Steven Hewitt

"WHEN you bring in a player, sometimes you pull out a plum or you get egg on your face." Well, Sammy McIlroy managed to pull out a few plums during the promotion season as he put together a squad that got Morecambe over the line and into the Football League.
All managers know that they are only as good as the players they are working with. They know that all eyes are on them to bring in the right ones to improve the side.

As McIlroy says, are they going to be plums to make a tasty pie, or leave you looking like you don't know what you are doing.

Two of the most important signings that McIlroy made for the Shrimps came at either end of the pre-season campaign.

It had been an unusual close season, what with Jim Harvey being replaced and McIlroy taking the full-time job – and all the fall-out that came with that move by the Shrimps board.

But when Craig Stanley was unveiled on a warm July day at Christie Park, it was a clear sign that the focus was forward to a new season and a new start.

Stanley came from Hereford and only a few weeks earlier had been a part of the Bulls side that knocked Morecambe out of the play-offs and went on to win promotion.

But he gave up his chance to go up with Hereford, instead agreeing a deal to join McIlroy at Christie Park.

On his arrival, Stanley said: "Sammy McIlroy's enthusiasm for the game and enthusiasm to get Morecambe into the League impressed me and sold the club to me."

He wouldn't be the last to express such sentiments.

Stanley went on to give whole-hearted commitment to the club, moving to the area and giving his all, all season long. With the number six on his back, he got to know every blade of grass on Christie Park in his amazingly energetic performances.

He was virtually ever-present going into March and with England National Game matches further crowding his schedule, it perhaps wasn't surprising that he was ready for a rest.

He dropped out of the starting line-up for eight games but, with two matches left of the season, he was back in, revitalised and ready to play his part in taking another side into the Football League.

That he did and at Wembley, produced one of his best performances of the season, driving the engine of the Shrimps midfield all afternoon.

Stanley was the first player to sign for McIlroy in pre-season and the last would also have a huge influence on the season.

Adam Yates appeared at right-back in the Shrimps' last pre-season friendly against Barrow. He signed a couple of weeks later from Leek and after that, only failed to start four games all season – again an amazing testimony to his fitness.

But there was more to Yates than Leek. He had started out at Crewe, another product of that renowned Dario Gradi production line.

And like everyone else whose development Gradi had overseen, Yates knew how to play football, he just wanted a chance.

He had been on loan at Halifax but really got his opportunity at Morecambe – and how he took it, becoming a key member of the defence on which Morecambe built their success.

To not lose a game all season when they had taken the lead was an incredible stat and one that Yates, with his lightning recovery speed to get back and make up for his, or his colleagues' errors, played his part in.

The role of full-back is an under-rated one in football. But they can have a huge influence over a team and how they play, both defending and attacking.

The Morecambe right side, with Yates supporting Garry Thompson, provided headaches for opponents all season.

And Yates didn't always need Thompson in front of him. At Altrincham on an October Tuesday, the Shrimps needed to bounce after being beaten 4-0 at Crawley three days earlier.

Fraser McLachlan put them 1-0 up but when Thompson was sent off, how would the Shrimps react – especially after the Crawley loss and with their influential right side now hampered?

No need to worry. Yates just played the role of two men, tackling back and getting forward like a man possessed.

The Shrimps were solid and just for good measure, Yates led a counter-attack and crossed for Danny Carlton to make it 2-0 – job done and three points secured.

Performances like that earned Yates, like Stanley, a call-up to the England National Game XI and left McIlroy reflecting on how two of his transfers had borne fruit.

If a manager is going to bring in the transfers that will make a difference, knowing any new signing is reliable is key. It's like if you want a plumber, you get one in that you know will do a good job for a good price.

When McIlroy brought in Neil Sorvel and Danny Adams, he knew what he was getting. He had had Sorvel in his side when he took Macclesfield out of the Conference and Adams in his defence.

He knew they could help the players who had been knocking on the promotion door for years, to get them through the door and into the League.

Sorvel played a pivotal role in the run-in, bolstering the midfield after Dave Perkins' departure. Sorvel is a players' player, perhaps not as appreciated by fans as more high-profile players, but his team-mates value him more than most.

Adams came in at a key time, filling in at centre-half when Chris Blackburn was out before making the left-back spot his own during the crucial final games of the season.

'Steel' was what McIlroy wanted to bring to Morecambe – both Sorvel and Adams did that.

And goals were what McIlroy's final signing of the season brought. Matty Blinkhorn signed on a Friday and scored after 15 minutes of his debut the next day.

On loan from Blackpool, he relished the chance to play first-team football. After that debut goal he was quiet but a pep talk from McIlroy got him going again and he finished his spell at Christie Park with eight goals in 12 games during the key month of March.

His goals took the Shrimps to the brink of the play-offs but a groin injury coupled with a recall to Bloomfield Road meant he missed the rest of the season.

He was there at Wembley though, sharing in the success, and a few weeks later, he had signed permanent forms with the Shrimps, and could share in the Football League experience.

17th February 2007

Morecambe 2 Cambridge United 2

(Bentley 60, Lloyd 81) (Chillingworth 27, Adameno 73)

MORECAMBE boss Sammy McIlroy took a swipe at the boo-boys and said he was "proud"of his injury-hit team after a late goal saved them from defeat at Christie Park.

McIlroy responded to a "small" band of critics who rounded on him during the game saying they should be "proud of what they have seen" after a catalogue of injuries which has threatened to disrupt the Shrimps' play-off ambitions. With Michael Twiss and Chris Blackburn joining the likes of Fraser McLachlan and Jamie Burns on the treatment table, McIlroy said he was forced to play Danny Carlton, Wayne Curtis and Adam Yates when all were not match fit. He said: "Those three lads were not fit but they wanted to play for me and for the club. They gave absolutely everything for Morecambe and I was proud of every single one of them." He added: "There are groups of people here who seem to want us to fail and I can't

Garry Hunter goes for goal against Cambridge.

understand that. I have noticed it and some of the players have noticed it too. Our home form hasn't been as good as we would have liked but we are up against it at the minute. One thing I do know, however, is that everyone here on and off the pitch is giving their all and they deserve support."

McIlroy also paid special tribute to Paul Lloyd whose late strike earned the Shrimps the point. Moments after coming off the bench Lloyd tried his luck with a long-range shot. He certainly didn't hit it as sweetly as he would have liked but Cambridge keeper Shane Herbert dived too early and the ball crept into the net off the foot of the right-hand post. It was a good time for Lloyd, allegedly a target for Jim Harvey at Forest Green, to make his mark. Cambridge had taken the lead for a second time eight minutes earlier when Charles Adameno curled a shot through a crowd of players from the edge of the area past Steven Drench's right hand.

Earlier the Shrimps, who had still only won four games at home that season, had enjoyed the majority of the possession and created the better chances but could not find a way past impressive young keeper Herbert.

He saved comfortably from Michael Howard's long-range effort before producing one of the saves of the season to deflect a sweetly-struck Garry Thompson drive.

Herbert than saved well again after a neat run and shot from midfielder Garry Hunter. Moments later Cambridge took a shock lead on 27 minutes when Daniel Chillingworth latched onto Ged Brannan's rare error to slide the ball past Drench from close range.

Morecambe almost hit back immediately with Curtis sending a looping header over the bar from Craig Stanley's cross. Later Cambridge ended the half on top, though, as Pitt drilled a fine effort inches over from the edge of the area.

The second half saw Morecambe up the tempo with the returning Carlton providing a sharpness up front that had been missing recently.

Twice he came close with a volley that looped onto the netting and another effort which sent Herbert scrambling to his right to tip away at full stretch.

Then came one of the most crucial moments of the game when Cambridge's Jon

SAMMY McIlroy has moved to ease his player crisis by bringing in experienced defender Danny Adams ahead of the trip to Forest Green on Saturday. With Chris Blackburn still injured, McIlroy's squad was trimmed even further when both Jim Bentley and Ged Brannan picked up their fifth bookings of the season last week against Cambridge. That means they will both miss Forest Green leaving young Danny Meadowcroft as the club's only recognised centre-half. Signing Adams until the end of the season will ease the situation, said McIlroy, who has worked with the 31-year-old at both Stockport and Macclesfield. He said: "He has a lot of experience and is a tremendous professional. I know he can do a job for us. He has had other offers, including some from league clubs, but he has answered my plea of mercy."

Brady missed a golden opportunity to put Cambridge 2-0 ahead.

Put through one on one with Drench, he pulled a shot wide when clear on goal.

It was a miss that proved vital. Within minutes Morecambe were level when skipper Jim Bentley ghosted into the box to head a Carlton corner past Herbert.

Three minutes later, the Shrimps had a golden chance to take the lead as Curtis broke free down the left but with Carlton screaming for a square ball into the area, he went for goal and skewed his shot well wide of the target. In the end, the Shrimps had to settle for another Christie Park draw and travel to Forest Green on Saturday looking to get their play-off campaign back on track.

Morecambe: Drench 6, Yates 7, Howard 7, Bentley 7, Brannan 6, Stanley 7, Hunter 7 (Walker 80), Sorvel 7, Curtis 6 (Lloyd 80), Carlton 7 (Watt 90), Thompson 8. Unused subs: Meadwocroft, Davies. Booked: Yates, Bentley, Brannan.

Cambridge United: Herbert, Collins, Pitt (Adameno 69), Morrison, Duncan, Bridges (Page 69), Brady, Brown, J Simpson, R Simpson (Smith 86), Chillingworth. Unused subs: Purser, Crane.

Referee: D Coote.

Attendance: 1,493.

Man of the match: **Garry Thompson.**

24th February 2007

Forest Green Rovers 1 Morecambe 3

(Lawless 11) (Lloyd 22, Carlton 36, Thompson 87)

MORECAMBE recorded a morale-boosting victory over Jim Harvey's Forest Green Rovers side to register their 10th away win of the campaign.

Sammy McIlroy's side claimed only their second win of 2007 after coming from behind to beat Rovers. The win came at a vital time for the Shrimps after a dip in form in recent weeks and injuries and suspensions to leading players. McIlroy was forced to shuffle his pack with a rare start for Danny Meadowcroft and a Conference debut for Paul Lloyd. New signing Danny Adams was also drafted in at centre-half and the changes seemed to affect the Shrimps in the early stages. Forest Green dominated the opening stages against a disjointed Shrimps but as the game wore on Adams inspired his new side with a superb debut at the back. But it was Garry Thompson who perhaps made the most telling contribution of the afternoon, making two goals and scoring the other, in a victory that lifted the Shrimps to sixth in the table.

The win looked a long way off at the beginning of the game, however, as Forest Green started superbly. Keeper Steven Drench was soon in action and made two fine saves in the first five minutes as he reacted sharply to turn away free-kicks from Kevin Nicholson and Simon Clist that skimmed along the wet surface.

Clist then came close again with a curler that hit the crossbar as the home side pushed forward relentlessly. Their pressure soon paid off with a bizarre goal on 11 minutes. Defender Alex Lawless launched the ball forward from just inside the Morecambe half. Drench came to collect but the ball bounced at a sharp angle over his head and into the net. Drench redeemed himself moments later, however, when Clist played in Les Afful behind the Morecambe defence. The former Exeter striker looked sure to score but Drench stayed tall and produced a vital save at a vital time.

Only after that miss did Morecambe come to life. The midfield finally gained some possession and Thompson became more and more influential down the right wing.

It was Thompson's pace that brought the Shrimps back into the game as he provided an equaliser in Morecambe's first attack of note. After steaming past Nicholson, he sent in a cross which former Shrimps keeper Ryan Robinson could only palm away and Lloyd, who almost joined Forest Green on loan a few weeks ago, slotted home the loose ball from six yards out. Nine minutes before the break, Thompson came to the fore again. Put through by Craig Stanley's diagonal pass, he chipped the ball into the danger area and Danny Carlton rose smartly at the far post to head past Robinson.

Morecambe had a golden chance to

extend their lead three minutes into the second half. Carlton teed up Lloyd who looked certain to score a second but was denied by a fine Robinson save. Carlton then misdirected a free header from a good cross before Forest Green, led by the excellent Adriano Rigoglioso, stepped up the pace in the search for an equaliser. Rigoglioso himself forced Drench into a neat save with a shot from distance. He then set up substitute Danny Carey-Bartram with a delightful through ball that was wasted by the striker as his poor first touch allowed Drench to make a sharp block. Fellow sub Paul Stonehouse was unfortunate to see a sweetly-struck shot cannon back off the underside of the crossbar. Then Thompson calmed Morecambe's nerves with a superb third, curling a 30-yarder past Robinson to clinch the points in fine style. It was the perfect way for Thompson to end a fine individual performance and the perfect finish to the game for McIlroy's side.

Morecambe: Drench 7, Yates 7, Howard 7, Meadowcroft 7, Adams 8, Thompson 9, Stanley 7, Sorvel 7, Lloyd 7, Carlton 7 (Burns 80), Curtis 7 (Hunter 86). Unused subs: Davies, McLachlan, Walker. Booked: Meadowcroft, Stanley, Carlton.
Forest Green Rovers: Robinson, Lawless (Preece 62), Jones, Hardiker, Nicholson, Williams (Stonehouse 59), Brough, Clist, Afful, Rigoglioso, Beesley (Carey-Bertram 55). Unused subs: Harrison, Lamb. Booked: Brough, Jones, Lawless.

Referee: A Turner.
Attendance: 1,292.
Man of the match: **Garry Thompson.**

"Thompson was fantastic on Saturday. His strength and pace put them under pressure and his goal was top drawer."
Sammy McIlroy

MORECAMBE start a busy period of nine Conference matches in 28 days with manager Sammy McIlroy in a positive mood. McIlroy saw his side come back from 1-0 down at Forest Green to beat Jim Harvey's side 3-1, despite being without several first team regulars. Now with Jim Bentley and Ged Brannan available and Chris Blackburn almost fully fit, McIlroy heads into Saturday's game at home to St Albans with only Michael Twiss on the treatment table. And the Shrimps' boss is likely to need all his squad during what is a hectic month of March. He said: "We are looking good on the injury front but from now until the end of the season we will need all the squad. We have nine games coming up, which is unbelievable, and if we play well we can pick up points." Fraser McLachlan and Jamie Burns were due to continue their comebacks from injuries with starts in last night's Lancashire United Cooperatives Challenge Cup Semi-Final at Marine. Both were substitutes on Saturday – a game where McIlroy was delighted to see his team come through.

27th February 2007

Marine 1 Morecambe 0

Lancashire United Co-operatives Challenge Cup Semi-Final.

MORECAMBE crashed out of the Lancashire United Co-operatives Challenge Cup after this shock defeat at UniBond side Marine. Despite coming close on a host of occasions, the Shrimps failed to test Marine keeper Chris Parry. They paid dearly for their lack of a killer touch when Danny Brookfield scored the only goal of the game nine minutes after the break. It was a goal that earned the Mariners a place in the final against Burscough, who beat Fleetwood. The Shrimps played a number of first-teamers looking to gain match fitness after recent injuries and some of the younger members of the squad. They produced some neat football in the first half, dominating the early proceedings and piling on the pressure. Jamie Burns, making his way back from a hamstring injury, looked the Shrimps' main threat throughout and almost scored on a couple of occasions with shots that flew just inches wide. Jason Walker hit the side netting with a 25-yard effort and Keiran Walmsley, back from his loan spell at Stalybridge Celtic, forced Parry into a neat tip over.

The second half saw Marine find their feet with the dangerous Nicky Young not too far away with an audacious 40-yard volley which almost caught out Scott Davies before they took the lead. There was more than a hint of offside when Young received the ball wide on the left but his cross was perfect for Brookfield to run onto at the far post and slot past Davies. The goal gave Marine a boost of confidence and they were rarely troubled in the second period. Burns should have done better with a close range header when free in the box and Michael West volleyed straight at Parry after some neat work from Walker. However, it was the home side that came closest to scoring again. Veteran Peter Cumiskey saw a cheeky 30-yard lob curl just wide six minutes from time and Davies reacted sharply to save from Ian Latham's excellent late effort as the Mariners finished on a high.

Marine: Parry, Dever, McDermott, Farley, Connolly, Hussin, Brookfield, Parle, Young (Lynch 65), Cumiskey, Latham. Unused subs: Nesbitt, Brazier, Rice, Barnes.
Morecambe: Davies, Walmsley, Langford, Brannan, Blackburn, McLachlan, West, Hunter, Walker, Pickersglil (McLuckie 72), Burns. Unused subs: Ball, Helm, Wisdom, Kelly.
Referee: I Rose.

3rd March 2007

Morecambe 2 St Albans City 0

(Blinkhorn 15, Thompson 90)

MORECAMBE striker Matty Blinkhorn took just 15 minutes of an impressive debut to score as the Shrimps sealed their fifth home win of the season on Saturday.

Although it was a result that boss Sammy McIlroy admitted 'flattered' his team, there is no doubt that the points were vital in the Shrimps' continuing quest to reach the play-offs. There were some good signs with the performances of newcomers Blinkhorn and Danny Adams but also some moments of frustration with some awful final passes at crucial moments. Against better sides that could have proved fatal but St Albans, struggling in the relegation zone, failed to strike at the heart of the Morecambe defence.

There was no doubt the Shrimps deserved the points. The victory was spurred by Blinkhorn who took just 15 minutes to make an impression. He was signed on loan from Blackpool on Friday as a replacement for unlucky injury-victim Paul Lloyd. The 22-year-old was thrown straight into the side by McIlroy and it proved to be a good decision as Blinkhorn linked well with Danny Carlton and showed he could be a very useful addition to the play-off hopefuls. A second goal two minutes into injury-time from Garry Thompson gave the score a somewhat flattering look against a battling St Albans side but the Shrimps were happy to win at home for the first time since December.

The Shrimps started brightly with a

Matty Blinkhorn makes a quick impression with an early goal on his debut.

Blinkhorn gets a pat on the back from his new team-mates.

Wayne Curtis header cleared off the line by Patrick Ada from Carlton's corner. The winger was also denied by two superb defensive clearances from Gary Elphick and Djoumin Sangare who both played well.

Sangare also found himself in a dangerous position after a corner was only half cleared but fortunately for the Shrimps, his volley was well over the bar.

The Shrimps' early pressure paid off when Blinkhorn opened the scoring.

Again Curtis was involved, finding Thompson with a far-post cross which was drilled back across the six-yard box for the onrushing Blinkhorn to slide home.

Morecambe continued to press but St Albans threatened on the break with a Chris Seeby volley sailing just past the left-hand post and a poor final shot from John Hastings after he had managed to turn away from Adams.

The second half was an end-to-end affair with both sides lacking the quality to take advantage of the space they were afforded. On several occasions Morecambe had men over but their final ball was poor all too often. Blinkhorn and Thompson were guilty of wasting opportunities with poor crosses, although skipper Jim Bentley was unlucky not to connect with one decent cross from the latter. St Albans also had chances themselves, the best being for substitute Chris Watters late in the game. Morecambe's usually ultra-reliable Adam Yates lost control on the edge of his own box, letting Watters in on goal. Luckily his poor shot was easily saved by Steven Drench. The Morecambe keeper was also in action again late on with a fine save from Ram Marwa after the midfielder broke into the box to connect with Matt Hann's left-wing cross.

The visitors' resistance came to an end when Morecambe added a late second.

Thompson latched onto a long through-ball and let fly from the edge of the area with a shot that shocked Paul Bastock as it flew into the bottom right-hand corner. The final whistle came seconds after to mark a welcome, and long overdue, home win for the Shrimps who climbed to sixth in the Conference table and maintained the pressure on those above them.

Morecambe: Drench 7, Yates 7, Howard 7, Bentley 7, Adams 7 (Blackburn 81), Thompson 7, Stanley 7, Sorvel 7, Curtis 7 (Brannan 83), Blinkhorn 8, Carlton 7 (Burns 73). Unused subs: Davies, Hunter. Booked: Thompson.
St Albans City: Bastock, Seeby (Simon Martin 68), Elphick, Sangare (Basse 83), Deen, Hann, Marwa, Ada, Clarke, Hastings, Buari (Watters 68). Unused subs: Perks, Roddis. Booked: Buari, Ada.

Referee: J Waugh.
Attendance: 1,415.
Man of the match: **Matty Blinkhorn.**

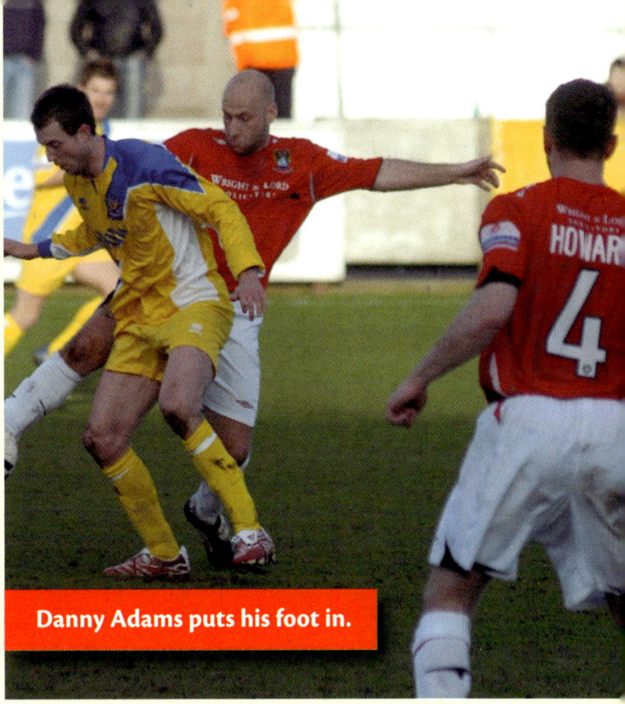

Danny Adams puts his foot in.

Sammy McIlroy decided against recalling David McNiven from Stafford last Friday, but he has not ruled him out of his play-off push. He said: "I have got a 24-hour recall on him but it would have been disrespectful to Stafford to call him back on Friday so near a match.

"We are monitoring him and he has been scoring goals, which is good. He will be fitter for playing games, it is no use bringing him back to sit on the bench."

There has been good news on Michael Twiss' knee injury. The Shrimps' top-scorer is back jogging and could return before the play-offs. McIlroy said: "At the end of this month, it will be a clearer picture. If we can get the points between now and then, if he comes back in it will be like signing another player."

6th March 2007

Rushden and Diamonds 2 Morecambe 2

(Rankine 32, Kelly 65) (Hope 73 og, Curtis 75)

MORECAMBE came back from two goals down to snatch an important point at Rushden and Diamonds.

An early Matty Blinkhorn cross was just too far ahead of Curtis and a neat 25-yard effort from Danny Carlton sailed just over the bar. Wayne Curtis was denied an opening goal when he saw a deflected shot come back off the post. Carlton then looked sure to score on the half hour but somehow failed to convert Garry Thompson's excellent cross.

The Shrimps looked favourites to score but then suddenly found themselves a goal down. The dangerous Michael Rankine used his height well to head Danny Williams' right-wing cross into the bottom right-hand corner of Drench's goal.

Rankine became the centre of attention with another free header well held by Drench and two similar efforts that just beat the crossbar. The Shrimps began the second half brightly. Curtis fired an effort from the edge of the bar just wide of the right-hand post and the hard-working Blinkhorn shot wide at full stretch. Despite dominating for long periods again the Shrimps looked to be set for a pointless outing. Little Marcus Kelly nipped in between two Morecambe defenders to head past Drench from eight yards out to make it 2-0.

Morecambe had other ideas though and pulled one back on 73 minutes with a freak own goal. Rushden skipper Chris Hope somehow managed to head Carlton's right-wing corner over his own keeper. The goal gave the Shrimps a clear lift and two minutes later they were level. Neil Sorvel played in Curtis with a delightful ball and the winger made no mistake with a cool finish to lob the advancing Scott Tynan.

Both sides then had chances to take all three points. Rushden defender Mark Allbrighton should have done better than head wide from close range.

Then in the final minute, Morecambe came close themselves. Garry Thompson, who came to life in the second half, waltzed past Paul Watson but saw his well-struck shot well saved at the near post by Tynan to deny what would have been a memorable win.

Morecambe: Drench 7, Yates 7, Howard 7, Bentley 7, Adams 7, Thompson 7, Stanley 8, Sorvel 7, Curtis 7, Blinkhorn 7, Carlton 7. Unused subs: Davies, Brannan, Blackburn, Hunter, Burns. Booked: Adams.
Rushden and Diamonds: Tynan, Watson, Ashton, Hope, Allbrighton, Kelly, Mills (Bostwick 64), Woodhouse, Williams (Tomlin 82), Rankine, Jackson. Unused subs: Baker, Beardsley, Goodliffe.

Referee: G Scott.
Attendance: 1,701.
Man of the match: **Craig Stanley.**

10th March 2007

Morecambe 1 Crawley Town 0

(Thompson 34)

A GOAL from Garry Thompson saw Morecambe seal their second successive home win and moved them up to fourth in the Conference table.

The in-form Thompson scored his third goal in four games and his ninth of the season with a superb strike on 34 minutes to give the Shrimps a vital three points. After struggling at Christie Park all season, it was the Shrimps' second home win in succession and in truth it should have been by a greater margin. Danny Carlton missed several opportunities to extend the lead. On the bright side, though, he and Matty Blinkhorn have quickly established a partnership that has begun to see the Shrimps look far more threatening up front. With Garry Thompson and Wayne Curtis hitting form on the wings as well, the Shrimps got a bite up front that had been missing at times that season. At the back, Danny Adams and Jim Bentley looked strong as the Shrimps kept their second successive Christie Park clean sheet.

It was Thompson who looked the Shrimps' most dangerous player in front of goal. He was unlucky not to add to his tally when he hit the post on 15 minutes with another well-struck shot. He also came close 10 minutes from half-time with a left-foot shot that was scrambled away to safety by Crawley keeper Ben Hamer at full stretch.

Carlton was in the thick of the action all afternoon. Although he drew a blank, the

SHRIMPS' boss Sammy McIlroy has been impressed with how his side have started their mad March run of games. The Shrimps will play nine games in March with a hectic run of midweek and Saturday games, ending on Easter Monday at home to Halifax Town (April 9). But having seen his team pick up seven points out of nine in the month ahead of last night's home game with Altrincham, McIlroy has praised his players. He said: "The players are getting tested to the limit but they are responding. Their fitness is good and their attitude has been fantastic – full credit to them. The players have battled on and have been 100 per cent committed to get us where we are at the moment – with a chance to go higher with the games in hand."

ROAD TO WEMBLEY? Morecambe could be one of the first teams to play at the new Wembley. The Conference are considering the possibility of playing the play-off final at the 90,000 capacity stadium on May 20, the day after the FA Cup Final. The League are expected to make a decision later this week. Morecambe's Sammy McIlroy said: "It is an incentive for us but our main objective is to get in the play-offs first of all."

fact he found himself in so many goal-scoring positions was a positive to take from the game. Twice Carlton headed straight at Ben Hamer from left-wing crosses after volleying over an excellent Adam Yates cross from 12 yards out on four minutes.

Carlton was then given a golden chance to extend the Shrimps' lead on 52 minutes when put through by Neil Sorvel. His lob beat the onrushing Hamer but unfortunately bobbled wide of the left-hand post. Blinkhorn then came close to scoring his second Shrimps' goal on 57 minutes with a shot that was cleared off the line and Curtis was unlucky to see a delightful late shot curl inches over the crossbar.

While the Shrimps dominated the chances chart, their failure to add a second gave Crawley hope. The visitors battled to the death in search of an equaliser with Danny Bulman drilling a fine shot over on 82 minutes and Lee Blackburn forcing Steven Drench into a neat save from a free-kick. Sorvel's challenge on left-back Darius Charles led to a big penalty appeal and Drench reacted well to dive at the feet of Rendell as the game came to a close. In the end, the Shrimps held on relatively comfortably to take three more vital points in their quest to seal a play-off place.

Morecambe: Drench 7, Yates 7, Howard 7, Bentley 7, Adams 7, Thompson 8 (Hunter 79), Stanley 7, Sorvel 7,Curtis 7, Blinkhorn 8, Carlton 6 (Burns 86). Unused subs: Davies, Brannan, Blackburn.
Crawley Town: Hamer, Hiley (Blackman 74), Okuonghae, Woozley, Charles, Evans, Bulman, Bull, Blackburn, Benyon, Rendell. Unused subs: Tolfrey, MacLeod, England, Marshall.

Referee: C Harwood.
Attendance: 1,374.
Man of the match: **Garry Thompson.**

13th March 2007

Morecambe 0 Altrincham 1

(Little 19)

SAMMY McIlroy said he would be recalling David McNiven from his loan spell at Stafford in an effort to spark his misfiring Shrimps.

After watching his side produce one of their worst performances of the season to go down to a shock 1-0 home defeat against struggling Altrincham on Tuesday night, the Shrimps' boss admitted that he would have to look at every option available to him ahead of Saturday's difficult trip to Exeter. Speaking after the game he said: "We have picked up a couple of small knocks and I might have to look at bringing David back. He's in great form at Stafford and will have picked up some vital match fitness. He will be extremely confident after a hat-trick against Gravesend and he could yet play a vital part for us."

The ball just wouldn't go in the net for Morecambe against Altrincham.

Tuesday saw the Shrimps second best for long periods against a willing but limited Altrincham. The Robins defended resolutely but the lack of creativity in the final third, with Garry Thompson unable to break free of two markers, was a worry for McIlroy.

In the end, a goal from veteran Colin Little on 19 minutes was enough to give the Robins their third successive victory as the Shrimps suffered their first defeat in six games on a highly frustrating evening. Little showed a real eye for goal after first effort was well saved by Steven Drench but he reacted quickly to latch on to the rebound and slot it past the helpless Morecambe keeper. The goal came just seconds after Drench had made a wonderful save low to his left to tip away Chris Senior's close-range header that was destined for the bottom left-hand corner. Morecambe showed brief glimpses of their recent form but Danny Carlton was unable to take the chances that came his way. One run ended with a good block from Stuart Coburn and another good shot on the turn was well saved by the Altrincham keeper who then excelled again with a neat block from Matty Blinkhorn's snapshot.

The second half saw Morecambe dominate possession and pile on the pressure.

Blinkhorn came close again with a near-post volley and Neil Sorvel dragged a shot wide from the edge of the area. The busy Blinkhorn almost embarrassed Coburn with a lob from 30 yards after the keeper had a rush of blood and rushed from his goal to clear. As time wore on Craig Stanley shot horribly wide and Wayne Curtis headed a Thompson free-kick over from six yards. It looked like it was going to be one of those nights for McIlroy's outfit. As they pushed forward they left gaps at the back and Altrincham should have taken advantage and extended their lead. Little did well to cross from the left for Senior who missed a golden chance to shoot past Drench.

Luckily his miss was soon forgotten as Altrincham celebrated another vital win in their quest for Conference safety. For Morecambe it really was a night to forget.

Morecambe: Drench 7, Yates 6, Howard 5, Bentley 6, Adams 6, Thompson 6, Stanley 6, Sorvel 5, Curtis 6, Blinkhorn 7, Carlton 5 (Burns 70). Unused subs: Davies, Brannan, Hunter.
Altrincham: Coburn, Rose, Band, Munroe, Peyton, Bushell, Chalmers, Lawton, Senior (McFadden 79), O'Neill, Little (Thornley 90). Unused subs: Talbot, Thomson, Scott.

Referee: M Brown.
Attendance: 1,403.
Man of the match: **Steven Drench.**

17th March 2007

Exeter City 1 Morecambe 0

(Logan 73)

MORECAMBE suffered their second successive defeat when they went down to a wonder goal at St James's Park.

Richard Logan was the hero for Exeter with a superb volley 17 minutes from time which condemned Sammy McIlroy's outfit to their second 1-0 defeat of the week.

The result saw the Shrimps drop out of the play-off zone with Exeter gaining valuable ground on their rivals. In truth Morecambe never looked like winning this game. But they also never looked like losing it on a day that was high in expectation but low in quality. Both sides struggled to find any fluency on a dry, bobbly pitch and both sides seemed to struggle with nerves.

McIlroy made three changes to the side that lost in midweek against Altrincham with the recalled David McNiven starting up front but given no service. McNiven was left to fend for himself for much of the game and provided some decent moments. In the first half he produced an audacious shot on the turn from 30 yards which almost caught out Exeter keeper Paul Jones. Late in the second half he did well to work himself an opening but was unlucky to see his shot deflected over by Chris Todd's desperate late tackle. Elsewhere the Shrimps' forward play was disappointing. Garry Thompson and Jamie Burns failed to threaten down the wings and there was little creativity in midfield.

The latest results have highlighted a lack of firepower for Morecambe – even in games where they have dominated the play the Shrimps have failed to create enough chances, a problem McIlroy says he and the players fully acknowledge.

"Defensively I am quite happy. We are keeping things tight and restricting opponents to very few opportunities," the manager told The Visitor. "On Saturday it was a case of both defences playing well and I thought it would take a bad error or a moment of brilliance to settle it. It was going towards a nailed on nil-nil when their sub hit a wonder strike. But we know we're not creating enough chances. I'm not putting the blame on midfielders or strikers independently, they have to combine properly to make the openings."

Exeter were equally as poor however with only rare forays on the Morecambe goal. Jon Challinor looked sharp up front and forced Drench into a good save in the first half with a well struck shot from Wayne Carlisle's right-wing cross. Drench had to react sharply again at the start of the second half to block at the feet of Lee Phillips after one of the best moves of the game put the Grecians through. It was a match that had 0-0 written all over it until Logan scored a stunner just minutes after coming off the bench. A long ball should have caused the Morecambe defence few problems but skipper Jim Bentley, hampered by a niggling calf injury, failed to clear and Logan took full advantage with a wonderful, dipping volley which gave Drench no chance.

A stunned Morecambe briefly threatened a comeback. Jamie Burns had the best chance to pull one back when he ran on to Neil Sorvel's fine pass but the ball bobbled at a vital time and he drilled his effort over. It was then a tale of two crosses as Burns' dangerous left-wing effort flew across the six yard box. It just needed a touch before Danny Carlton wasted a glorious opportunity with a weak final ball when Morecambe had men over in the box. Chris Blackburn did threaten to break into the box but was hauled back by the neck by Billy Jones. It was a decision that somehow went unpunished, much to the fury of boss McIlroy whose frustration was clear for all to see at the end of a big afternoon.

Morecambe: Drench 7, Blackburn 6, Howard 6, Bentley 6, Adams 6, Thompson 5, Stanley 5, Sorvel 6, Burns 5, Blinkhorn 6, McNiven 7. Unused subs: Davies, Brannan, Carter.
Exeter: P Jones, B Jones, Richardson, Edwards, Todd, Buckle (Cozic 40), Carlisle, Elam, Gill, Phillips, Challinor (Logan 69). Unused subs: Rice, Taylor, Stansfield.

Referee: D Sheldrake.
Attendance: 3,530.
Man of the match: **Steven Drench.**

AFTER his side's second successive defeat, Shrimps boss Sammy McIlroy called on his midfelders and strikers to 'get it together' for a run-in to the play-offs.

But preparations were hampered by injuries to two key players.

Skipper Jim Bentley took a kick to the shin at Exeter on Saturday and Michael Howard got a knock in training on Monday – both were doubtful for the Aldershot match. With Conference play-off positions changing hands weekly and the Shrimps having seen their 'games in hand' advantage whittled away recently, every point from now to the end of the season will be crucial.

20th March 2007

Morecambe 2 Aldershot Town 1

(Blinkhorn 8, Sorvel 19) (Hudson 83)

MORECAMBE'S play-off hopes received a timely boost with a thrilling win over Aldershot on Tuesday night.

After two successive defeats, the Shrimps returned to winning ways thanks to two wonder goals and a superb performance from goalkeeper Steven Drench. The points looked secure when Morecambe blasted their way into an early two-goal lead with wonder strikes from Matty Blinkhorn and Neil Sorvel. They went on to battle to the death in the face of a spirited fightback from the Shots which saw them score one late goal and come close to another on several occasions.

The game could not have started any better for Morecambe as Blinkhorn scored his second goal for the Shrimps with a superb strike on eight minutes.

The on-loan striker let fly with a dipping volley from 30 yards which flew past Nikki Bull's right hand and curled into the top right-hand corner. Garry Hunter, in the side for the rested Craig Stanley, then came close with a volley that just cleared the crossbar. Neil Sorvel then added to Morecambe's lead with a stunning strike of his own to put the Shrimps 2-0 up on 19 minutes.

The play then swung from end to end with the shell-shocked Shots fighting back strongly. Kirk Hudson saw a shot deflected inches wide of the left-hand post and Drench saved superbly from John Grant who looked set to score after running onto Darren Barnard's excellent throughball. Dean Smith and Jonny Dixon both fired efforts wide before Grant came close again with a shot that beat Drench low to his right but came back off the post. At the other end, Morecambe had chances of their own.

Neil Sorvel blasts Morecambe 2-0 up after only 19 minutes.

At full-time, Sammy McIlroy make sure his players kept their focus.

Wayne Curtis thought he had made it 3-0 but was foiled by an offside flag.

Garry Thompson forced Bull into a good save low to his right and Chris Blackburn volleyed onto the roof of the net.

The second half belonged to the Shots who peppered the Morecambe goal from the restart when Drench made possibly the save of the season to tip Dixon's dipping volley onto the crossbar. Drench then saved well from Molesley and a close range Grant header but was finally beaten seven minutes from time when Kirk Hudson drilled a shot through his legs to set up a nervous finale. Danny Carlton wasted a glorious chance to seal the points when he missed the target with only Bull to beat. He was almost made to pay when Grant's snapshot from 25 yards shaved the left-hand post with Drench beaten. In the end the Shrimps held onto their lead to take three more important points in their play-off push.

Morecambe: Drench 9, Yates 7, Adams 6 (Curtis 30), Bentley 7, Blackburn 7, Thompson 7 (Brannan 84), Hunter 8, Sorvel 7, Burns 7, Blinkhorn 7, McNiven 7 (Carlton 74). Unused subs: Curtis, Lloyd. Booked: Bentley.
Aldershot: Bull, Smith, Barnard (Winfield 90), Day, Molesley, Grant, Williams (Soares 61), Hudson, Charles, Beckford, Dixon (Pritchard 70). Unused subs: Scott, Wells.
Referee: D Richardson.
Attendance: 1,165.
Man of the match: **Steven Drench.**

24th March 2007

Burton Albion 2 Morecambe 1

(Shaw 27, Clare 29) (Curtis 80 pen)

MORECAMBE'S rollercoaster season continued when they suffered their third defeat in four games to Burton Albion.

The Shrimps only had themselves to blame with defensive errors at critical times gifting Burton their second victory of the season over Morecambe. For long periods, Morecambe were the better team and played the better football but they were punished for their errors with two goals in two minutes, enough to see the Brewers take the three points. It was yet another frustrating afternoon for Sammy McIlroy's side who dropped out of the play-off zone as they lost to one of their main rivals for the second week in a row. Once again results elsewhere went their way though, and the race for the play-offs was set to go all the way in what was due to be an exciting, and fruitful, final few weeks of the season.

Morecambe started well enough and Matty Blinkhorn almost gave the Shrimps an early lead with a shot that was well turned away by veteran keeper Kevin Poole. Garry Hunter then volleyed a smart effort inches over the crossbar after a superb piece of skill put him through. Burton, who beat Morecambe 1-0 on the opening day of the season at Christie Park, came back strongly with Aaron Webster heading Keith Gilroy's cross just wide and Darren Stride heading against the woodwork after ghosting into the Morecambe box at the far post. As both

SAMMY McIlroy was left frustrated in his bid to strengthen his squad for the play-off run-in after Southport pulled out of a deal for Carl Baker. The Shrimps boss was keen to bring in the attacking midfielder, who has impressed in the Conference this season, despite playing in a struggling side. A deal was understood to be close ahead of the loan deadline last Thursday, but Southport pulled out. Despite the setback, McIlroy was happy with the squad he has until the end of the season. He said: "I was in for Baker again but unfortunately it didn't happen. We need to put that to bed now and I am happy with what I have got left and we have to get on with it."

sides looked to gain the upper hand, Burton were gifted an opener following a mistake by Jim Bentley.

The Morecambe skipper saw a low through-ball roll past his left foot and presented Jon Shaw with a free run on goal. The striker kept his cool well and slotted home past the helpless Steven Drench. Two minutes later it was 2-0 with an equally sloppy goal from Morecambe's viewpoint. Keith Gilroy shook off Garry Thompson's weak challenge and crossed to the far post. Danny Adams missed the cross and somehow well-known Conference goalgrabber Daryl Clare had been left on his own to head past Drench from eight yards out.

From there Morecambe dominated but struggled to break through a solid Burton defence. David McNiven did find a way past Poole with a shot that was cleared from under his own posts by Stride and Hunter drilled an effort wide of the left-hand post.

Blinkhorn directed a header weakly wide after the Burton defence failed to clear their lines as the Shrimps piled on the pressure before the break. Morecambe continued their onslaught in the second half. Poole did well to spot the danger and race from his goal to save at the foot of Blinkhorn after a neat Hunter through-ball and the Burton keeper reacted well to save from McNiven's long-range effort. Adam Yates was unlucky to see a well-struck curler from distance just fly past the left-hand post and substitute Wayne Curtis saw a golden chance go begging as he hesitated over a shot and allowed a Burton defender to clear at full stretch.

The Shrimps were then given a lifeline when Stride handled Hunter's bouncing throw-in and Curtis took the chance to give his side hope with a cool penalty.

The pressure continued with Burton on the back foot. Despite their best efforts, though, there was no way back for the Shrimps who dropped vital points at a vital time against vital opponents.

Morecambe: Drench 7, Yates 7, Adams 6, Bentley 6, Blackburn 7, Thompson 6 (Carlton 74), Hunter 8, Sorvel 8, Burns 6 (Curtis 46), Blinkhorn 7, McNiven 7. Unused subs: Stanley, Brannan, Davies. Booked: Bentley, Thompson.
Burton Albion: Poole, Brayford, Stride, Austin, Webster, Nicholls (Corbett 65), Holmes, Carden, Gilroy, Shaw (Tinson 87), Clare (Harrad 77). Unused subs: Ducros.

Referee: A Haines.
Attendance: 1,732.
Man of the match: **Garry Hunter.**

27th March 2007

Morecambe 2 Northwich Victoria 1

(Blinkhorn 19, Blackburn 71) (Mayman 69)

CHRIS Blackburn was Morecambe's goal hero as he earned three valuable points at Christie Park against Northwich Victoria.

The defender pounced on a loose ball in the Northwich box just two minutes after Danny Mayman had levelled for the visitors with a superb strike which stunned the home fans. It was a goal that could prove vital at the end of the season and it was a goal that took the Shrimps back into the play-off spots. Results went their way with defeats for Exeter and York and a draw for Burton.

After three defeats in the last four games, the Shrimps got back on the right track.

They started the game brightly with Paul Lloyd sidefooting Carlton's cross inches wide of the post and Blackburn heading an Adam Yates free-kick just off target. The visitors then came close themselves when Chris Smith headed a Michael Byrne free-kick wide of the left-hand post. The Shrimps went on to take the lead when Matty Blinkhorn beat Connett to Carlton's corner to head home from close range. He came close to doubling his tally with a shot at full stretch well saved by Connett after a flowing Morecambe move involving Carlton, Garry Hunter and Wayne Curtis.

The second half saw Northwich step up the pace and they started the period well with former Morecambe player Matty Shaw testing Steven Drench at his near post. Paul Brayson was later denied by the crossbar after nipping in between Jim Bentley and Drench to lob the ball goalward.

Morecambe then took charge again. The ever-threatening Blinkhorn made Connett save sharply low to his right with a near-post header. Blackburn then clipped a shot over at the far post after Bentley flicked on another dangerous corner by Carlton. Midfield duo Garry Hunter and Neil Sorvel both came close before Northwich scored a shock equaliser. Blackburn did well to head clear but the ball fell to Mayman and he lashed a stunning volley into the top right-hand corner of Drench's net.

The Vics' joy was short-lived however as the Shrimps regained the lead two minutes later to set up a frantic finale. Michael Byrne and Carlos Roca both missed the target from the edge of the area. Mayman then almost added a second on 87 minutes with a volley which curled just wide with Drench beaten. Morecambe came close to a third with

Jim Bentley keeps a close eye on his man.

substitute David McNiven heading Wayne Curtis' cross the wrong side of the right hand post as Morecambe clinched a vital three points.

After the game, Sammy McIlroy praised Chris Blackburn's contribution. He said: "Chris was tremendous all evening and fully deserved his goal. He has defended superbly at one end and is always a threat when he gets into the box at the other end and his goal could be an important one for us."

Morecambe: Drench 7, Yates 7, Adams 7, Bentley 7, Blackburn 8, Lloyd 7 (Burns 75), Hunter 7, Sorvel 7 (Stanley 76), Curtis 7, Blinkhorn 7, McNiven 7 (Carlton 74). Unused subs: Davies, Brannan. Booked: Blinkhorn.

Northwich Victoria: Connett, Battersby, Roberts, Charnock, McCarthy, Mayman, Carr, Smith (Roca 77), Byrne, Brayson (Dean 83), Shaw. Unused subs: Senior, Warburton, Barwick. Booked: Battersby, Roberts.

Referee: M Matadar.
Attendance: 1,315.
Man of the match: **Chris Blackburn.**

31st March 2007

Morecambe 2 Woking 0

(Blinkhorn 15, 48)

MORECAMBE sealed their second home win of the week to climb to third in the Conference table.

On-loan goal ace Matty Blinkhorn was the star of the show with two well-taken goals to give the Shrimps the upper hand on teams challenging for the play-off spots. With just six games to go, including a vital trip to Stevenage on Saturday, the Shrimps held their destiny in their own hands.

After three defeats in four games before the last week, there were certainly a few nerves around Christie Park. However, the Shrimps' successes and shock defeats for York and Stevenage meant the play-offs were now a very real possibility. The game saw the Shrimps come up against a Woking side who sacked manager Glenn Cockerill just days previously. The result never really looked in doubt once Blinkhorn had opened the scoring on 15 minutes. After swapping passes with David McNiven he slotted home a shot past Cards' keeper Nick Gindre. If other Morecambe players had been as clinical, this could well have been one of the biggest victories of the season.

Skipper Jim Bentley was unlucky not to put his side 2-0 up after his volley from a corner was cleared off the line but Wayne Curtis was guilty of squandering several opportunities. His first saw a deft lob beat Gindre but bounce just the wrong side of the post before a second effort from a similar position brought a good save from the keeper. Garry Thompson then dragged a shot wide before Blinkhorn finally made the pressure count with an exquisite second three minutes into the second half.

Blinkhorn latched on to a long through ball and after seeing Gindre well off his line lofted a left-footed effort into the empty goal from 20 yards out. As the pressure continued Blinkhorn was denied a hat-trick by a Gary MacDonald goalline clearance before Gindre saved well again from Garry Hunter and Curtis. McNiven was unlucky to see a long-range curler just beat the crossbar as the Shrimps looked to increase their lead.

Although second best for long periods, Woking did come close on a number of occasions with Steven Drench forced into the save of the afternoon when he did well to turn away Giuseppe Sole's 26th-minute free-kick, but all too often the visitors were denied by a strong and well-organised Morecambe defence. The Cards produced a final flurry with Jason Pearce and Craig McAllister heading just wide and Drench saving well from a close-range Olly Berquez volley. There was no way through for the struggling visitors, though, who seemed to lack confidence in the final third. For Morecambe however, the confidence was rising and with Blinkhorn maintaining his run, there was promise of some exciting games ahead.

McIlroy confirmed this week that he would have the services of Matty Blinkhorn until the end of the season, including the play-offs, as long as Blackpool don't need him.

He said: "Matty has been tremendous for us and he took his goals brilliantly on Saturday – they were real striker's goals. Blackpool have got a call-back which I hope never happens. If he keeps doing what he is doing, then we will all be delighted."

Morecambe: Drench 7, Yates 7, Adams 7, Bentley 7, Blackburn 7, Thompson 7, Hunter 7, Sorvel 7 (Stanley 85), Curtis 7, Blinkhorn 8, McNiven 7 (Brannan 83). Unused subs: Davies, Lloyd, Burns. Booked: Adams.
Woking: Gindre, Osano, Hutchinson, MacDonald, Bunce (Lambu 56), Pearce, Murray, Smith (Berquez 78), Sole (Marum 78), Webb, McAllister. Unused subs: Bittner, Green.

Referee: J Collin.
Attendance: 1,466.
Man of the match: **Matty Blinkhorn.**

Jim Bentley rises highest at a set-piece.

3rd April 2007

St Albans City 0 Morecambe 2

(McNiven 38, Blinkhorn 80)

MORECAMBE secured another three priceless points with a 2-0 win at struggling St Albans.

In the end some quality finishing and superb goalkeeping from Steven Drench gave the Shrimps a vital three points as once again teams challenging them for a play-off place suffered defeats. On 10 minutes, centre-half Djoumin Sangare was guilty of wasting a golden opportunity when he headed Ahmed Deen's right-wing corner wide at the far post when unchallenged. Twelve minutes later, the home side came close to opening the scoring again when midfielder Lee Clarke raced into the box to connect with Malik Buari's cross. He was then denied by a superb save from Drench who somehow got down low to his left to keep the ball out. Drench had to be at his best again two minutes later. He denied Clarke once more with a shot from distance that the in-form Morecambe keeper did well to hold on to.

After a sluggish start, Morecambe burst into life after the half hour. Skipper Jim Bentley headed wide before the Shrimps took the lead with a welcome goal for David McNiven on 38 minutes. The striker, who has worked hard with no reward since returning from his loan spell at Stafford, raced onto a long ball and powered past Gary Elphick before shooting under the onrushing Paul Bastock. Garry Thompson came close to extending the Shrimps' lead three minutes later with an audacious volley from 30 yards out that almost caught out Bastock but curled inches over the bar.

The home side started the second half sharply with substitute Matt Hann losing control of the ball when in a good position and right-back Chris Seeby seeing a shot deflected for a corner. Seeby tried his luck again from distance with a volley and Clarke should have done better with a free header before Shrimps' defender Chris Blackburn produced a vital last gasp clearance to deny Hann a shot on goal.

Wayne Curtis and Thompson both drilled in shots that forced Bastock into saves. Matty Blinkhorn then scored his sixth goal since joining the Shrimps as he nipped in between defender and goalkeeper to lob a loose ball into the empty net and cap another good performance from Sammy McIlroy's in-form side.

Morecambe: Drench 8, Yates 7, Adams 7, Bentley 7, Blackburn 7, Thompson 7, Hunter 7 (Stanley 85), Sorvel 8 (Brannan 85), Curtis 7, Blinkhorn 7, McNiven 7 (Burns 80). Unused subs: Davies, Lloyd. Booked: Blinkhorn.
St Albans: Bastock, Seeby, Elphick, Sangare, Deen, Marwa (Davis 77), Buari, Watters (Hann 45), Lopez (Cracknell 77), Archer, Clarke. Unused subs: Perks, Basse.

Referee: S Tomlinson.
Attendance: 619.
Man of the match: **Neil Sorvel.**

7th April 2007

Stevenage Borough 3 Morecambe 3

(Nurse 27, Morison 48, Hakim 51) (Curtis 45, Fuller 53og, Thompson 66)

MORECAMBE moved a step closer to sealing a play-off spot with this thrilling draw at Broadhall Way.

The Shrimps staged a superb fightback to come back from 3-1 down to level the scores and take a well-earned point, which took them level with Oxford on 72 points.

Stevenage began sharply with top-scorer Steve Morison soon causing problems, heading a Craig Dobson corner wide and being denied a shot on goal by Adam Yates' last-gasp covering tackle. Morison saw a weak volley cleared off the line by Danny Adams before the home side were gifted an opening goal on 27 minutes. John Nurse took advantage of hesitation between Chris Blackburn and goalkeeper Steven Drench to stab the ball over the line.

Morecambe then raised their tempo. Matty Blinkhorn volleyed wide from 25 yards before the Shrimps equalised in injury time. David McNiven played in Garry Thompson and his cross was bundled home by Wayne Curtis at the near post.

The game then burst into life with a scintillating second half.

Morecambe were forced to replace the injured Drench with Scott Davies and the young keeper had the worst possible start as he was beaten twice in quick succession.

The Shrimps were unfortunate not to take the lead on 47 minutes when a brilliant effort from McNiven crashed against the underside of the crossbar.

But within seconds, Stevenage went ahead as Blackburn failed to clear. Dangerman Morison stabbed the ball past Davies for his sixth goal in four games against Morecambe that season. Three minutes later, Stevenage extended their lead to 3-1 when substitute Paul Hakim volleyed home and the game looked over.

But Morecambe had other ideas and they hit back quickly. Stevenage right-back Barry Fuller headed into his own net as he tried to divert Jim Bentley's goalbound header. The pressure continued with Blinkhorn heading Adam Yates' cross wide before the Shrimps scored a dramatic equaliser. Thompson showed great strength to muscle past John Nutter and stroke the ball through a crowd of players.

Morecambe: Drench 6 (Davies 46), Yates 7, Adams 7, Bentley 7, Blackburn 6, Thompson 7, Hunter 8, Sorvel 7, Curtis 7, Blinkhorn 7 (Stanley 83), McNiven 7 (Carlton 75). Unused subs: Brannan, Burns. Booked: Hunter, Blinkhorn.
Stevenage Borough: Julian, Fuller, Nutter (Batt 69), Gaia, Henry, Beard, Dobson (Hakim 46), Lewis, Cole, Morison, Nurse. Unused subs: Potter, Oliver, Guppy.

Referee: A Hendley.
Attendance: 1,845.
Man of the match: **Garry Hunter.**

9th April 2007

Morecambe 4 Halifax Town 0

(Blinkhorn 39, 89, Sorvel 60, Thompson 87)

MORECAMBE had one foot in the play-offs this week after storming to a Bank Holiday Monday win over struggling Halifax Town.

Three second-half goals gave the Shrimps another valuable three points which maintained their third place position with three games of the normal season to go.

Once again Matty Blinkhorn was the Shrimps' star. He added another two goals to make it eight from 12 matches since joining on loan from Blackpool at the beginning of March. It was Blinkhorn who popped up at the vital time to give the Shrimps the lead in the final stages of the first half. He doubled his tally with a superb strike two minutes from time. He could have had a hat-trick had he not somehow managed to miss an open goal from six yards out. The miss was soon

Garry Thompson rounded off a good day with the fourth.

forgotten as the Shrimps were left celebrating their sixth win in the last seven games at Christie Park.

Halifax came into the game with the worst away record in the Conference with just three wins and 15 goals from 20 outings. They started brightly, though, and came close to scoring on four minutes when Danny Forrest's close-range header was cleared off the line by Garry Hunter. Steve Torpey, who scored against the Shrimps at the Shay earlier in the season, looked lively on the left and showed no lack of confidence as he saw two efforts fly just wide of the target. After being second best for a long spell, the Shrimps burst into life when Blinkhorn opened the scoring on 38 minutes. He ghosted in at the far post to head home Garry Thompson's left-wing free-kick which flew across the Halifax six-yard box with the visiting defence stood watching.

The goal gave Morecambe a clear lift and they started the second half sharply. The pressure soon paid off when Neil Sorvel kept his cool to slide home Danny Adams' superb throughball on the hour claiming his second goal for the club. Halifax tried in vain to get back into the game with a Torpey free-kick flashing dangerously across the Morecambe six-yard box and a well-struck Forrest drive superbly tipped over by debutant keeper Scott Davies. The action was all then in the Halifax half as the visitors' confidence crumbled visibly. Wayne Curtis forced former team-mate Craig Mawson into a great save before skewing the rebound wide from six yards out.

But the Shrimps moved further ahead with a third goal three minutes from time.

Danny Carlton's corner was flicked on at the near post by Curtis and Garry Thompson scored at the far post.

A minute later, the rout was completed. Blinkhorn took advantage of some poor defending from Adam Quinn to stroke the ball into the empty net from 25 yards out completing a fine day in front of a large,

Morecambe: Davies 8, Yates 7, Adams 7, Bentley 7, Blackburn 8, Thompson 7, Hunter 7 (Stanley 74), Sorvel 8 (Brannan 75), Curtis 7, Blinkhorn 8, McNiven 7 (Carlton 69). Unused subs: Lloyd, Burns.
Halifax Town: Mawson, Toulson, Cresswell, Quinn, Doughty, Uhlenbeek (Killeen 46), Kearney, Billy (Stamp 68), Torpey, Campbell (Thompson 67), Forrest. Unused subs: Wright, Trotman. Booked: Kearney.

Referee: K Evans.
Attendance: 2,412.
Man of the match: **Matty Blinkhorn.**

McIlroy said: "That was fantastic and was just what we wanted. It's a real confidence booster to be scoring goals at this stage of the season. We had a good crowd on and it was great to do a good performance for them. It was a great atmosphere today and great for the fans to see us score four goals."

Matty Blinkhorn chipped in his second goal from 30 yards.

14th April 2007

Weymouth 2 Morecambe 1

(Beavon 37, James 53 pen) (Carlton 41)

MORECAMBE'S play-off party was spoiled by a spirited Weymouth side who failed to read the script.

With the sun shining brightly and a large group of holidaying Shrimps fans making the journey to the Wessex Stadium, this was supposed to be the game that assured Morecambe their place in this year's play-offs. After just one defeat in six, the Shrimps came up against a home team with one point from the last five games and on the end of a 7-0 hammering by Cambridge and two further heavy defeats. But the formbook was well and truly thrown out of the window as Morecambe produced one of their most insipid performances of the season.

Their normal fluent passing game was nowhere to be seen. They lacked pace, ideas and even a bit of passion as the home side won almost every second ball and surprisingly dominated the midfield battle.

It was a performance that left boss Sammy McIlroy scratching his head and one that will give him plenty of food for thought this week. Despite the poor performance however, the Shrimps can count themselves unlucky to have lost the game to a controversial penalty. Danny Adams seemed to get the ball when he challenged Stuart Beavon on 53 minutes but after some hesitation, the referee pointed to the spot.

Ironically, and perhaps more annoyingly for the Shrimps, the referee failed to make the same brave decision just 30 seconds earlier when Danny Carlton was crudely bundled over in the box by Brian Dutton – only for the man in the middle to wave play on. Former Hereford skipper, and penalty expert, Tony James, stroked the penalty past Steven Drench's left hand and Morecambe could not find a way back in the game.

Weymouth produced the early pressure with Simon Weatherstone firing over in the first minute. Next Rafael Nade, who caused the Morecambe defence problems all afternoon, almost took advantage of some early hesitation by Chris Blackburn.

Stuart Beavon saw a good run end with a shot beaten down by Jim Bentley before Weatherstone forced Steven Drench into a neat save with a well-struck 25-yarder.

On 19 minutes, James wasted a golden opportunity when he headed straight at Drench from eight yards out. Only after the early scares did Morecambe hit first gear.

Garry Thompson shot weakly wide from

the right hand side before Wayne Curtis forced Jason Matthews into a great save from a header after the Shrimps' free-kick defied a defence looking for offside. Blackburn looped a shot onto the top of the Weymouth net from Thompson's corner and the Shrimps looked set to take charge.

Then they were hit by a swift Weymouth counter-attack. Nade was left in space on the right and delivered a cross which was met by the unmarked Beavon who headed past the helpless Drench.

Four minutes later however, the scores were level. A Thompson corner was headed back across the Weymouth box by Bentley, Blackburn flicked on and Danny Carlton rose well to direct a header past Matthews. Two minutes later, the Shrimps came close to taking the lead with a curling free-kick from the unlucky David McNiven hitting the foot of the post with the Weymouth keeper beaten low to his left. The game then turned on a minute of controversy in the second half with the two successive penalty appeals that went Weymouth's way.

In the final stages, Neil Sorvel blasted wide from a great opening and McNiven volleyed wide on the turn after a good Paul Lloyd flick for the Shrimps. But it was the home side who came closest to scoring when former Shrimp Conal Platt volleyed a great chance over from close range on 73 minutes and then forced Drench into a good save in the last minute. In the end Morecambe simply did not do enough and they knew they would have to perform much better in the final two games of the campaign – and hopefully the play-offs.

"It was very disappointing, we didn't play to our capabilities. It was a bit of a shock really because, more than anything else, I couldn't see it coming.
"We know we let everyone down, myself, my assistant and the team are all together and we are not going to point the finger at individuals.
"We had good support down there and we didn't like sending them back with an inept performance but these things happen in football and it is about how we respond."

Sammy McIlroy

Morecambe: Drench , Yates 6, Adams 6, Bentley 6, Blackburn 6 (Brannan 75), Thompson 6, Hunter 6 (Stanley 73), Sorvel 6, Curtis 6 (Lloytd 53), Carlton 6, McNiven 6. Unused subs: Davies, Burns. Booked: Blackburn
Weymouth: Matthews, Crittenden, Barnard, Dutton, James (Cottrell 59), Robinson, Weatherstone, Phillips (Ironside 90), Coutts, Nade, Beavon (Platt 73). Unused subs: Jones, Crawley. Booked: Dutton, Phillips.

Referee: A Turner.
Attendance: 1,206.
Man of the match: **Steven Drench.**

21st April 2007

Kidderminster Harriers 0 Morecambe 1

(Thompson 41 pen)

MORECAMBE'S hopes of a place in the Football League were still very much alive after they sealed their place in this year's Conference play-offs.

A Garry Thompson penalty was enough to seal the victory the Shrimps and their supporters wanted so badly, extending their season for the third time in four years. There was no doubt there were more than a few nerves in the air at Aggborough both on the pitch and in the stands. Although Morecambe could not find the second goal they wanted to put the game beyond doubt, they held firm to keep the dream very much alive.

It was a result that understandably delighted boss Sammy McIlroy who said he was 'proud' at his side's achievements. He said: "After last week's disappointment at Weymouth I asked for a response and I certainly got it. We have battled all the way and everyone involved with the club, the players, the officials, the backroom staff and the supporters can feel proud of what has been achieved so far." Thompson deserved full credit for his spot-kick. He had to endure an agonising delay to take it after Kidderminster keeper Scott Bevan was sent off for hauling the Morecambe winger down in the box as he raced through. Bevan was replaced by sub keeper Steve Taylor but after about three long minutes he was beaten by Thompson's perfectly-placed effort. In the end it was enough to spark celebrations among the large band of Shrimps' supporters who had travelled to the game and who could then look ahead to another nervous extension to the season.

Morecambe always looked the sharper against these FA Trophy finalists who were looking for a double in the year over the Shrimps. On seven minutes, striker Danny Carlton volleyed Adam Yates' long ball wide of the right-hand post and the recalled Craig Stanley drilled a 25-yard effort just wide. Paul Lloyd then broke free of former Blackburn defender Jeff Kenna and fired over. Kidderminster then produced their first real threat when the diminutive Simon Russell lobbed just over from distance and drilled a right-footer wide. Morecambe hit back with Ged Brannan shooting straight at Bevan before the penalty decision gave the Shrimps a valuable half-time cushion.

The second half saw Morecambe dominate the pressure but fail to score the

The Shrimps could be facing either Oxford, York, Exeter or Burton in the first leg of the play-offs next Friday with the second leg the following Monday or Tuesday.

McIlroy said: "We will see who it is but whoever it is it won't be an easy game. But having said that, I am sure they will be thinking the same about us. I am not frightened of any of them. We have fighting chance of getting to Wembley and getting into League Two."

second goal they desperately wanted to calm the nerves against the spirited 10 men. Thompson volleyed over the bar from a precise Carlton corner and the Shrimps' goal-scorer was denied on two more occasions. First he forced Taylor into a wonderful save with a volley on the turn and then he saw a goalbound effort cleared off the line by Michael Blackwood. Morecambe keeper Steven Drench was a virtual spectator as Kidderminster failed to produce a single shot on goal until injury-time. It was a nailbiting moment for the Shrimps' large band of travelling supporters but as the ball sailed over the bar, they were able to celebrate a winning afternoon.

Morecambe: Drench 7, Yates 7, Adams 7, Bentley 7, Blackburn 7, Thompson 7, Stanley 7, Sorvel 7, Brannan 8, Lloyd 7, Carlton 7 (Burns 90). Unused subs: Davies, Howard, McLachlan, McNiven. Booked: Brannan. **Kidderminster Harriers:** Bevan, Kenna, Creighton, Whitehead, Blackwood, Smikle (McGrath 78), Sedgemore, Hurren, Russell (Taylor 41), Constable, Christie (Reynolds 72).Unused subs: Hay, Brady. Sent off: Bevan.

Referee: A Rodda.
Attendance: 1,654.
Man of the match: **Ged Brannan.**

SAMMY McIlroy wants to see a party spirit at Christie Park on Saturday to celebrate the Shrimps reaching the play-offs. But he will tell his players that he wants to 'go out on a high' with a win over Grays to seal third spot in the Conference. Morecambe's 1-0 win at Kidderminster last Saturday ensured the Shrimps will be in the play-offs for the second year running – barring a mathematical miracle. But McIlroy – who could have Michael Twiss at his disposal – doesn't want his side to switch off with the final positions to be confirmed.

28th April 2007

Morecambe 1 Grays Athletic 0

(Lloyd 2)

MORECAMBE ended their Conference campaign on a high with a narrow victory over gallant Grays.

The Shrimps took the three points to finish the season level on points with pre-season title favourites Oxford. It was a feat that delighted triumphant boss Sammy McIlroy who said he was "proud" of his players. Said McIlroy: "I always said the season was a marathon and not a sprint and over 46 games we have deserved to finish where we have. The players have been magnificent this season and I am very proud of them. Our main objective was to get into the play-offs and we have done that and now we move on to our next objective which is to win the play-offs."

Paul Lloyd was the man to earn the Shrimps their victory against Grays Athletic with a goal in the second minute. It certainly wasn't a pretty strike, but it proved to be an important one. Adam Yates deserves the credit for the assist with a great cross from the right which Lloyd stabbed goalwards past despairing defender Simon Downer.

Many thought that would be the cue for the party to start but things didn't quite go to plan as Grays then took charge. Justin Edinburgh's side created a number of chances but failed to test Morecambe keeper Steven Drench. Defenders Downer and Jamie Stuart both wasted excellent first-half opportunities to get back into the game.

Downer volleyed a Stuart Thurgood over from close range and Stuart directed a free-header wide after getting in front of his marker. Thurgood forced Drench into a neat save from a curling free-kick and the Morecambe keeper reacted well shortly after to save from Dennis Oli's close-range shot. The Shrimps' defence, well marshalled by Jim Bentley and Chris Blackburn, had to be at their best with superb last-ditch tackles to deny Grays clear chances.

In the second half, Ashley Nicholls and substitute Leroy Griffiths both fired into the side netting in the final stages and the former shot straight at Steven Drench when he should have done much better. At the other end, Morecambe struggled to build on their superb start. The returning Michael Twiss came close to marking his first game since February with a goal. He drilled Danny Carlton's neat lay-off wide and Neil Sorvel forced Knowles into a scrappy save with a shot he held on to at the second attempt. Carlton then came close with a header after some superb work by Twiss.

The second half saw Grays push forward again with Thurgood shooting over. Aaron O'Connor then produced an effort on the

Michael Twiss returned to the line-up after injury.

turn that Drench did well to hold on to.

Morecambe hit back again with Carlton outpacing Downer but shooting straight at Knowles and Twiss forcing the Grays keeper into a stop after a neat run.

As the game came to a close, the visitors wasted two further opportunities with O'Connor shooting straight at Drench after a poor clearance and Nicholls blasting an effort into the side netting when he should have done much better.

In the end the Shrimps did enough to hold on for their seventh home win from their previous eight Christie Park games.

Morecambe: Drench 7, Yates 7, Adams 7, Bentley 7 (Brannan 46), Blackburn 7, Lloyd 6 (Burns 67), Stanley 7, Sorvel 7, Curtis 6, Twiss 7 (McNiven 84), Carlton 6. Unused subs: Davies, Howard. Booked: Blackburn, Carlton.
Grays Athletic: Knowles, Sambrook, Stuart, Downer, Thurgood, Oli (Rhodes 88), O'Connor, Tonkin, Martin, Bodkin (Griffiths 55), Nicholls (Harding 84). Unused subs: Bayes, Barness.

Referee: S Cummings.
Attendance: 2,303.
Man of the match: **Chris Blackburn.**

York Play-offs

GED BRANNAN has his sights set on finishing his top level playing career at Wembley and giving his two sons a day they will never forget. The popular former Tranmere and Wigan man says he intends to concentrate on the coaching side of the game after the summer. Brannan almost joined Southport at the turn of the year to become Paul Cook's assistant but the Sandgrounders sacked his former Accrington team-mate and he stayed at Christie Park, much to the delight of boss Sammy McIlroy. Now he is looking forward to the play-offs and a possible Wembley date. Brannan said: "I have played at Wembley before and it is an unforgettable experience but this time it would be extra special. "I have two young boys now and I would love to take them with me and make it a special family occasion. Now we are in the play-offs I can't see any reason why we can't do it this year. On our day, I don't think there is a better team in the Conference and I am hoping the experience of players like myself, Jim Bentley, Michael Howard, Danny Adams and Neil Sorvel can stand us in good stead.

He added: "It is my intention at the moment to finish playing at the end of the season so it would be great to finish on a high."

Sammy McIlroy said: "I didn't want Ged to join Southport and although I was disappointed for him that it fell through in the way it did I am delighted to have kept him. He is a valuable member of the squad and is always totally reliable. The young lads look up to him and he is a true professional."

Brannan showed his versatility on Saturday by coming on in place of centre-half Jim Bentley. But Bentley said after the game that he would be fit to start the first leg at York on Friday night. And the Shrimps' skipper has urged fans to make themselves heard at the KitKat Crescent. He said: "They came out in force at Hereford last year and they gave us great support and I hope they can do the same again on Friday. The lads really appreciate it and it gives them a real lift. We want to go all the way this year not just for ourselves but also for the fans. This is my fifth year here and the third time we have reached the play-offs and I dearly want to give them something to cheer about."

Bentley said his side will be stronger for the defeat at Hereford.

He said: "It was awful because we all know we deserved better and the referee played a big part in the final result. It took a while to recover from that but we are back there now and we want to go one step further. It would be a dream for me to play at Wembley and I know a lot of the other lads feel the same way."

4th May 2007

York City 0 Morecambe 0

A SOLID rearguard action from the Shrimps left Monday's second leg finely poised.

The Shrimps' defence produced a superb performance to hold out a York side who dominated possession but struggled to produce many real clear-cut chances. When Billy McEwen's side did threaten they were denied time and time again by the Morecambe defence where Chris Blackburn was magnificent and Adam Yates provided two vital last-gasp challenges. When York did get a shot in on goal, Steven Drench stood tall and helped give Sammy McIlroy's side the platform they wanted for the home game. Despite all York's pressure, it was the Shrimps who came closest to a goal when Wayne Curtis' 74th-minute close-range effort from Jim Bentley's knock down was superbly saved by Tom Evans.

York started brightly with Craig Farrell flashing a free-kick wide and Craig James forcing Drench into an uncomfortable save with a swerving free-kick.

The Morecambe fans then had their hearts in their mouths when skipper Bentley seemed to get away with a push on Clayton Donaldson as York's top scorer threatened to run on goal. The Shrimps' only effort of note in the first period came when Michael Twiss struck a sweet free-kick straight at Evans five minutes before the break.

York maintained the pressure in the

SAMMY McIlroy was delighted to be going back to Christie Park with a 0-0 draw from the play-offs first leg at York.

McIlroy said:" We didn't want to be going back with a deficit. The back four did brilliantly with Ged Brannan doing a great job in front of them. Our plan did work.

"Chris Blackburn was magnificent but as a back four I thought they were all superb. The midfield worked well but we know we can, and we will, play better with the ball on Monday. I was disappointed that we didn't keep the ball better but look at the situation, the atmosphere, the occasion and you can understand that. We were a bit edgy. You can have all the experience in the world but when that whistle goes, and 7,000 people are screaming, it can get to you. It was difficult but we knew it was going to be difficult, that is why we set our team out the way we did."

Shrimps' skipper Jim Bentley was also pleased with the result.

He said: "We had our game plan to set our stall out and we worked extremely hard."

second half with Drench forced to react sharply again to save an effort from the tricky Martyn Woolford. Blackburn produced a vital clearance as Donaldson looked set to poke home the rebound. Drench saved well with his legs from the York midfielder, Manny Panther. The home side then forged their best opening of the game when the Morecambe defence were caught out by a one-two on the halfway line. As Donaldson lined up his shot, however, Adam Yates came out of nowhere to produce a superb, and vital, block. The Shrimps began to threaten themselves in the closing stages with substitute Curtis seeing his close range volley tipped over by Evans and Michael Twiss making the keeper work with a neat turn and volley from 25 yards out.

York provided a brief late rally with Steve Bowey shooting and heading wide and Twiss scrambling away a Farrell volley as this intriguing clash came to an end.

The tension shows on the touchline.

The Visitor's player ratings:

Steven Drench: Was alert when called on and made two excellent stops. 8
Adam Yates: Amazing to think this is his first season. Booked. 9
Jim Bentley: Had his hands full with Clayton Donaldson. Booked. 7
Chris Blackburn: Amazing performance at the heart of the defence. 10
Danny Adams: Kept on his toes by the lively Woolford. Booked. 6
Garry Thompson: Struggled to get involved, perhaps due to hamstring. 6
Ged Brannan: Proved to be a nuisance to York before going off. 7
Neil Sorvel: Worked hard but didn't impose himself in midfield. 7
Craig Stanley: Tried to get forward but it proved to be a quiet night. 6
Michael Twiss: Little opportunity going forward but always a threat. 6
Danny Carlton: Lone striker found himself well marked by the York backline. 6
Subs:
Gary Hunter (Brannan 61) Brought an attacking edge
Wayne Curtis (Carlton 61) Great chance to score
Paul Lloyd (Thompson 84) Energetic when he came on
Unused subs: Davies, Howard.

York City: Evans, Lloyd, McGurk, Parslow, James, Bowey, Bishop, Panther, Woolford, Donaldson, Farrell (Brodie 90). Unused subs: Gamble, Peat, Convery, Greenwood.

Booked: James.
Referee: G Lewis.
Attendance: 6,660.
Man of the match: **Chris Blackburn.**

7th May 2007

Morecambe 2 York City 1

(Curtis 41, 47) (Bowey 20 pen)

MORECAMBE produced one of the greatest victories in their history to move a step closer to a place in the Football League.

Two goals from Wayne Curtis sealed the Shrimps' place in the play-off final at Wembley on May 20, much to the delight of their huge support. There were tears of joy from some of the Shrimps' more experienced fans who had twice before seen their side fall just short at this stage.

After being the bridesmaids, the Shrimps have finally attained bridal status with everyone now hoping the confetti will be raining down on a day of celebration at the newly-refurbished stadium. The Shrimps' players earned their chance of glory after showing their determination once again to come from behind after conceding an early penalty which also saw them lose their first-choice goalkeeper.

The Morecambe defence was caught out by a long ball over the top from Manny Panther. Clayton Donaldson ran on to the ball but was caught out by a combination of Steven Drench and Chris Blackburn and as he

Steven Drench is treated after dislocating his elbow and ending his season.

Wayne Curtis heads Morecambe level in the 40th minute.

crashed to the floor, the referee pointed to the spot.

Fears that Drench may have been sent off as he was stretchered off with a dislocated elbow were thankfully dispelled as youngster Scott Davies was called on. Davies' day began badly after being beaten by Steve Bowey's coolly-taken spot-kick. But his afternoon was soon to improve as Morecambe raised their game and began to unsettle the visitors.

The Shrimps always looked threatening from set-pieces and that proved to be their route back into the game. With half-time approaching, Adam Yates delivered a free-kick into the box and Curtis nipped in front of his marker to direct a looping header over York keeper Tom Evans, who was in no man's land off his line. The goal gave the crowd a clear lift and Morecambe continued to pressure York after the break, with Curtis earning hero status with a second goal just after the restart. For probably the first time in the tie, the York defence was all at sea as the Shrimps outnumbered the visitors. Craig Stanley provided the perfect ball for Curtis who

Wayne Curtis' second goal puts Morecambe on the way to Wembley.

WE'RE on our way to Wembley!

Wayne Curtis netted twice to send Shrimps fans singing into the Morecambe streets and contemplating their trip to the new national stadium on Sunday, May 20.

It had been a nervy affair from the kick-off of the first leg at York until the moment referee, Mr East, prompted the wild celebrations at Christie Park by blowing the final whistle that signalled victory for the home side.

York could claim, justifiably, to have been the better side in three of the four halves of this semi-final. But Morecambe got on top when it counted, defended superbly and – having lost out in two previous play-offs at this stage after outplaying both Dagenham and Hereford – their fans will feel no guilt this time.

Chief executive Rod Taylor said: "It was a great result and a fabulous occasion and the fans were simply amazing. They supported the team brilliantly and were fantastically well behaved. We got some great comments from the people from Sky TV who said that if all football was like the experience they'd had at Christie Park, it would be in a far better state."

The club, of course, has a 100% record at Wembley having won the FA Trophy in their only other appearance at the old stadium against Dartford in 1974.

And plans are now underway for organising a mass exodus of thousands of Morecambe fans to London. Seat prices for Wembley have been kept to a reasonable £25 for touchline seats and £20 behind the goal. Children's prices are £10 and disabled fans can get in for £20 with a carer going free.

The Visitor's **player ratings**

Steven Drench: Hugely unfortunate to get injured after such a good year. 7
Adam Yates: Was superb again with timely tackles and solid headers. 8
Jim Bentley: Led from the front with a commanding performance. 8
Chris Blackburn: Made just one mistake in the whole tie. Superb. 9
Danny Adams: Improved on Friday and kept Woolford quiet throughout. 7
Paul Lloyd: Full of energy down the right and sent over several crosses. 7
Craig Stanley: Slipped up for penalty but made amends with assist. Booked. 7
Neil Sorvel: Consistently broke up York's attacks as they pushed on. 7
Wayne Curtis: Match-winner with his two memorable goals. Booked. 9
Michael Twiss: Was dangerous when able to find space. Booked. 7
Danny Carlton: Worked the channels and gave everything in the second half. 7
Subs:
Scott Davies (Drench 20): Assured performance. Booked.
Gary Hunter (Lloyd 64): Plenty of challenges in midfield.
David McNiven (Curtis 77): Worked hard in attack.
Unused subs: Brannan, Howard.

York City: Evans, Lloyd, McGurk, Parslow, James (Peat 53), Bowey (Convery 55), Bishop, Panther, Woolford, Donaldson (Brodie 77), Farrell. Unused subs: Gamble, Greenwood.
Booked: McGurk.

Referee: R East.
Attendance: 5,567.
Man of the match: **Chris Blackburn.**

was left in acres of space on the left-hand side. His first two efforts were well saved by Evans but he still had the time to pick his spot with a third attempt which looped over Evans and into the empty goal.

York then seemed to run out of steam and ideas. Billy McEwan made the shock decision to replace the influential Bowey with Mark Convery. Although the substitute did try his luck from distance with a shot that curled wide of the left-hand post, York's biggest failing was perhaps the failure to test Davies with only Craig James producing a weak shot on goal. It was the Shrimps who came closest to adding to the scoreline at the death. Danny Carlton was unlucky to see a flick from Curtis's cross just beat the left-hand post before the same player tested Evans with a volley.

The four minutes of added time only added to the tension as the Shrimps held on to book their day out at Wembley; a day that will never be forgotten.

airman Peter McGuigan and director n Parker enjoy the moment.

Scott Davies came off the bench, got booked, was beaten by a penalty but responded brilliantly to help Morecambe to victory.

The Morecambe squad celebrate reaching Wembley.

Wembley

MICHAEL TWISS has battled his way back to fitness in time for the Shrimps' play-off campaign and now he is focussed on the 'job to do' at Wembley on Sunday. The striker had looked like missing the push for promotion with a knee ligament injury. But he managed to get back to play the final match against Grays and the semi-final with York. And with 90 minutes to go in the season, he doesn't want to miss out on promotion again. He said: "There were a lot of things going around with people saying I was not going to make it. But I knew that I could get back and be involved at the latter end of the season. We know we are at Wembley but there is a job to do. To play there and lose won't be a happy feeling but if we come away with a win it will be a lot better."

WAYNE CURTIS has been having sleepless nights since scoring the two goals that set up Morecambe's trip to Wembley on Sunday. That was the highlight of his career so far but he is hoping that Sunday's match eclipses it. He said: "The two goals against York are the most pleasing in my career but I must now look ahead to performing for another 90 minutes. I have over 100 friends and family from Barrow offering their support. I couldn't sleep Sunday night thinking about the day so the emotions are certainly building." Curtis has been involved three times in play-off quests for the Shrimps but this year is different. "We are due a bit of luck and if we do what we have been doing then we will give ourselves the best possible chance, especially with the experience within the squad that we have this time. We are so close to the club's major goal and better prepared than ever."

JIM BENTLEY will be a proud man when he leads out Morecambe for Sunday's big game at Wembley. And it won't just be a special day for the Shrimps' hero, but for all his family. He said: "It's going to be a massive day and great for us as players and great for the town. But there is the small matter of a football match and one that we are going down there to win and to give our all. I left Manchester City 10 years ago with the intention of getting back in to the Football League and it has taken until now to get this opportunity. I have worked hard here and at Telford and this is a massive opportunity for us and we are going to do everything we can to take it." Bentley's dad, Jack, played twice at the old Wembley for Telford losing to Macclesfield 2-0 in 1970 and scoring in Telford's 3-2 win over Hillingdon in 1971. "He used to tell me all about it. I was proud to say my dad played at Wembley and now it's my turn and my son will grow up and say his dad played at Wembley."

CRAIG STANLEY knows what it's like to win the Conference play-offs – and he wants to do it again. The midfielder left Hereford for Morecambe last summer after helping the Bulls to promotion by beating Halifax at the Walkers Stadium in Leicester.

Now his focus is on doing the same with the Shrimps.

"I came here to get promotion, that is the reason why I came here.

"I was on the other side against Morecambe last year. They pushed us very hard and I knew with the team they had and with a few added players, they'd be pushing for honours and it has worked out well for the club.

"The only difference is the incentive of playing at Wembley but at the end of the day it is still just one game to go and the main thing is we win the game.

"We're confident we can get the win on Sunday. We know it is going to be a hard game because Exeter are a good team. But if we play as well as we can, we are more than confident we can win the game."

Stanley will know one of his rivals on Sunday very well. "I lived with Adam Stansfield and his wife for a year at Hereford. He is one player that we do need to watch out for.

"I have had a text from him but we are both preparing for the game and when it comes to it, there's no friendship, we are there to win the game.

"It's about us and if we play as we can, we are more than capable of winning the game and getting promotion."

Stanley was on the bench at Walsall for a couple of games but has never played in the Football League.

"I would have liked to have played in the League with Hereford but it didn't work out, now hopefully it can happen this year.

"At the end of the day, if you don't want to play at the highest level you can then I don't think you should be playing football."

MORECAMBE will play in their blue away kit on Sunday after losing the toss to Exeter to be the 'home' team.

MORECAMBE will have three goalkeepers with them at Wembley – all with different tales to tell about these last couple of weeks. First choice is between Scott Davies and loanee Chris Neal with the former likely to get the nod as replacement for the unfortunate Steven Drench. Drench, of course, misses the climax of a season in which he's played a massive part because of the injury he sustained when making a challenge, and giving away a penalty, in the home leg of the semi-final. And, though both fit keepers are excited about the prospect of playing on Sunday, they both spare thoughts for the unlucky Drench. "He should be out there playing in the final," says his understudy and friend Davies. "We wouldn't even be there if it hadn't been for him this season. About 20 clean sheets and superb saves that have meant we've won games we could have drawn or drawn ones we should have lost have been a big part of why we've got to this final. I train with him every week and room with him on away trips and he's a great lad and a fantastic keeper. Drenchy has said to us that we've got to go and win it for him and that's what we'll be trying to do."

Drench himself has had emotional ups and downs since the semi-final but says he's now looking forward to the day himself. "I have been distraught at not being able to play. I made an honest challenge for the ball and can't understand why there was even any talk about me being sent off. I thought the ref got it right and was pretty good all game. I've been to the doctor and it looks like I'll be back training in six to eight weeks. I hope I can get back fully fit and be playing for Morecambe next season in the Football League."

MORECAMBE'S footballers travel to Wembley for the biggest game of their careers knowing they are in touching distance of their Football League dream. Manager Sammy McIlroy and his players will leave Morecambe tomorrow, Thursday, stopping off at their training camp for two days before heading to Wembley on Sunday.

And the Shrimps boss is hoping his players won't freeze in front of the biggest crowd that most of them will have played in front of. "It's all about what happens on the day at Wembley. You can play at Wembley 10 times and on one day anything can happen. I watched the Trophy final and Stevenage never came out of the dressing rooms and were soon 2-0 down, but they got a goal back and turned it around.

"These things happen at Wembley. We have to be composed and hope no-one freezes. Wembley can affect players, any type of players. The game will pass by in no time at all," he added. McIlroy played in three FA Cup finals at Wembley with Manchester United and managed Macclesfield to FA Trophy victory there in 1996. But he has not been to the new stadium yet and is excited at the prospect of taking the Shrimps there on Sunday – and hopefully into the Football League.

"It means a lot to me. It's a fantastic achievement that Morecambe have got to the play-off finals and it ranks with everything I have done in football. When the final whistle went against York, that was the greatest moment of my life – that is how it felt.

"For Morecambe to be a Football League club will be fantastic, for the town, for the chairman, and the directors and the players. The players will never have a better opportunity to be a League player. The icing on the cake is that it is at Wembley."

McIlroy is waiting on Garry Thompson to see if he will recover from the hamstring injury that kept him out of last Monday's match. "He is getting daily treatment and has come on in leaps and bounds so the signs are good for him," said McIlroy.

McIlroy will have options available to him when he selects his side.

"We had a fantastic spirit at Macclesfield and that took us a hell of a long way. We have something similar here at Morecambe. It's very, very hard for me to pick 16 players when everyone is fit – that is how good the squad is. It's difficult to keep 18 or 19 players happy when everyone is fit." He knows he will have to break Morecambe's duck against Exeter, which has gone on for eight games in the Conference.

"It's going to be a tough game," he said. "I felt Exeter deserved to win against Oxford. Our games have been very close, 2-2 here and we lost down there in very difficult conditions. I expect it to be close again. They are very close as two units. They have got decent players who can win games and we have too.

"One piece of magic from a certain player can do it." McIlroy's assistant, Mark Lillis, has drawn up a special training programme to prepare for the final, using the experience and contacts he gained while with Premier League Derby County.

Lillis said: "We are a big family and on the day we need all the family members to stick together. We are preparing right. We wrote on the board in the changing rooms 'No regrets.' If you know as a coach that you have done all the preparation and playing for a massive game, then it is up to the players to get us over the line."

20th May 2007

Exeter City 1 Morecambe 2

(Phillips 8) (Thompson 42, Carlton 83)

DANNY Carlton wrote his way into Morecambe's record books with a stunning strike to send Morecambe into the Football League for the first time in their history.

The striker produced a wonderful left-footed effort which flew past Exeter keeper Paul Jones and into the top right-hand corner of the goal with seven minutes to go, sparking huge celebrations among the estimated 12,000 Morecambe fans who had made this most memorable of journeys. It was a goal worthy of gracing any stage in the world and by far the best moment of a big Wembley weekend that produced an awful FA Cup final. But closer to home it was a goal that people in pubs and clubs in Morecambe will be talking about for years to come. It was a perfect way to cap a remarkable day and seal the Shrimps' goal of League football.
So often they had promised to fulfill that goal only to see the dream fade away.
But then, after years of knocking on the door, the Shrimps were allowed to join the party and by the look of the faces of the fans at the final whistle, there are many who would be joining them.

Perhaps the most noticeable aspect of the game was the way Sammy McIlroy's side kept their composure after going down to a disappointing early goal, when Lee Phillips headed past young keeper Scott Davies. To concede after eight minutes was a far from perfect start and it could have been even worse if Adam Yates had not reacted sharply to stop a dangerous left-wing cross from reaching the busy Phillips.

But then after a shaky opening 10 minutes, Morecambe began to dominate with Carlton, playing his best game for some time, at the centre of everything. Up front on his own, he ran for every ball and ran directly at defenders causing them all sorts of problems. He first came to the fore with a shot from the edge of the box that was well saved by Exeter keeper Jones, the first of a series of fine saves he was to make.

Garry Thompson forced the Exeter number one into a good tip away and Wayne Curtis headed straight at the stopper from eight yards out. Exeter rallied briefly with young Davies, in for the injured Steven Drench, tipping Phillips'well-struck shot round the post. Jones was somewhat fortunate when he parried a cross against team-mate Edwards and the ball bounced back into his arms. His best moment, though, came when he saved a Curtis penalty on the half-hour.

Carlton's pace was too hot for Chris Todd who sent him tumbling in the box, but Curtis, normally deadly from the spot, failed to strike the ball as he intended. Jones then saved well, before reacting sharply to save the rebound as the semi-final hero followed up his kick.

Jones could only stem the tide for so long as Morecambe continued to ask all the questions with some slick, passing football. It finally paid off when Exeter left-back Billy Jones made a hash of a clearance on the edge of his own box. The ball rolled into the path of Thompson and he produced the neatest of finishes to put the Shrimps level with three minutes to go to the break. The half ended with Morecambe in the ascendancy as Twiss drilled a shot just wide of the left-hand post and the Grecians were grateful for the half-time whistle. The Shrimps started the second half brightly but when Exeter boss Paul Tisdale gambled with two early substitutions, his side found a new gear with a different formation. Shrimps' supporters were given a scare when Adam Stansfield closed down Davies' attempted clearance and the relief was palpable as the ball bobbled wide of the target. The incident seemed to kick-start

Exeter who began to spread the ball around well but never really tested the Morecambe goal. James Mackie came on for former Morecambe ace Lee Elam and produced a neat run and shot that drifted just wide of the right-hand post and Davies stood up well to block from Stansfield. Just as the game looked to be heading for extra-time, Carlton popped up to score the most memorable goal of his career.

A long ball forward should have caused few problems, but as Rob Edwards and Steve Tully hesitated, Carlton raced onto the ball, turned inside and fired an unstoppable shot into the top corner from the edge of the area. The goal sparked scenes of joy among the Morecambe fans and on the bench, with

SETANTA

Speedy
No.1 FOR TOOL HIRE
zerosevenmobile.com
BLUE SQUARE PREMIER L

The Visitor's player ratings

Scott Davies: Kept his cool after conceding and made several good saves. 8
Adam Yates: Nervous early on but came on in leaps and bounds. 9
Jim Bentley: Ran through a brick wall for the Morecambe cause. 9
Chris Blackburn: Early goal was a setback but responded magnificently. 9
Danny Adams: Never shirked a tackle and kept possession well. 8
Garry Thompson: A menace to Exeter defence and took his goal superbly. 9
Craig Stanley: Saved his best for big occasion with a towering performance. 9
Neil Sorvel: Was crucial in first half as the Shrimps won midfield battle. 8
Wayne Curtis: Always a threat on left and recovered from penalty miss. 8
Michael Twiss: Not at his best after injury but gave everything for the team. 8
Danny Carlton: Unsappable energy and WHAT A GOAL! 10
Subs:
Gary Hunter (Twiss 72): Always busy and gave his all.
Ged Brannan (Thompson 86): Helped close the game out.
David McNiven (Carlton 88): Intelligent in dying minutes.
Unused subs: Neal, Howard. Booked: Carlton.
Exeter City: P Jones, Tully, B Jones, Todd (capt), Edwards, Carlisle (Logan 53), Taylor, Gill, Elam (Mackie 56), Phillips (Stansfield 37), Challinor. Unused subs: Richardson, Buckle. Booked: Todd. Sent off: Gill Referee: Michael Oliver. Assistant referees: Nick Hobbis, Barry Holderness.

Attendance: 40,043.
Man of the match: **Danny Carlton.**

Sammy McIlroy's soon-to-be-legendary slip as he celebrated with relish. When Exeter's Matt Gill was sent off for aiming a headbutt at Craig Stanley in injury-time, the game was won. Morecambe had sealed their place in the Football League on a day that no-one with any connection to the town, no matter how large or small, will ever forget.

A Dream Come True

ALL THE Morecambe players were united in their joy at achieving the club's ambition of reaching the Football League.

Phrases such as 'unbelievable', 'over the moon' and 'stuff of dreams' were in abundance as the reality slowly began to sink in.

For captain Jim Bentley, who has missed out twice before in the play-offs, it was a proud day.

He said: "We came here to win today and we've done it – I'm absolutely made up.

"I left Manchester City 10 years ago and have spent five years at Telford and five years here and finally I'm back in the League.

"They came out of the traps well to be fair. The lad Phillips who scored got a good goal and played well so when he went off, I was quite pleased.

"But slowly we warmed to the game, knocked the ball around well and created chances. Their goalkeeper did very well and at the end of the day, it is all about the result.

"We talked before the game about the spirit we had had this season, it had seen us through against York and it was the same again today.

"It was all about the spirit. You need that as well as football ability to get you through."

Bentley knows more than most the pain that those at Christie Park have been through in recent years and had a word for his predecessor as skipper, Stewart Drummond.

"Stewie came close and he was one of the best players I have played with but I have stepped up to be captain and nothing gives me greater pleasure than being captain and leading Morecambe into the Football League."

He is looking forward to Friday's open top bus parade and presentation night.

"I know a lot of the people who follow the club and it will be a great chance to talk to them about the day. I know what it means to them and to get the town into the Football League. I am made up for myself, my family, the board but most of all for the fans," he added.

Bentley's partnership with Chris Blackburn in the heart of the defence was again superb.

He said: "I'm delighted for everybody. The fans were fantastic and it's a great feeling – almost unexplainable, but on the other hand, commiserations to Exeter, it's gutting for them.

"Even when we went 1-0 down to a poor goal, I still fancied us to score and not concede again."

Craig Stanley had the déjà vu of winning a second successive play-off final.

He said: "It was a tough game. In the first half, I thought we dominated even though they went ahead.

"We had enough chances to have won two games and if we had taken our chances the game would have been finished.

"But fair play to Exeter, in the second half, they were the better team. Adam Stansfield came on and Richard Logan and they went four up front. It was tough for us and it was very tiring because it was a massive pitch.

"But we battled hard and got the goal and I always thought that whoever scored the second goal, would win the game."

Stanley was doing his best to catch up Danny Carlton when he fired in the stunning winner.

"The pass put him in behind and he did what he did. He deserved it, he worked the channels well.

"It's unbelievable, it's not really sunk in yet – playing at Wembley and winning the game. Hopefully now I can stay and play in the Football League – I know I'm good enough.

"I love the club and enjoy the football here, which is why I came to the club. Sammy and Mark have got me playing the way I can play."

This time last year Adam Yates was playing in the UniBond League with Leek Town.

Now he is an integral part of Morecambe's promotion-winning side, a team who have not lost a game all season after going ahead.

He said: "The amount of times we have come back in games and to do it today at Wembley is unbelievable. To go up automatically would be tremendous but to do it at Wembley is even better.

"It's an unbelievable record. It shows the character we have got and the players in the squad. We knew that we have gone behind before but come back and get a win or a draw.

"That calmed us today and we started to play and could have been three or four up."

Another of the club's younger players is Scott Davies, who was given the chance in goal due to Steven Drench's injury.

"I just kept working hard and hoped the day would come. Today was the day and now we can celebrate making history.

"It's everybody's dream, you don't have to say anything else other than it's Wembley.

"Obviously, we had got a few nerves but what player wouldn't get nerves. Now we have got to savour the moment, it is the biggest moment in any player's career."

Davies didn't forget his friend and team-mate.

"This is for Drenchy, he has worked hard and kept us in games through the season."

And not for the first time this year, Davies had to recover from a disappointing start.

"Every time I have played, apart from having a goal-kick, the first thing I have done is to pick the ball out of the net. But you have got to carry on and we showed character to come back."

David McNiven has played for several clubs, both in England and Scotland, but Morecambe was special, he said.

"The team spirit here is the best I have known at any club. No matter who is playing every single player is all together.

"Our aim this year was to get promoted and this is probably better than winning the League. Today will have generated a lot of money for the club and I would take going up this way next year.

"I'm keen to kick on now. We've got a good team and teams that have come up have proved they can do it.

"We knew we had played well enough to win the game, we were the better team."

Mattie Blinkhorn was watching, unable to play having gone back to Blackpool after his loan spell was ended.

He said: "It's unbelievable and I'm buzzing for all the lads. I am just happy to have played a little part in getting them there."

And a final word to a man who has seen the Shrimps at close quarters, Fraser Eagle coach driver Steve Blackston.

He said: "It's out of this world.

For me personally it is a dream come true and I am over the moon for the lads. They have been focussed and have always been on the game all the time.

"I was offered another team at the start of the season but I chose to go with Morecambe and I am glad I did."

GOOD LUCK
to
THE SHRIMPS!
MORECAMBE

MORECAMBE
Marching to Wembley
2007
PLAY-OFF FINAL
WEMBLEY
MORECAMBE
MORECAMBE
GARDENS

MORECAMBE F.C.

MORECAMBE
WEMBLEY
MORECAMBE

MORECAMBE F.C.

The Visitor
R&B
Morecambe
832132
SOLD
Wayne's Wembley World
CURTIS FIRES MORECAMBE INTO PLAY-OFF FINAL
The match...the interviews...the tension ...the glory...and how to get your tickets for the final, see pages 3, 52, 53, 54, 55 & 56

Thank you from the Chairman

On behalf of the Board of Directors I would like to thank everyone who travelled down to the new Wembley stadium for the Conference play-off final against Exeter City last Sunday. The support given to the team was absolutely fantastic and the scenes at the end of the match will live in everyone's memory forever.

It was, without doubt, the greatest day in the history of Morecambe Football Club and I am sure the celebrations will continue for a few more weeks or even longer! The fact that there were over 11,000 Morecambe supporters in attendance was absolutely amazing and gives all of us the confidence that we can look forward to a very exciting future in the Football League.

I can assure everyone that whilst the objective of achieving Football League status has been achieved, we are not going there just to make up the numbers. We remain an ambitious club and already have plans for significant progress, both on and off the field.
We need to strengthen the playing squad and Sammy will have the necessary funds available in order to do so. We will build a stronger infrastructure off the field to ensure we maximise every opportunity to allow Morecambe Football Club to be a strong contender in the Football League.

But what we need more than anything else is your continued support. Our average home gate last season was 1,750 and we really need to convert some of the 11,000 fans who travelled to Wembley to become regular supporters of Morecambe Football Club.

The attraction of Football League at Christie Park has to have a positive impact on our attendances. I would urge those supporters at Wembley who do not attend Christie Park on a regular basis to turn up in great numbers next season to support the team in the Football League.

Maybe we can recreate some of the magic atmosphere that we experienced at Wembley. An average gate next season of over 2,500 must be our target. We need your support to help us to continue our progress within the Football League.

Congratulations to Sammy, Mark, the players and backroom staff, not only for a wonderful season but also for a Wembley experience that will live forever.

Finally, on a personal note, I would like to thank each and every one of you who gave the team such magnificent support. Let us all look forward with confidence to life in the Football League!

Peter McGuigan
Chairman
Morecambe FC

What a Goal!

DANNY CARLTON said he had never felt before like he felt when the ball hit the back of the net to earn Morecambe promotion.

The striker has become an adopted Morecambrian since moving over from Leeds to join the Shrimps.

He said: "To score the winner in the first play-off final at Wembley is just unbelievable – you can't ask for more.

"The ball came through Rob Edwards, I just got across him and the legs were a bit tired and I didn't fancy running past him so I went for it and it went in the top corner.

"That is what we wanted at the beginning of the season. We have done it the hard way but we are in the League now.

"The roar when we came out with more than 10,000 fans cheering us on put hairs up on the back of the neck.

"Next season, I don't think it is as big a step as everyone thinks. Yeovil are doing well and they were in the Conference a few years ago, so why not us?"

Garry Thompson, like Carlton, has been in two unsuccessful play-off campaigns with the Shrimps.

"We have had to sit and watch this day in the past. It just shows the spirit of the lads that we went down but came back really strongly.

"I'm just so proud to have got a goal. I didn't know a lot about it. The left-back had gone to clear and it just came to me. I tried to get it on target and it went in.

"We had chances in the first half and the penalty, then had to weather the storm a bit before Danny took his goal really well."

Thompson thanked Dave Edge and his team for helping him back to fitness in time for the match.

Now he is looking ahead to next season.

"We went to Swindon this year in the FA Cup and were unlucky that day, they scored a penalty late on that shouldn't have been a penalty.

"If we prepare right, have a good pre-season there is no reason why we can't go into it and do well, maybe back-to-back promotions."

The Bus Trip Home

MORECAMBE'S players turned it on at Wembley and the town turned out back home to celebrate the biggest achievement in the club's 87-year history.

The response of the local public in welcoming home the triumphant heroes on their open-topped bus tour round town last night left club players, management and officials almost speechless. Seafront hotels and pubs were adorned with flags and posters and crowds gathered at numerous points along the route.

Chief executive, Rod Taylor, told *The Visitor* after the parade: "That was beyond my wildest dreams – absolutely amazing.

"There was a great send-off from Christie Park, then the streets were lined right along Lancaster Road and up Broadway and we thought 'that's marvellous'.

"Then, when we turned into the town hall it took our breath away – there were hundreds and hundreds of people.

"And it continued right up the prom to a rousing reception at The Carleton – it's a scene I'll remember for the rest of my life and I'm sure the team will as well."

Shrimps manager, Sammy McIlroy, echoed the emotion saying: "The public response was magnificent and it really opened a lot of people's eyes about the support we have.

"I was totally surprised and delighted and I know the players were – they felt really proud about what their achievement has meant to the people of Morecambe."

New Stadium

by Glen Cooper

WEMBLEY hangovers had only just subsided when Morecambe fans' thoughts were drawn to visiting another superb new stadium – but this one hadn't been built yet. Club chairman Peter McGuigan called press, local and national, to Christie Park to reveal that, hopefully in time for the start of the 2009/10 season, Morecambe would have its own 21st century venue on largely unused land at Westgate in the town.
The new multi-million pound, 6,000 capacity stadium would, said Mr Mcguigan, not only be desirable but 'absolutely essential' to secure the long-term future of the club.

The plans include selling Christie Park, probably for housing, and creating a sports complex at Westgate including two training pitches and a gym. The pitches would also be used for a major expansion of the club's Football in the Community scheme involving local schools and community groups.

There would also be a number of retail outlets leased to national chains and, possibly, a new hotel within the complex.

The naming of the new ground would depend on the ability of the club to attract a major sponsor but the legacy of Christie Park benefactor, JB Christie, would live on by the naming of the access road to the venue as 'Christie Way'.

The land at Westgate would be bought from Lancaster City Council.

It is currently used by Westgate Wanderers Youth FC with whom the club has since been negotiating compensatory arrangements.

Plans for the expansion of Christie Park, submitted in 2006, would be abandoned and the new stadium would be built with the scope for expansion in the event of crowds increasing significantly.

A proposal for a temporary bar area behind the existing north stand at Christie Park would still go ahead in the interim.

Announcing the ambitious plans, MFC chairman Peter McGuigan told The Visitor: "Despite our success at Wembley and in gaining promotion, we made our biggest ever financial loss as a club during the last season.

"Going into the League has always been our aim but it does bring with it a whole new landscape in terms of costs. We have no scope to expand the way we really want to at Christie Park.

"Westgate would allow us the room we want to develop the footballing side of our business, including the new training facilities we so desperately need, as well as offering the potential to establish other streams of income without which I would have serious concerns for the future of this club.

"It would also allow us to increase the amount of work we do with the community, offering at least six nights of community use of excellent new sporting facilities."

The land at Christie Park was originally given to the town by fan and benefactor JB Christie on the understanding that it always be used for recreational and sporting purposes.

This issue dominated the debate the last time a move away from the ground was contemplated about 20 years ago.

Then the land was being offered for a new retail park – a plan that eventually subsided when the company looking to develop the site got into financial difficulties.

The actual wording of the Christie covenant allowed for the land to be returned to public recreational use 'if the football club ceases to exist'.

Looking to the Future

by Glen Cooper

WHEN all the hysteria and excitement of Morecambe's Wembley triumph had died down – though it will remain a fantastic 'life landmark' memory for all who experienced it – the business of facing a future in the Football League really began to sink in. From ground improvements, new security facilities, strengthening the playing squad – down to the nitty gritty of new arrangements for press access and the use of Football League logos and 'image rights' – there was no doubt the club had been launched into a whole new footballing world.

Having secured his place in the club's folklore by becoming Morecambe's top Conference scorer in the run-up to Wembley, Wayne Curtis, the man who shot them to the final, was rewarded by being given the honour, when he extended his contract, of being the first player to sign for the club as a Football League player.

Wembley hero Danny Carlton stepped up a division by joining long-time admirers Carlisle, and Chris Blackburn ended weeks of speculation about his future by putting pen to paper at Swindon.

Carl Baker, a long-term McIlroy target, was signed from Southport for what was then a club record (undisclosed sum but believed to be up to £50,000).

Matthew Blinkhorn, who had impressed during his loan spell towards the end of the season, soon also came in from Blackpool for a fee which a tribunal finally set at £15,000.

Dave Artell, whom Chester fans voted their player of the season for 2006/7 but who couldn't secure an improved contract at the Deva Stadium, joined to supplement a Blackburn-less central defence.

Jon Newby, a journeyman striker who submitted a courteous hand-written letter asking for a trial at Christie Park was granted his wish and performed well enough pre-season to secure a deal.

Joe Lewis, the young Norwich City goalkeeping prospect who had represented England at age-group level, was signed on loan as regular stopper Steven Drench continued his recuperation from injury.

Within a couple of weeks of the start of the 2007/8 season midfielder Damien Allen, with whom McIlroy and Lillis had worked at Stockport, also joined the club following a period playing in Belgium with Royal Antwerp.

The management team said it was now happy with the squad, having assembled a group of players that boasted a blend of youth and experience and cover in every position.

But amid all this shuffling the big news – indeed, Wembley aside, the biggest news to hit the town for years – was the announcement that the club intended to move to a new purpose-built stadium at Westgate.

Christie Park would be sold, probably for housing development, and the proceeds would go a long way to creating the new multi-million pound venue which would also include training facilities, retail outlets and, possibly, a hotel.

Concerns over the covenant that had been placed on the existing ground by benefactor, JB Christie, seemed to have been allayed when the original wording was analysed to reveal a clause that stated the land should return to public recreational use only 'if the football club ceases to exist'.

Club officials were happy that, were Mr Christie still alive, he would be shoulder to shoulder with them backing the new development. He was a fan of the team, first and foremost, and would be delighted with the prospect of helping secure its long-term future via the new stadium, they said.

As attention turned back to the action on the pitch fans gave their predictions for the coming campaign – with most opting for a mid-table finish.

As the new season got underway The Shrimps opened with a home game in front of 3,663 fans who saw a hard-fought 0-0 draw against a powerful looking Barnet side.

But, though it was steady if unspectacular, consolidation in the first few matches in the League (highly satisfactory in itself), few could have predicted the new euphoria this team was about to produce in the cups.

An amazing yet fully deserved victory in Morecambe's first ever Carling Cup appearance – away at neighbours Preston – was followed by a simply stunning 3-1 win, again on the road, at once mighty Wolverhampton Wanderers.

That cup run was to end in emphatic, though (to the hundreds of vociferous travelling Shrimps fans) not disheartening, defeat by 5-0 at Sheffield United but by then the glory – and worldwide attention – had already been secured.

Top-of-the-bill coverage on regional and Sky TV ensued and Morecambe were well and truly on the footballing map.

There were (as this book was written) also notable wins in the Johnstone's Paint Trophy at Tranmere and at home to Port Vale.

Could we allow ourselves to dream of another trip to Wembley?

Whatever the outcome of that particular adventure, the first steps on a long (we hope) journey into the serious, grown-up world of League football has begun.

Strap yourselves in and let's enjoy the ride!

Appendix Match Statistics 2006-07

DATE	OPPONENTS	HT	FT	PT	POS	ATTN	Goalkeeper					
12/08	**BURTON ALB**	0-0	0-1	-	18	1907	Drench	_Brannan(80)**_	Blackburn	Bentley	Howard	Thompson(89)*
15/08	NORTHWICH	1-0	2-0	3	10	1346	Drench	Yates	Meadowcroft	_Blackburn_	Howard	Thompson
19/08	WOKING	0-0	1-1	1	9	1222	Drench(72)*	Yates	Meadowcroft	Blackburn	Howard	Thompson
26/08	**STEVENAGE**	1-2	3-3	1	12	1524	Robinson	Yates	Meadowcroft	Blackburn	Howard	Thompson
28/08	HALIFAX TN	0-1	1-1	1	11	1908	Robinson	Yates	Meadowcroft	Blackburn	_Howard_	Thompson (35
02/09	**WEYMOUTH**	1-0	2-0	3	9	1333	Robinson	Yates	**Meadowcroft**	Blackburn	Perkins	Thompson
09/09	**OXFORD UTD**	0-2	0-3	-	13	2314	Robinson	Yates	_Meadowcroft_	Blackburn	Perkins	Thompson(67)
12/09	YORK CITY	2-0	3-2	3	10	2233	Drench	_Yates_	_Brannan_	Blackburn	_Perkins_	**Thompson**
16/09	DAGENHAM	1-1	1-2	-	12	1237	Drench	Yates	Brannan	_Blackburn_	Perkins	Thompson
19/09	**TAMWORTH**	0-0	0-0	1	12	1248	Drench	Yates	Brannan	Blackburn	Perkins	Thompson
23/09	**KIDDIE**	0-0	0-1	-	12	1495	Drench	Yates	Brannan	Blackburn(88)**	Perkins	Thompson(71)
30/10	GRAYS	0-0	1-0	3	11	1056	Drench	Yates	_Brannan_	Blackburn	Howard	Twiss
02/10	**RUSHDEN**	0-0	1-0	3	11	1252	Drench	Yates	Brannan	Blackburn	Howard	Twiss
07/10	**CRAWLEY**	0-2	0-4	-	11	890	Drench	Yates	Brannan	_Blackburn_	Howard	Twiss
10/10	ALTRINCHAM	1-0	2-0	3	10	1087	Drench	Yates	Brannan	Bentley	Howard	_Thompson_
14/10	EXETER CITY	1-1	2-2	1	10	1582	Drench	Brannan(59)**	Bentley(29)*	Blackburn	Howard	Yates
21/10	ALDERSHOT	_1-0_	_1-0_	3	8	2394	Drench	Yates	Brannan	Blackburn	Howard	Rigoglioso(90)*
28/10	MOOR GREEN	0-0	2-1	C	-	550	Drench	Yates	Brannan	_Blackburn_	Howard	Rigoglioso
04/11	**GRAVESEND**	_1-0_	_1-0_	3	7	1429	Drench	Yates	_Bentley_	Blackburn	Howard	Thompson(87)
11/11	**KIDDIE**	1-0	2-1	C	-	1673	Drench	Yates	Bentley	Blackburn	Howard	Thompson
18/11	CAMBRIDGE	1-0	3-1	3	6	3142	Drench	Yates	Bentley	Blackburn	Howard(87)***	Thompson
25/11	**FOREST GREEN**	1-1	1-1	1	6	1561	Drench	Yates	Bentley	_Blackburn_	Howard	**Thompson(71)**
02/12	**SWINDON TN**	0-0	0-1	C	-	5942	Drench	Yates	_Bentley_	Brannan	Howard(89)**	Stanley
09/12	STAFFORD	1-0	1-0	3	6	1374	Drench	Yates	Bentley	Blackburn	Howard	Stanley
16/12	YORK CITY	0-0	2-1	C	-	1017	Drench	Yates	Bentley	Blackburn	Howard	Stanley
19/12	**HOLKER OB**	3-0	AB	C	-	187	Davies	Smith	Brannan	Meadowcroft	Langford	Platt
21/12	**HOLKER OB**	2-0	3-0	C	-	167	Kelly	Smith	Brannan	Meadowcroft	Lloyd	Platt(82)**
26/12	SOUTHPORT	0-1	2-1	3	6	1804	Drench	**_Yates_**	Bentley	Blackburn	Howard	Twiss
30/12	TAMWORTH	0-0	1-0	3	5	1029	Drench	Yates	_Bentley_	Blackburn	Howard	Stanley
01/01	YORK CITY	0-1	1-3	-	6	2203	Drench	Yates	Bentley	**Blackburn**	Howard	Hunter(67)**
06/01	OXFORD UTD	0-0	0-0	1	6	5489	Drench	Yates	Bentley	Blackburn	Howard	Hunter
13/01	**MANGOTSFIELD**	1-0	5-0	C	-	859	Drench	Yates	Brannan	Blackburn	**Howard**	**Hunter(64)***
16/01	**LANCASTER**	1-0	5-0	C	-	772	Davies	Leigh	Meadowcroft	Langford	Wisdom	West(83)**
20/01	**DAGENHAM**	1-0	1-1	1	6	1711	Drench	Yates	Bentley	Blackburn	_Howard_	Curtis
23/01	**SOUTHPORT**	0-0	0-0	1	6	1484	Drench	Yates	Bentley	Blackburn	Howard	Curtis(59)**
27/01	STAFFORD	2-0	3-0	3	5	957	Drench	**Yates**	Bentley	Blackburn	Howard	**Twiss**
03/02	**STEVENAGE**	0-1	1-1	C	-	1134	Drench	Yates	Bentley	Blackburn	Howard	Twiss
06/02	STEVENAGE	0-0	0-0	C	-	1056	Drench	Yates	Bentley	Blackburn	Howard	Twiss
10/02	GRAVESEND	1-1	1-2	-	6	1156	Drench	Brannan	Bentley	Blackburn(41)*	Howard	_Hunter_
17/02	**CAMBRIDGE**	0-1	2-2	1	6	1493	Drench	_Yates_	**_Bentley_**	_Brannan_	Howard	Thompson
24/02	FOREST GREEN	2-1	3-1	3	6	1292	Drench	Yates	Adams	Meadowcroft	Howard	Thompson
27/02	MARINE	0-0	0-1	C	-	190	Davies	Walmsley	Brannan	Blackburn	Langford	West
03/03	**ST ALBANS**	1-0	2-0	3	6	1415	Drench	_Yates_	Bentley	Adams(82)***	Howard	**Thompson**
06/03	RUSHDEN	_0-1_	_2-2_	1	5	1707	Drench	Yates	Bentley	_Adams_	Howard	Thompson
10/03	**CRAWLEY**	1-0	1-0	3	4	1374	Drench	Yates	Bentley	Adams	Howard	**Thompson(79**
13/03	ALTRINCHAM	0-1	0-1	-	5	1403	Drench	Yates	Bentley	Adams	Howard	Thompson
17/03	EXETER CITY	0-0	0-1	-	6	3515	Drench	Blackburn	Bentley	Adams	Howard	Thompson
20/03	**ALDERSHOT**	2-0	2-1	3	4	1166	Drench	Yates	Bentley	Blackburn	Adams(25)*	Thompson(83)*
24/03	BURTON ALB	0-2	1-2	-	6	1732	Drench	Yates	_Bentley_	Blackburn	Adams	_Thompson(74_
27/03	**NORTHWICH**	1-0	2-1	3	4	1315	Drench	Yates	Bentley	**Blackburn**	Adams	Curtis
31/03	**WOKING**	1-0	2-0	3	3	1466	Drench	Yates	Bentley	Blackburn	_Adams_	Thompson
03/04	ST ALBANS	1-0	2-0	3	3	658	Drench	Yates	Bentley	Blackburn	Adams	Thompson
07/04	STEVENAGE	_1-1_	_3-3_	1	3	1845	Drench	Yates	Bentley	Blackburn	Adams	**Thompson**
09/04	**HALIFAX TN**	1-0	4-0	3	3	2412	Davies	Yates	Bentley	Blackburn	Adams	**Thompson**
14/04	WEYMOUTH	1-1	1-2	-	3	1206	Drench	Yates	Bentley	_Blackburn(73)*_	Adams	Thompson
21/04	KIDDIE	1-0	1-0	3	3	1654	Drench	Yates	Bentley	Blackburn	Adams	Thompson
28/04	GRAYS	1-0	1-0	3	3	2310	Drench	Yates	Bentley(h/t)*	_Blackburn_	Adams	Curtis
04/05	YORK CITY	0-0	0-0	C	-	6660	Drench	_Yates_	_Bentley_	Blackburn	_Adams_	Thompson(85)*
07/05	YORK CITY	1-1	2-1	C	-	5567	Drench(20)*	Yates	Bentley	Blackburn	Adams	Lloyd(70)**
20/05	EXETER CITY	1-1	2-1	C	-	40,043	Davies	Yates	Bentley	Blackburn	Adams	**Thompson(88**

Key: (80)*, **, *** - substitutes used and time. _Brannan - booked_ _Howard - sent off_ **Twiss - goalscorer**

					Substitute	Substitute	Substitute	Substitute	Substitute
Stanley	*Hunter(65)**	Perkins	Carlton	Twiss	Yates**	Rigoglioso*	Meadowcroft	McNiven***	Davies (gk)
Stanley	Hunter	Perkins(63)*	Carlton	**Twiss 2**	Rigoglioso	Brannan*	McNiven	*McLachlan***	Davies (gk)
Stanley	Hunter	Perkins(83)***	Carlton(74)**	Twiss	Brannan***	**McNiven D****	McNiven S	Mclachlan	Davies (gk)*
Stanley	Hunter	Curtis	**Carlton**	**Twiss 2**	Rigoglioso	Brannan	McNiven	McLachlan	Davies (g/k)
Stanley	Hunter	Curtis(70)**	Carlton	**Twiss**	Rigoglioso	Brannan*	McNiven **	McLachlan	Davies (g/k)
Stanley	Hunter	**Curtis**	Carlton(80)*	Twiss	Rigoglioso	Brannan	McNiven*	McLachlan	Drench (g/k)
Stanley	Hunter	Curtis	Carlton	Twiss	Howard	Brannan	McNiven*	Mclachlan	Drench (g/k)
Stanley	Hunter	Curtis(78)*	Carlton(84)**	**Twiss 2**	Howard*	Meadowcroft	McNiven	McLachlan**	Davies (g/k)
Stanley	Hunter	Curtis(77)*	**Carlton**	Twiss	Howard	Meadowcroft	McNiven*	McLachlan	Davies (g/k)
Stanley	Hunter(77)**	Howard(60)*	Carlton	Twiss	Meadowcroft	McNiven	McLachlan**	Shaw*	Davies (g/k)
McLachlan	*Hunter*	Twiss	Carlton	McNiven	Howard	Meadowc't**	Smith	Shaw*	Davies (g/k)
tanley(70)*	McLachlan	*Perkins*	Carlton	***McNiven***	Hunter*	Thompson	Meadowcroft	Shaw	Davies (g/k)
Stanley	McLachlan	*Perkins*	**Carlton(75)***	McNiven(84)**	Hunter*	Thompson	Meadowcroft	Shaw**	Davies (g/k)
Stanley	McLachlan(80)***	Perkins	Carlton(23)*	McNiven(53)**	Hunter***	Thompson	Meadowcroft**	Shaw*	Davies (g/k)
Stanley	**McLachlan(75)***	Perkins	**Carlton**	Twiss	Hunter*	Meadowcroft	McNiven	Shaw	Davies (g/k)
Stanley	McLachlan(68)***	Perkins	**Carlton**	Twiss	Meadowcroft*	McNiven***	Lloyd **	Smith	Daviers(g/k)
Stanley	McLachlan	Perkins	Carlton(22)*	Twiss	Meadowcroft**	McNiven**	Smith	Shaw	Davies(g/k)
Stanley	McLachlan(40)*	Hunter(75)***	**McNiven(70)****	*Twiss*	Curtis**	Meadowcroft	Smith*	Shaw***	Davies(g/k)
Stanley	Perkins	Curtis	Rigoglioso(82)*	*Twiss*	Brannan	McNiven	Platt**	McLachlan*	Davies(g/k)
McLachlan	Perkins	**Curtis**	Rigoglioso	**Twiss**	Hunter	Brannan	McNiven	Platt	Davies(g/k)
tanley(82)**	Perkins	**Curtis(72)***	Rigoglioso	**Twiss 2**	Brannan***	McNiven	Platt*	McLachlan**	Davies(g/k)
Stanley	Perkins	Curtis	Rigoglioso(71)*	Twiss	Brannan	Platt*	McLachlan	Burns*	Davies(g/k)
Mclachlan	Perkins	Twiss	Rigoglioso	Thompson(88)*	McNiven	Platt*	Smith	Burns**	Davies(g/k)
McLachlan	Perkins	Twiss	Rigoglioso(75)*	**Thompson**	Curtis**	Brannan	McNiven	Burns*	Davies(g/k)
Lachlan(55)**	Perkins	**Twiss**	Rigoglioso(72)***	Thompson(53)*	**Curtis** *	Brannan	Platt**	Burns***	Davies(g/k)
Hunter	Walmsley	Burns	**Curtis**	**McNiven 2**	Lloyd	West	Pickersgill	Kelly	Davies(g/k)
unter(82)*	Walmsley	Burns	**Curtis 2**	McNiven	West*	Pickersgill	Langford**		
Stanley	*Perkins*	Rigoglioso(78)**	Curtis	Platt(69)*	Brannan	McNiven**	McLachlan	Burns*	Robinson(g/k)
unter(89)**	McLachlan	Burns(69)*	Curtis	Twiss	Rigoglioso*	Brannan**	McNiven	Walmsley	Robinson(g/k)
Stanley	McLachlan(67)***	Twiss	Rigoglioso(48)*	Twiss	Brannan***	McNiven*	Lloyd	Walmsley**	Robinson(g/k)
Stanley	*Brannan*	*Curtis*	Twiss	McNiven(87)*	Rigoglioso	Meadowcroft	Walmsley	McLachlan	Davies(g/k)
anley(72)***	Perkins	**Twiss 2**	Curtis	McNiven(64)*	Rigoglioso*	Meadowcroft	McLachlan***	**Walker****	Davies(g/k)
Valmsley 2	McLachlan	**Walker(75)***	Rigoglioso(85)***	**Jarvis**	Pickersgill***	Baker**	**Taylor***	Bell	Anderson
Stanley	Brannan	Hunter(85)*	Twiss	***Thompson***	Rigoglioso	McNiven	McLachlan	Walker*	Davies(g/k)
Stanley	Brannan(59)*	Hunter	Twiss	Thompson	Meadowcroft	McNiven**	McLachlan	Walker*	Davies(g/k)
Stanley	Sorvel	Hunter	Watt(70)*	**Thompson(84)****	Curtis	Brannan*	McLachlan	Walker**	Davies(g/k)
Stanley	Sorvel(86)**	Hunter	Watt(67)*	**Thompson**	Brannan	Meadowcroft	Carlton*	Walker**	Davies(g/k)
Stanley	Sorvel	Brannan(102)**	Hunter	Thompson(96)*	Meadowcroft	Carlton	Watt**	Walker*	Davies(g/k)
Stanley	Sorvel(78)**	Thompson	Twiss	*Walker(79)****	Meadowcroft*	Lloyd**	Watt***	Langford	Davies(g/k)
Stanley	Sorvel	Curtis(79)*	Hunter(79)**	Carlton(87)***	Meadowcroft	**Lloyd****	Watt***	Walker*	Davies(g/k)
Stanley	Sorvel	Lloyd	Curtis(86)**	Carlton(81)*	Hunter*	McLachlan	Burns**	Walker	Davies(g/k)
McLachlan	Hunter	Burns	Pickersgill(70)*	Walker	Ball	Helm	McLuckie	Wisdom	Kelly(g/k)
Stanley	*Sorvel*	Curtis(82)**	**Blinkhorn**	Carlton(73)*	Hunter	Brannan**	Blackburn***	Burns*	Davies(g/k)
Stanley	Sorvel	Curtis	Blinkhorn	Carlton	Hunter	Brannan	Blackburn	Burns	Davies(g/k)
Stanley	Sorvel	Curtis	Blinkhorn	Carlton(85)**	Hunter*	Brannan	Blackburn	Burns**	Davies(g/k)
Stanley	Sorvel	Curtis	Blinkhorn	Carlton(79)*	Hunter	Brannan	Blackburn	Burns*	Davies(g/k)
Stanley	Sorvel(75)*	Burns	Blinkhorn(75)**	McNiven	Hunter*	Curtis	Brannan	Carlton**	Davies(g/k)
Hunter	**Sorvel**	Burns	**Blinkhorn**	McNiven(73)**	Curtis*	Brannan***	Carlton**	Lloyd	Davies (g/k)
Hunter	Sorvel	Burns(45)*	Blinkhorn	McNiven	**Curtis***	Brannan	Carlton**	Lloyd	Davies (g/k)
Hunter	Sorvel(74)***	Lloyd(74)**	**Blinkhorn**	Carlton(73)*	Stanley**	Brannan	McNiven*	Burns***	Davies(g/k)
Hunter	Sorvel(84)**	Curtis	**Blinkhorn 2**	McNiven(82)*	Stanley**	Brannan*	Lloyd	Burns	Davies(g/k)
unter(85)***	Sorvel(85)**	Curtis	***Blinkhorn***	**McNiven(80)***	Stanley***	Brannan**	Lloyd	Burns*	Davies(g/k)
Hunter	Sorvel	**Curtis**	*Blinkhorn(83)****	McNiven(76)**	Stanley***	Brannan	Carlton**	Burns	Davies(g/k)*
unter(73)**	**Sorvel(77)*****	Curtis	**Blinkhorn 2**	McNiven(69)*	Stanley**	Brannan***	Carlton*	Lloyd	Burns
unter(73)***	Sorvel	Curtis(53)*	Carlton	McNiven	Stanley***	Brannan**	Lloyd*	Burns	Davies(g/k)
Stanley	Sorvel	Lloyd	*Brannan*	Carlton(89)*	Howard	McNiven	McLachlan	Burns*	Davies(g/k)
Stanley	Sorvel	**Lloyd(80)*****	Twiss(78)**	Carlton	Howard	Brannan*	McNiven**	Burns***	Davies(g/k)
Stanley	Brannan(61)*	Sorvel	Twiss	Carlton(61)**	Howard	Hunter**	Curtis*	Lloyd***	Davies(g/k)
Stanley	Sorvel	Curtis(75)***	Twiss	Carlton	Howard	Hunter**	Brannan	McNiven***	Davies(g/k)*
Stanley	Sorvel	Curtis	Twiss(75)*	**Carlton(88)*****	Howard	Hunter *	Brannan**	McNiven***	Neal(g/k)

Appendix

Appearances season 2006-07

Surname	Forename	League, incl play-offs			FA Cup			FA Trophy			Lancs Cup			Total		
		apps	sub	gls	apps	sub	gls	apps	sub	gls	apps	sub	gls	apps	sub	gls
Adams	Danny	19												19		0
Baker	Gary											(1)		0	(1)	0
Bentley	James	34		1	2			3						39		1
Blackburn	Chris	42	(1)	3	2			4			1			49		3
Blinkhorn	Matthew	12		8										12		8
Brannan	Gerard	18	(15)		2			2			2			24	(15)	0
Burns	Jamie	4	(10)			(1)			(1)		2			6	(12)	0
Carlton	Danny	30	(5)	8					(1)					30	(6)	8
Curtis	Wayne	30	(3)	8	1	(1)	1	1	(1)	1	1		2	33	(5)	12
Davies	Scott	2	(3)								2			4	(3)	0
Drench	Steven	43			3			4						50		0
Gray	Shaun															
Howard	Michael	31	(1)		3			4		1				38	(1)	1
Hunter	Garry	27	(10)		1		1	3		1	2		1	33	(10)	3
Jarvis	Paul										1		1	1		1
Kelly	Tiernan										1			1		0
Langford	Andrew										2	(1)		2	(1)	0
Leigh	Andy										1			1		0
Lloyd	Paul	5	(5)	3							1			6	(5)	3
McLachlan	Fraser	10	(5)	1	3			1	(1)		2			16	(6)	1
McLuckie	Phil											(1)		0		0
McNiven	David	13	(17)	3	1		1	1			1			16	(17)	4
Neal	Chris															
Meadowcroft	Daniel	7	(5)	1							2			9	(5)	1
Perkins	David	20			2			2						24		
Pickersgill	Thomas										1	(1)		1		
Platt	Conal	1	(3)			(1)			(1)		1			2	(5)	
Rigoglioso	Adriano	7	(3)		3			1	(1)		1			12	(4)	
Robinson	Ryan	4												4		
Shaw	Matthew		(4)			(1)								0	(5)	
Smith	Jonathon					(1)					1			1	(1)	0
Sorvel	Neil	22		2				2						24		2
Stanley	Craig	40	(6)	2	2		1	4						46	(6)	3
Taylor	Aaron											(1)	1	0	(1)	1
Thompson	Garry	37		12	2			3		1				42		13
Twiss	Michael	33		10	3		3	4		3				40		16
Walker	Jason	1	(4)						(3)	1	2		1	3	(8)	2
Walmsley	Kieron		(1)								3		2	3	(2)	2
Watt	Jerome	1	(2)					1	(1)					2	(3)	
West	Michael										2	(1)		2	(1)	0
Wisdom	Danny										1			1		0
Yates	Adam	46	(1)	2	3			4						53	(1)	2

FIGURES IN BRACKETS ARE USED SUBSTITUTE APPEARANCES

Dedicated to the people of the Blenio Valley

Contents

Author's acknowledgements

My first thanks must go to Roy Guest, the last managing director of the United Carlo Gatti, Stevenson and Slaters Company, whose father worked man and boy for the Company. Roy Guest was a mine of information during my early researches and has remained a counsellor ever since.

Next my very warm thanks to the Gatti/Corazza family, Mary Wynne Williams, Louis Corazza, David Corazza and Giovanni Borri who have all helped me with reminiscences or advised me in some way.

My researches have taken me several times to Switzerland and the Blenio Valley, where I enjoyed the hospitality of the late Pino Peduzzi and the expert help of Professor Giorgio Cheda, Dr T. Martinoli and Paolo Jacomelli. My sad lack of Italian has been supported by the translations of Polly Buston, Rosemary Stevenson and Maddelena Fagandini.

In Norway, my colleague Gundel Krauss Dahl has pursued my ice interests over several years and from a chance meeting in the Oslo Maritime Museum, Goethe Goethesen has given me invaluable expert help on the Norwegian ice trade. My thanks to them all.

The late Messrs Dadomo and Rimoldi, together with Messrs Gallinari, Marney and Dadomo all generously offered information and anecdote on their lives as ice men working for the Gatti Company. Mr Forster of the Lowestoft Ice Company introduced me to artificial ice-making and Mr Witteens, from Diplomis, to the archive film on Norwegian ice production.

My thanks to my solicitor, Ian Harley, who advised me over Carlo Gatti's will and to Peter Jacomelli. From the day I first lunched at his restaurant – Valchera's in Richmond – seven or eight years ago, I have been asking him questions!

I appreciate the help received from the Westminster Libraries, particularly the Central Library and the Victoria Archive Library, the Holborn Local History Library, Lambeth Archive Library, the Maritime Museum, Greenwich, the Victoria and Albert Museum Library, Kragero Museum, the Archivo Historico at Bellinzona, and the Royal Archives at Windsor Castle, by whose kind permission I have quoted from Queen Victoria's Exhibition Diary.

Final thanks to Peter Barber of the British Library, to whom I first sent my manuscript, and whose stringent but encouraging remarks forced me to extend and complete my research; to Maureen Barsby and Caryl Knight who have assisted in the typing and preparation of the text and to Sally Jeffery, the designer, who has brought the publication to fruition.

Introduction

In 1982, I was training overseas students in television production at Visnews in London. One of my students chose to script and direct a short video on the Regent's Park Canal in London – a waterway now more used for leisure than industry. In the course of some historical research, I came across this comment on the uses of ice from the Canal in the 19th century.

> Mr Carlo Gatti – a Swiss Italian emigrant who came to Britain in 1840 – started up an ice parlour and used the ice he took from the many ponds and rivers in the area for his business during the summer. He held the ice contract on the Regent's Park Canal and stored ice in wells 60 feet deep of which several existed at Wharf Road near King's Cross . . . The measure of the success of this venture was that ultimately Mr Gatti was importing a quarter of a million tons of ice from Norway in a fleet of wooden sailing ships.

This comment interested and intrigued me so much, I have been researching the life of Carlo Gatti on and off for the last eight years.

It has not been easy. Gatti's humble commercial beginnings are difficult to identify. Official records, the National Census, the Register of Births and Deaths, the Postal Directories, etc., give sparse details. Trade magazines, which one would expect as a valuable source of information, were non-existent in the 1850s to 70s and only commenced ten to twenty years later.

Then there was the problem of separating fact from the many myths about Carlo Gatti – family myths and myths which have grown up in the Blenio Valley. Sometimes they have been surprisingly accurate, sometimes illusion. There was also the problem of separating Carlo Gatti's achievements from those of his nephews, Agostino and Stefano, and his own daughter, Rosa, although, of course, they were closely interlinked. In the past, this has led to great confusion.

The more I discovered about Carlo Gatti, his courage, ingenuity and business acumen, the more I felt he deserved a biography, but after a couple of years, I realised that, although he was well known and recognised in the latter part of his life, my researches, at least, could not provide a full and rounded picture of this remarkable man. Hence this memoir which records all the sources I have discovered but which poses many more questions.

But to begin the story, one must go back to Carlo Gatti's homeland, the Ticino, in Switzerland.

Figure 1 The Blenio Valley, from Dufour's Map of Switzerland, 1858

1 The Blenio Valley

Carlo Gatti was brought up in the Blenio Valley in the Ticino, the only Italian-speaking canton in Switzerland. The Ticino lies south of the Alps and borders Italy; in fact, its southern tip lies only 50 kilometres from Milan. Nowadays the Ticino is a centre of tourism – the Tuscany of Switzerland – with a million and a half tourists a year. It is also a great throughway, from the Gotthard Pass to Italy, for thousands of business and commercial interests.

It is a strikingly beautiful country of high mountains in the north, picturesque villages, groves of chestnuts, little mountain chapels, shrines and rugged castles, and in the south, serene lakes with almost tropical vegetation. Today it has a particular charm and relaxed Italian ambience for all who visit, but in earlier times it was a rather different place.

Conquered by the Swiss in the 15th and early 16th centuries, various areas were ruled as mini-colonies by the older German Swiss cantons, until 1803 when the republic and canton of Ticino was created. Its creation was an uneasy one of alp and lake, town and country, secular radicals and Catholic conservatives and for much of the 19th century, its political life was stormy. Added to that, many Ticinesi continued to look to Milan and the Lombardy plain as their natural and cultural home – as in some senses they still do today.

A poor country, known as the poorest in Europe, neglected and exploited in the earlier years, it became one of those areas where emigration became a way of life and a way of survival to many. From the 16th century, Ticinesi emigrated to Milan, Rome, Turin, and later on to Paris, St Petersburg and Vienna. Architects, sculptors, artists, fine craftsmen and even bankers, left to seek wider opportunities; and they were joined by many looking for work in humbler positions.

In the 19th century, when the Ticino had become a full and independent member of the Confederation, emigration continued. Like modern emigrants, men from a certain area or valley would seek work together in a particular town or country and, building up a network of family and neighbourly connections, would recruit succeeding generations of their own people to come over and join them. Ticinesi were to be found in Italy, France, Germany, Britain, North and South America and Australia.

Poverty was the greatest cause of emigration and poverty and isolation were to be found principally in the Alpine valleys of which the Blenio Valley was one. Locked in on the north by the mountains, an impenetrable barrier, crossed only on foot by packhorse or by stage-coach, it was a valley where much of the land was poor and the terrain difficult to work. Primitive agricultural methods, property divided into small unproductive plots, made for a harsh life, which was often plagued by natural disaster. It was conditions like these which drove many of the Bleniesi from their homes to seek their fortunes elsewhere.

From the 16th and 17th centuries, the rural poor went to Italy as cooks, stablehands, porters or chestnut-sellers. A century later, many took on more skilled tasks, particularly chocolate-making. Frederico Bruni in his book *I cioccolatieri, dall'artigianato all'industria*[1] finds traces of the Bleniesi in the 18th century all over Europe, in Milan, Nice, Marseilles, Frankfurt and London. This craft with its allied trades in confectionery, café and restaurant-keeping was to become the principal source of income for the central and upper valley of the Blenio. From the lower part of the valley, men emigrated to become shop and hotel keepers, ice cream makers and sellers and particularly chestnut sellers. The chestnut-sellers from Malvaglia were famous in Paris.

From their harsh and unrewarding rural life, the Bleniesi brought a capacity for hard work, sacrifice and ingenuity and it was these virtues which enabled them to survive the hardships of the rapidly growing industrial cities of Europe and beyond. And they never forgot their homeland. The object of emigration was first, to send money home to help and support their families and second, to amass enough capital to return to build their little 'palazzo' in their village and reap the rewards of their labours.

The number of small 'palazzos' in the villages of the Blenio are a physical record of how many emigrants achieved their aim. Among these emigrants, Carlo Gatti stands out as supremely successful, together with Monico and Pagani, both of whom came first to work for him.

2 The Gatti family

Much research remains to be done in the Ticino on the origins of the Gatti family, but it has been established as one of the oldest families of the Blenio Valley – *vincina e patrizia* – and there are brief references to the Gattis in documents from 1400 to 1600. As *patrizi*, the individual family members, whether rich or poor, possessed considerable rights, privileges and power in their community. In the 18th century, the Gattis were landowners on a small scale and some were educated professional men, serving the community as lawyers, as mayor and parish priest and, in the case of Carlo's grandfather, as a judge. Living in a poor isolated region, however, they were not wealthy people.

Carlo's immediate family lived in Marogno, a hamlet close to Dongio, and part of the original modest house still remains, derelict now, but attached to the larger house Carlo built for himself later on.

As a young man in his twenties, Carlo's father, Stefano (1776–1842) turned to commerce for a career, seeking his fortune in Paris, where he arrived in the turbulent revolutionary years (1795–1800), when Napoleon was making his bid for power. Together with his partner, Righenzi, he set up a successful wholesale business in the chestnut trade and, it is said, in fruit. Stefano married Apollonia de Righetti from the Valley and they had six children, Giacomo, Giuseppe, Giovanni, Apollonia, Caterina and Carlo.

At this stage, for the sake of clarity, it is perhaps important to mention the principal members of Carlo's family, who were influential in his life or who played a part in his career in London, with which this memoir deals.

Giacomo (1804–63), his eldest brother, was a very erudite man, spending some of his academic studies in Greece. He became the parish priest of the village of Castro in the Valley and spent the greater part of his life there, much loved and respected.

Giuseppe and Giovanni were two other older brothers. Like Giacomo, both would have received the same initial schooling in the local Church school. Giuseppe (1807–73) served in the Swiss Army as a lieutenant – all his life he carried the nickname Ul Tenent. He, too, was much respected and was elected Councillor of the Grand Council of the Ticino, 1839–48. He married Caterina Andreazzi and had ten children, one of whom married his cousin, Rosa, who was Carlo's daughter. This son died as a young man.

Of Giovanni (1809–76) little is known except that he was a cultivated person with up to date ideas. He married Maria Gatti and had five children of whom his two sons, Agostino and Stefano, are an important part of the London story.

Both Giuseppe and Giovanni joined their father in Paris and worked there for many years. One can assume from this that their mother probably stayed in the Valley to care for the younger children. The situation varied amongst these emigrant families. Some wives went with their husbands, others stayed at home and made visits. Children were often left with grandparents or aunts and uncles for long periods, but there was much journeying back and forwards, in spite of a long hazardous journey, first by stage-coach and steamer and later on by train. Giuseppe would have had to make routine visits to attend the Grand Council.

Both the sisters, Apollonia (1814–94) and Caterina (?–?) married men involved in the Paris wholesale business. One married a Righenzi, one an Appolonari, and it was they and their husbands who bought out Giuseppe and Giovanni, when they decided to join Carlo in London.

Two cousins, Agostino (1811–?) and Gaspero (1813–52) probably preceded Carlo to London. They made artificial flowers and feathered goods and had two shops there, one in Coppice Row, Holborn and the other in Lambeth.[2]

As for Carlo (1817–1878), much depends on hearsay. He went to the Church school, was a poor pupil and showed no love of learning. He played truant often, preferring to mix and play with the village boys. Finding him so undisciplined, his teacher, Don Giacomo Martinoli, took a cane to him. The beating was so severe that Carlo never returned to school. At the age of 13, he set off, probably in the company of a group of chestnut sellers, to walk to Paris to his father and brothers. It was a journey of over 600 miles. On arrival, he was put to work in the business.

In 1839, at the age of 22, he married Maria Marioni, a village girl from Castro. They were married in Castro by his brother Giacomo, the priest there. By that time, Carlo must have grown into the tall, broad man who earned the nickname Gatton.

(see Appendix I: The Gatti family.)

3 The Gattis in Paris

The bill in Figure 2 records the family business, Righenzi and Gatti, at 84 rue Montmartre. It is dated 1843, a year after Stefano died and when presumably Giuseppe and Giovanni joined the other partners in running the firm. It was a wholesale business – a *Magasin de Marrons de Lyon, de Luc, Turin et toutes éspèces* – delivering to the provinces and abroad.

In the 19th century and indeed in earlier times, chestnuts were used widely by chefs and high class confectioners for desserts and sweetmeats, for instance, *marrons glacés*; but at the same time they were a staple food for poor people in certain areas in France, Italy and Spain, where they were boiled, roasted or ground into flour. Roast chestnuts, too, were a winter favourite in towns and cities all over Europe. To the Ticinesi, the chestnut was the very 'staff of life'.

The Magasin de Marrons at number 84 was situated in the south end of the rue Montmartre where it ran into Les Halles, the great market of Paris. It was one of the oldest streets in Paris and ran north to the Abbaye de Montmartre from which it took its name. In Carlo's time it was a street of 18th and 19th century houses, once residential, but at its southern end taken over by merchants as shops and warehouses.

The presence of the King's and later the Imperial Messageries – a central staging post for passengers, parcels and mail – also meant that the street had a large number of hotels or furnished rooms to accommodate messengers, couriers and travellers.[3]

Today there is no number 84. If the numbering of the street has remained the same, it must have stood close to the Messageries and have been demolished or amalgamated into the modern number 86 on the corner of rue Leopold Bellon when new modern roads were laid down.

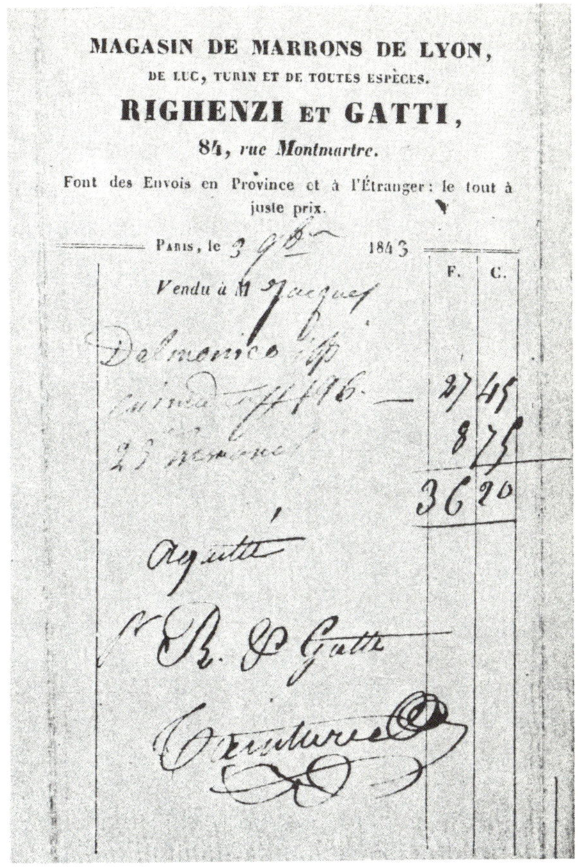
MAGASIN DE MARRONS DE LYON,
DE LUC, TURIN ET DE TOUTES ESPÈCES.
RIGHENZI ET GATTI,
84, rue Montmartre.
Font des Envois en Province et à l'Étranger: le tout à juste prix.
Paris, le 3 9bre 1843
F. C.
Vendu à M
27 45
8 75
36 20

Figure 2 Parisian bill

We do not know if the Gatti family lived at number 84, but what we do know from hearsay is that, as Carlo grew up, he did not prove a success in the business and that he left it, to the relief of his brothers, in his early twenties. Pino Peduzzi claims in *Pionieri Ticinesi* that he went to London at that age, but I do not think this can be substantiated.[4] Although obituaries are often inaccurate, one which states 'Though he lived in Paris no less than 18 years, his finances do not seem to have particularly prospered in the great capital of France . . .'[5] to me is more convincing and is not the sort of statement a writer would manufacture. It goes on 'He began life in London, as he did in Paris, selling roast chestnuts . . .' so it seems likely he left the family business and started to work on the streets.

Carlo would have been familiar with the chestnut sellers or *marroniers* since childhood. He would have seen them depart from the Blenio after the harvest and the new wine had been laid down and watched their return in the spring with money for their families and a bag of presents and trinkets.[6] This type of travelling life may have attracted his restless nature and accounts for hearsay that he built up gambling debts with Belgeri, the baker in Dongio, when he was at home in the village, much to the disapproval of his brothers. In Paris he may, too, have run a little kiosk or coffee stall or worked in a café. It is said he met Maria Marioni working in her father's café. This was probably in Paris not London. There are no Marionis recorded in London till 1856.[7]

Paris at that time was renowned for its café society, with over 4,000 cafés, serving the very rich, the literary and artistic and the ordinary man at the corner of the street. When Carlo's father came to Paris, the most famous cafés lay in the Palais Royal and one of these was the Café Corazza, run by the Corazza family who came originally from the Blenio Valley. These cafés were the forum of the French Revolution. If you wanted to know a man's political allegiance, all you had to do was to seek out his favourite café. The Jacobins were to be found at the Café Corazza. The Royalists at the Bourbon or the Mirabeau. Dantonists drank coffee at the Café Gilbert, the Enragés met at the Café Méchanique.

In the 1830s and 40s, cafés became more social than political institutions and Carlo would have had the opportunity of savouring café life, both as a customer and a member of staff. He would have relished their charms, but also learned the ways in which they were run and managed. During this period he must have lived a much harsher and less cultivated life than his more sophisticated brothers and mixed amongst very different companions.

4 Carlo Gatti comes to London

Writing in the *Daily Telegraph*, September 10th 1925, the Member of Parliament, the Rt Hon T. P. O'Connor, looked back to his youth fifty years earlier when he first frequented Gatti's restaurants in Adelaide Street and in Villiers Strcet where Carlo Gatti himself

. . . the presiding genius and founder of the family and the business could be seen almost nightly . . . This Gatti remained and was proud to remain what he was at the start. He took the keenest interest in his restaurant; he was capable, now and then, of taking his turn at watching the steak or the mutton chop on the big grill – of which he was one of the pioneers – as he sat gossiping with his cronies. He was very corpulent; and probably found his armchair, in the midst of his work and in sight of his growing wealth, the best form of relaxation.

Later Mr O'Connor goes on:

A transformation in the social life of London has been created by members of this family, for until the Gatti restaurants came, there was scarcely any provision for the large class whose means are between extreme poverty and great wealth. The only place at which to get a cup of tea or coffee in London was in those frowzy coffee houses, sadly declined from the coffee house which was in the days of Swift and other 18th century figures the resort of the aristocrats and the wits of that splendid age. It was the Gattis also who, besides producing finely ornamented and airy restaurants, introduced music at a meal – an unheard of novelty at the period when they began. These restaurants, in their well-chosen position, have been for two generations very popular, especially in literary and artistic circles, and the family must be regarded as one of the pioneers of the brighter, more comfortable London we have today, a transformation which can be appreciated by those, only, like myself, who had to find their frugal meals either in a coffee shop or the tap room of a humble public house.[8]

How did such a transformation come about and what is the story behind Carlo's unexpected success? Research suggests his early years in London remain something of a mystery, as indeed, does his date of arrival.

From 1793, all aliens were registered on arrival in Britain and the first time Carlo's name appears on a certificate of arrival is on July 2 1847 at Dover.[9] He was 30 and he came alone. His profession, which is difficult to decipher, appears to be mechanic and he has signed in a cramped schoolboy hand. It is possible that he could have come earlier in a group, where one man signed for the others. Strolling musicians, hawkers and other traders, often illiterate, were recorded that way. Nevertheless he probably came without his family in the first place. He had married Maria Marioni in 1839 and it seems certain that his first three children, Stefano, Maria Appolonia and Rosa, were all born in the Ticino.[10]

What is also certain is that he came to London a poor man and began by running a coffee stall and selling his *goffre* – a small kind of waffle sprinkled with sugar – and that he supplemented this in winter by selling chestnuts.[11] His equipment is likely to have been a good deal less sophisticated than the one illustrated in Figure 3, as this was the most up to date stall at the time. He went on to acquire various coffee stalls or kiosks and probably, during that time, lived in the poorer slum areas of Holborn, where there was already a small Italian community.

Holborn in the 19th century was an area of great contrasts. Behind the main shopping street lay the gentry's fine mansions in Hatton Gardens and Ely Place, and alongside these were the crowded streets and narrow courtyards which for many years were London's worst slums. Saffron Hill, known as the Rookery because of its crowded tenements, and Field Lane were the site of Fagin's den in Charles Dickens' *Oliver Twist*. Dickens, who lived in Holborn at one time, wrote about real life when he described Oliver Twist's first reaction to this area.

> A dirtier or more wretched place he had never seen. The street was very narrow and muddy and the air was impregnated with filthy odours . . . The sole place which seemed to prosper amid the general blight of the place were the public houses; and in them the lowest orders of Irish were wrangling with might and main. Covered ways and yards, which here and there diverged from the main street, disclosed little knots of houses, where drunken men and women were positively wallowing in filth.

The Irish were the first immigrants to Holborn. The Italians followed, forced like modern immigrants, to take the cheapest accommodation they could find in the poorer parts of the city. First of these were the itinerant musicians and street entertainers – the 1841 National Census records a Giacomo Gatti, a musician with two sons, living in Saffron Court – then came the artisans, figure makers, makers of picture frames, mirrors and barometers. Mazzini established a school there for poor boys in the 1840s and by 1870 the area was crowded with Italians and known as Little Italy.

Working as a chestnut seller on the streets of

Figure 3 Coffee stall, London, *c.* 1851

Paris, Carlo would have known poverty and squalor, but arriving in the slums of Holborn must have been a formidable experience. Such bad living conditions may account for the tragic deaths of his only son and baby daughter, Stefano and Maria Appolonia, aged nine and two, in 1849.[12]

But he and his family were not entirely alone. His cousins, Agostino and Gaspero Gatti, are recorded in 1847 as having two shops, in Coppice Row, Holborn and in Lambeth. They were manufacturers of preparations for artificial flowers and were probably established there some years earlier.

1849 saw a change in Carlo's fortunes. He joined forces with Battista Bolla who had premises at 129 Holborn Hill and they established a café-restaurant as Gatti and Bolla. Battista Bolla was a *chocolatier* from Castro and was said to be the first Bleniese *chocolatier* to come to London. He was to live and work at 129 Holborn Hill well into the 1870s.

By 1850, Gatti and Bolla had acquired another shop at 122 Holborn Hill and are recorded as Chocolate Manufacturers.[13] And in 1851, the National Census records Carlo as living in the Parish of St Andrew at 129 Holborn Hill with his wife, Maria, and his daughters Rosa, aged five, and Clara, ten months, together with Battista Bolla, Julian Bolla, aged fifteen, and eight workmen from Switzerland, one of whom was a Corazza.

See Appendix II for the names of workers living in Gatti households, 1851–1881.

5 Gatti and Bolla

The line drawing in Figure 4 of a section of Holborn Hill is part of a pictorial record made by John Tallis in *Streets of London*, 1838–46, and is an accurate picture of the street in Carlo's time. Number 129 sits on the corner of Leather Lane, the seat of one of London's oldest markets. It lies on the boundary of the City of London. Number 122, Carlo's other shop, lies to the east of Leather Lane.

Number 129 has a double frontage with two shop windows, living accommodation above and attics where the workmen must have slept. There are also cellars where ice could have been stored. Two doors down is the Bell and Crown which became Ridlers Hotel. The photograph in Figure 5 shows Ridlers Hotel just before it was demolished and includes number 129 with its fascia still intact some 50 years later. It reads:

B BOLLA. ESTABLISHED GATTI AND BOLLA IN 1849
CAFE RESTAURANT

So clearly Bolla was there first. The rate books confirm that he was there in 1848 but with aplomb Carlo has begun his first takeover!

Gatti and Bolla soon became well known in Holborn Hill, for an obituary states that in 1849 Carlo revisited Paris:

> . . . whence he immediately returned with a machine for manufacturing chocolate. The machine was an old and rusty one, but that was all he could get with the money at his disposal.
>
> With patience and a will, he and Battista Bolla, whom he had interested in the business, set themselves to place it in working order . . . and began the manufacture of chocolate before the very eyes of the public at the house numbered 129 Holborn Hill. Neither the chestnuts or the goffre had, however, been given up for the new business. They were sold side by side with the chocolate. And this chocolate, it is fair to add, obtained an Honourable Mention at the Great Exhibition in 1851.[14]

The Illustrated Cyclopedia, 1851, also notes that at the Great Exhibition there was 'a model in motion of an apparatus for grinding and preparing nuts (cocoa nuts) and those who walk down Holborn may see the real apparatus in action.'

It appears Carlo's flair for business was beginning to develop. By putting the machine in the shop window, he was attracting attention and custom. One can almost imagine it. Bolla at the back of the shop in charge of the whole chocolate-making operation and Carlo at the front, chatting up the customers, serving chocolate and waffles and perhaps more substantial meals.

In the 1850s most chocolate manufacture was in drinking chocolate, which never caught on in Britain in quite the same way as it did on the continent. Cocoa, although rather an inferior drink, did become popular and would also have been served at Gatti and Bolla's. Chocolate as confectionery was not highly developed. Bolla probably made chocolate drops – plain or silvered – bonbons, and tablets of chocolate, but it was not until the 1860s that chocolates with different fillings, packaged in boxes, were

Figure 5 Holborn Hill, showing number 129 with date visible on fascia (top right)

introduced. The Gattis were to develop chocolate confectionery in later years.

The café probably served ice cream. Ice cream was a major attraction in Parisian cafés and Carlo's later reputation lay in 'coffee and ices'. In 1851, Henry Mayhew wrote 'the sale of ice cream in the streets was unknown until last summer, and was first introduced, as a matter of speculation, by a man who was acquainted with the confectionery business and purchased his ices from a confectioner in Holborn . . . The sale, however, was not remunerative'.[15]

This confectioner may have been Carlo Gatti. By this time he must have started his ice business, cutting ice on the Regent's Park Canal, so he would have had ice for ice cream-making. We shall probably never know, but it appears the time for selling ices on the street had not yet come!

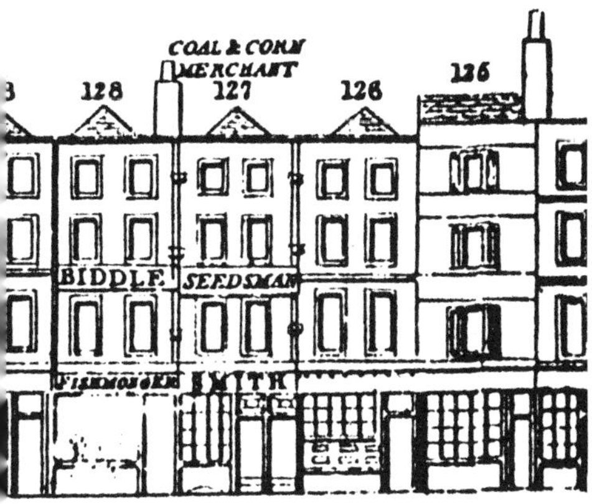

Figure 4 Holborn Hill in the 1840s. Number 129 can be seen to the left of Leather Lane.

6 The Great Exhibition, 1851

The Great Exhibition, master-minded by Prince Albert, was a celebration of Britain and her Empire and designed to show her position as the first industrial power in the world. It was housed in a magnificent Palace of Glass in Hyde Park, designed by Joseph Paxton.

The arrangements for the exhibition were under the control of Her Majesty's Commissioners and were financed primarily by public subscription. Men from industry, commerce, art and design were asked to submit machinery, articles or products of all kinds for consideration for exhibition. Local Committees were formed all over the country to which initial plans and drawings were submitted and these Committees had powers of selection and rejection. If an exhibit was accepted, the Committee then allotted space to the individual exhibitor within the space given by the Commissioners to that Committee.

Carlo may have submitted his plans for a working model of his machine to the Committee or he may have been asked to do so. The Committees were always on the look-out for new innovative ideas and the chocolate machine was clearly a novelty in Holborn. The model is recorded in the 1851 Exhibition Catalogue as follows:

Manufacturing Machines and Tools
Class 6 No 450
Gatti and Bolla 129 Holborn Hill Manufacturers
Model of a machine for the manufacture of French and Italian chocolate. The good qualities of the cocoa beans are intended to be retained by the process.

Class 6 was in the section of Machinery in Motion – a major element of the Exhibition on the ground floor.[16]

Queen Victoria herself took a tremendous interest in

Figure 6 The Palace of Glass in Hyde Park, 1851

the Exhibition. She wrote a regular journal of her daily visits to various sections. On June 16th she wrote:

> To the Exhibition . . . the whole time taken up with seeing machinery and most interesting it was. First we saw a very curious machine for cutting wood – a curvilinear sawing machine for timber for ships . . . Lithograph printing in colours and varnishing; sugar mills and sugar refiners of all kinds; mills for grinding wheat and linseed and for extracting oil from the latter; a machine for making biscuits. A large one, the largest in the exhibition, invented by Mr S. Russell, for crushing sugar cane and extracting the juice, another for cleansing corn and grain; coffee mills; a very curious machine for making chocolate; a very ingenious one for making cigarettes and wrapping them up in paper – all done by the same machine . . .[17]

It would be nice to think that 'the very curious machine for making chocolate' was Carlo's machine but it is much more likely that this was M. Herman's full-size 'complete and admirable set of machines employed for the manufacture of chocolate by which the cocoa beans are crushed after being roasted, mixed with sugar and the chocolate fully prepared for use.' This was a French machine and the description comes from the Juror's Report, which also states 'a mixing machine for chocolate is also exhibited by Messrs Gatti and Bolla'.

One can only assume Gatti and Bolla's model of the 'old and rusty machine' was not as up-to-date as M. Herman's. M. Herman, in fact, won the Council medal, a most prestigious award. There is no Honourable Mention for Gatti and Bolla, as his obituary suggested. The Honourable Mention went to A. and G. Gatti, Carlo's cousins.

Their exhibit was in Class 29 Miscellaneous Manufacturers and Small Wares. There were 74 exhibitors in wax, feathers, cambric and shells. The citation reads as follows: 'Honourable Mention, for artificial flowers and articles used in their manufacture, such as leaves, buds and other components of flowers; chiefly of common material, but very good in regard to colour, some of the tints being exceedingly bright and rich. The flowers are extremely accurate in their imitation of nature and are mostly well selected for the peculiar class of article. As cheap commercial productions, this collection deserves commendation.'

The display included an artificial cluster of sweet peas, made from white muslin and velvet, each piece shaded separately, flowers made of paper and patterns, comprising every colour and description of material, both before and after being made up as flowers.

Figure 7 Machinery Court at the Great Exhibition

These flowers would have been sold in the Gattis' shops in Coppice Row, Holborn and in Lambeth. Neither lay in rich or fashionable areas, so one can assume from the citation that the Gattis were serving a lower-middle and working class clientele. In days when many of these women had only one day dress and a Sunday best with perhaps two hats, which were worn over many years, wonderful changes were wrought each spring with artificial flowers and feathers; so women and girls with a sharp eye for fashion must have been the first to appreciate the artistry of the Gattis! We do not know if it was Agostino or Gaspero themselves who made the flowers or an unknown workman from the Valley.

The 1851 Census records Agostino living at 28 Bridge Road, Lambeth with his daughter Mary, aged three, born in Lambeth, and Clara Hilliard, a visitor from France, with her daughter Eugenia, aged two. Clara Hilliard was, in fact, Agostino's sister and her son, Luigi Adolfo, was born in London in 1854.

Unfortunately the Census records for Coppice Row have been damaged and we have no record of Gaspero who died in Strasbourg in 1852. Agostino died in Paris.[18] In 1863 there was a Madame Clarisse Gatti, Artificial Florist, at Bridge Road, and in 1877 Gatti A and G (G. H. Calderwood), manufacturers and importers of all kinds of materials for artificial flowers, are recorded at 20/21 Farringdon Road and Vineyard Walk. Whether Madame Clarisse was a relative or simply used the name I do not know, but it is pleasant to imagine that G. H. Calderwood, when he took over the firm, chose to keep the good name of Gatti as a sign of quality.[19]

7 Hungerford Market

In the year of the Exhibition, 1851, Carlo had established himself as a pastrycook at 29 and 40 Great Hall, Hungerford Market, off the Strand.[20]

Hungerford Market was an impressive market complex covering 52,890 square feet. Opened in 1833, it had been designed to compete with Covent Garden Market in fruit and vegetables and to break the monopoly of the Fish Market at Billingsgate, as well as offering other merchandise and providing several taverns. It consisted of two great quadrangles: the Fish Market which fronted onto the river and the new pedestrian suspension bridge, designed by Brunel, which was to bring shoppers from Lambeth and Southwark, and the Great Hall which had shops and stalls at ground and first floor level. Beyond the Great Hall lay an open space with a bus terminus which led out into the Strand.

In 1850, Henry Mayhew describes the shops in the Great Hall as follows:

> On the western side there are 9 butchers, 1 tripe-seller, 6 dealers in game and poultry, 2 butter shops, 1 pork, 1 milk-seller and 7 fishmongers, 1 cook shop, 1 ginger-beer seller, 2 toy shops, 1 print seller, 1 basket-seller, 1 confectioner, and 2 taverns. On the eastern side are 1 tavern, 1 hairdresser, 1 glass shop, 1 mealman, 3 potato shops, 11 fruiterers, 3 fruit and vegetable dealers, 2 greengrocers, 2 ginger-beer sellers and 6 fishmongers. In the middle avenue there are 1 dealer in wardrobe clothes, 1 boot and shoe-maker, 1 grocer, 1 hairdresser, 2 picture frame dealers, 2 milliners, 1 artist (profilist), 1 parasol and archery shop, 1 haberdasher and 1 fishing-tackle maker; altogether 74 shops and 3 taverns in the market and 6 shops in the arcade leading to the market.[21]

Rents varied from 4 shillings to £1 a week.

By 1853, Carlo had expanded his shops in the Market to 33, 34 and 65 Great Hall and had probably begun the sale of the Penny Ice Cream to the London public for which he was to become so famous. In the 1850s ice cream was a delicacy only for the rich. The excitement engendered among ordinary working people eating ice cream for the first time was enormous. As well as cool delight and refreshment, it found them spluttering, complaining of pain in their teeth, and for those who gulped it down all at once, fear for their very lives.[22]

Gatti's ices were served in little 'pastry shells'.[23] This may have been an adaptation of the famous *goffre*, or waffle mixture, which he served with coffee. Certainly it predated the cornet by almost 40 years.[24]

The penny ice was a great novelty and soon caught on. In later years it became all the rage and was developed not only by confectioners, but by hundreds of Italian ice cream sellers on the streets of London. These were the Hokey Pokey men – so called because to tempt their customers they would invite them to taste a little – *Ecco un poco*. 'A penny ice man could do a brisk trade even when his little customers were blue with cold'.[25]

Whether Carlo ever sent ice cream sellers into the

Figure 8 The opening of Hungerford Market, 1833. It was designed to rival the market at Covent Garden.

streets, we cannot be sure, but knowing his enthusiasm for seizing on a new idea, it seems very likely. We know that he supplied all the Hokey Pokey men in the Holborn area with their ice for freezing in the later years. What he did do, however, was to introduce the mass consumption of ice cream in Britain. This eulogy written in the 1880s gives a flavour of its popularity:

Hail to thee, thou Penny Ice! Thou didst steal amongst us in the summer to blunt the edges of our noonday heat, to puzzle and delight the tongue enamoured of thy perfumed pleasantness, to cool the parched throat that woke to new hope, and gaped in joy at feeling thy bland avalanches descend its sides, to thrill the whole baked being with shooting darts of delicious cold![26]

It was in Hungerford Market that Carlo also established his first real continental café, based on his experience in Paris. Red plush seats, cloths on the table, mirrors on the wall, coffee and ices accompanied by a little light music, all this created a stir in the poor man's West End. In fact, the café offered an entirely new venue for a new type of customer, which included families.[27]

While Carlo was embarking on these new developments, he had news that his brothers were to join him in London.

Figure 9 The riverside entrance to the Fish Market at Hungerford Market.

Figure 10 A new pedestrian bridge was built over the Thames to bring customers direct to the Market. The piers of that bridge remain part of Hungerford Railway Bridge today.

8 The brothers come to London

Exactly why Giuseppe and Giovanni decided to leave Paris for London and embark on entirely different careers, with a brother whom they had thought of in the past as a ne'er-do-well, remains unresolved. They would, of course, have heard of Carlo's coffee stalls, his establishment at 129 Holborn Hill, the shops at Hungerford Market and perhaps his local ice business, but all this was small-time business not huge financial success.

I suspect there were a number of factors leading to their decision. By then Carlo must have recognised the expansion of business and commercial interests in London and forseen the development of the café trade. It may have been he who urged them to come over. Or the brothers, having endured once more insurrection and the raising of the barricades in Paris in 1848 and fearing instability in the future, decided to 'cross the water' to a more settled country.

Yet another factor could have been *la maladie de l'encre*, a blight on the chestnut trees which from 1850 onwards began to sweep from Spain across south west France. It must, in later years, have seriously affected the *marron* trade, when millions of trees in France, Spain and Italy were wiped out.[28]

Or maybe it was news of the magnificence of the Great Exhibition and indeed the entry of Carlo's machine, which clinched their thinking! Whatever the reason, it must have been a radical change from the *marron* business, and in their first years in Britain they must have relied heavily on Carlo's advice and some good *chocolatiers* and confectioners from the Blenio Valley, whom they brought over to help them.

What was different about their arrival in Britain, compared to Carlo's, was that they came with capital, having sold out their business in rue Montmartre to their sisters and their husbands, Righenzi and Appolonari.

I do not know their date of arrival, but from the Rate Books we know that Giuseppe Gatti had premises at 13 Aldgate in the City in 1852 and the Postal Directories confirm him as a confectioner and chocolate manufacturer at that address. The census of 1861 confirms he lived there with his family.

In 1852, Gatti Bros were established as Chocolate Manufacturers in Haggerston and at an unknown date a Steam Works was established by Gatti Bros in Little George Street, Minories.[29]

But as Giuseppe and Giovanni were settling in their families and setting up businesses, a disaster befell Carlo in Hungerford Market.

Figure 11
The fire at Hungerford Hall

9 Great fire at Hungerford Hall

On March 18th 1854, the *Illustrated London News* carried an advertisement as follows:

> Hungerford Hall, Strand will open on Monday evening 20 inst at 8 o'clock the Great Moving Diorama of London showing the death of the Duke of Wellington, Lying in State in Chelsea College, the Magnificent State Funeral Pageant, Gorgeous Paraphernalia . . . and the imposing ceremonial in St Paul's Cathedral.
> Gallery 6d. Reserved Seats 1s. Stalls 1s 6d.

The Panorama was a popular event in the 1850s. Pictures were painted on a long canvas which was stretched in a convex semi-circle and moved slowly forward on rollers. Music, drums and general effects accompanied a narrator who described the events – in this case the epic State funeral of the Duke of Wellington. The canvas was illuminated from behind by open gas jets, which, when lit, could be dimmed or brightened according to the mood of the moment, and it was those jets which started the fire.

On April 1st *The Times* recorded that Hungerford Hall had been burnt out the night before. It was said that the two boys employed to light the jets had inadvertently started the fire and had perished in it. Not only was the Hall destroyed, scarcely a shop on either side of the Great Hall above had escaped damage and most of the roof was burnt away or broken.

Carlo's shop at number 31 suffered. The *Illustrated London News* states 'No 31 Messrs Gatti Confectioners. Great damage to stock in trade by water etc. Insured at the Union Fire Office.'[30] It is interesting to note that Carlo was insured. Very few others were, not even the owner of the Panorama, who had spent £2,000 to £3,000 on his painted canvas. Fire, of course, remained a tremendous hazard in the 19th century and the Hungerford Market Company and Carlo were fortunate that the London Fire Brigade, led by James Braidwood, was summoned to the fire.

Established only twenty years earlier, the Brigade, according to Fire Report 293, sent eight manual fire engines to the scene and were in process of bringing into action their brand new fire boat on the Thames, when the fire came under control.

What a task it must have been for the Company to

rebuild and refurbish both the Great Hall and Hungerford Hall and for the shopkeepers to set to rights their damaged shops. It may also have been a turning point for the Market for Hungerford Market had never been the success which the Company had hoped. It did not successfully compete with either Covent Garden or Billingsgate and the pedestrian bridge across the river failed to bring in enough customers. Even in 1851, Charles Knight in his *Pictorial Half Hours of London Topography* records that many of the shops were deserted and that it had not fulfilled its purpose.

One of the few growing successes, however, seems to have been Gatti's shops and café, and the refurbishment of Hungerford Hall offered just the expansion that Carlo and his new partners were looking for in 1857. Here one sees the first elements of the Café Concert.

On October 3rd 1857 the following advertisement appeared in the *Westminster News*:

> New Music Hall, Hungerford Market. Entrance opposite the Suspension Bridge. This elegant and spacious Hall has been redecorated after the most recherché models of the 'Parisian Saloons' forming one of the most charming and delightful Concert Halls in London. Here visitors will have the gratification of enjoying first class entertainment – a beautiful and well-lighted room – refreshments carefully selected and every arrangement for comfort. Open every evening at halfpast seven for Glees, choruses, Solos, Duets Comic character, Singing etc.

Although no mention is made of Gatti's name it is hard to believe that this advertisement does not refer to him. Certainly by the following year, 1858, Carlo had a licence for music for Hungerford Hall and a partnership had been formed between himself, his brother Giovanni and Giuseppe Monico covering all the shops in Hungerford Market, in Holborn and Whitechapel.

Giuseppe Monico came from the same village, Dongio, in the Blenio Valley. One presumes he came over at much the same time as the brothers. By 1858 he had already established a confectioner's shop in Knightsbridge.[31]

This new partnership was essentially a family affair with members from all three families living and working 'over the shop'. The 1861 census records that Carlo had moved into Hungerford Market and was living in 12 Upper Area – the residential part of the complex – with his wife Maria, his daughter Giaftian [sic] aged five, six servant/labourers, a confectioner and three others. In the Upper Hall were Agostino Gatti (20), Head Refreshment Room Keeper, and his three assistants Giacomo Monico (20), Stefano Gatti (16), Battista Monico (16), four waiters, one of whom was a Lucca Gatti, three cooks and a shopman, all from Switzerland. Giovanni had a house in or attached to Hungerford Hall.[32]

But hardly had they got established when they were threatened by the further decline and closure of the Market itself. About 1859, the Hungerford Market Company sold out to the South Eastern Railway who planned to bring the railway across the river into Charing Cross to serve both the West End and the City.

10 The coming of the railway

Hearsay has it that while serving coffee at his kiosk in the early days, Carlo met an indiscreet railway engineer who told him of plans to build a railway station at Victoria. Whereupon Carlo bought a plot of land on the site and was later compensated.

I have never found any references to Victoria in my researches, but this story may be true of Charing Cross. If it is true, then Carlo made a long term commitment, first in renting property in a number of shops in Hungerford Market and later in purchasing Hungerford Hall. He was installed there from 1851 or even earlier and was rewarded, with his partners, some eleven years later when the whole complex was destroyed to make way for the railway station and the hotel.

The Gattis and Monicos stayed to the last, but it is

obvious from this carping description that Hungerford Market was very run down as it prepared for its destruction.

For the rest there was a dreary makeshift aspect even in the corridors of the quadrangles where articles of real use were sold; but about the central hall there clung a number of extraordinary expositions of cheap prints, picture frames, walking sticks, shells and sticky sweet-stuffs from which by some inexplicable means certain people appear to obtain livelihoods in forlorn parts of the metropolis, so that when a prosperous penny-ice shop was opened, notwithstanding its own innate dinge, it gave an air of prosperity to the place which it had never possessed before. The adventurous dispenser of penny ices took pity on the poor hall, which had been opened for half a dozen purposes, and advertised as adapted to a hundred more, and having fitted it up after the fashion of a fifth-rate foreign café, threw it open as an annexe to his establishment for the consumption of his confections, and even added to its melancholy attractions a band of two violins, a harp and an octave flute, which disturbed or assisted, according to their idiosyncrasies, the digestions of the consumers, who were thinly scattered over the area.[33]

The xenophobic feeling in the 19th century against all things 'foreign' is well and truly registered here but the article does confirm that Gatti's was a popular café serving the lower orders of society with what was for them a great novelty – the penny ice cream.

It must have been a sad sight to see the magnificent buildings of the Market crumble before their eyes, but the prospect of compensation must have been equally agreeable. H. P. Clunn, writing in the *Face of London* in 1832, says of Hungerford Hall: 'This was afterwards appropriated by Messrs Gatti and Monico for the sale of ices and fitted up as a small foreign café with an orchestra and when the building was pulled down in August 1862 for the construction of Charing Cross Station, this firm received £7,750 compensation.' In modern day terms that would be about £262,570.

With this new influx of capital what would be the next development? In fact Carlo, who was always on the look-out for new enterprises, had already embarked on an entirely different business – the import of ice from Norway.

Figure 12 The demolition of Hungerford Market

Figure 13 Ice-cutting on a canal

11 Carlo Gatti, Ice Merchant (English and Foreign)

Collection and storage of ice must have been a familiar custom to Carlo Gatti. There would have probably have been communal village ice pits in the Ticino in the 19th century or extensive use of vaults and cellars. The *Encyclopaedia Britannica* of 1771 cites a saying 'the meanest person in Italy, who rents a house, has his vault or cellar for ice'. But the idea of storage and use of ice came late to Britain and then only for the benefit of the very wealthy.

From the early 17th century, the aristocracy and gentry with large estates began to build ice houses, which were filled each winter with ice from their lakes and ponds. The ice was used in the great houses to preserve food in the summer months, for iced drinks and ice cream and the cooling of rooms. It had medicinal uses too in the reduction of fevers.

In the 19th century, ice began to be introduced on a large scale for commercial use in the preservation of fish, both at sea and on land, and of meat; for servicing hotels, clubs and caterers and in providing the pleasures of cool drinks and ice cream to a wider public. From the 1850s onwards, ice chests were extensively advertised. Towards the end of the century, the introduction of the small ice chest for individual homes provided a further revolution. Although there was an established home market in ice, this revolution was achieved by the import of quantities of ice, first from America (Wenham Lake) and later almost entirely from Norway.

Hearsay has it that Carlo had a licence to cut ice on the Regent's Park Canal. The canal runs for eight and a half miles from Paddington to Regent's Canal Dock in Limehouse. What sections of the canal were covered we do not know, or where he stored his ice.

Figure 14 Regent's Canal Dock, Limehouse

He may have started selling his ice to the first and established London ice merchant, William Leftwich, who had an ice well on the canal at Upper James Street, Camden Town and who, no doubt, had a similar interest in the canal. Or he may have started by digging ice pits in the traditional way, selling to fishmongers and butchers in the summer months, and using small quantities of ice for his ice cream making. There were cellars below the house in 129 Holborn Hill.

The first formal date we have in the Postal Directories is in 1860: 'Carlo Gatti Ice Merchant 12 Upper Area Hungerford Market 2 New Wharf Road'.

New Wharf Road lies alongside the Battlebridge Basin on the Regent's Park Canal at King's Cross. There would also have been ice storage facilities in the vaults of Hungerford Market near the Fish Market.

A Norwegian colleague of mine, Goethe Goethesen – an expert on sailing ships and Norwegian cargoes – has unearthed a letter from J. G. Dahll in London, written September 29th 1856 to his brother J. M. Dahll in Kragero, Norway. In it he states: 'he has made a contract with C. Gatti, Ice Merchant, to deliver in February, March or April next year, 400 tons of ice. Guaranteed thickness 8 inches. Payment 50% cash and the rest on 3 months . . . .? Price 17/- (shillings) a ton'.[34] He also states that Gatti has promised him all his business for the summer time. Goethesen writes that the conditions are unclear but he gets the impression that Dahll is keen to try to keep Gatti as a customer. In fact the Dahlls did get a permanent contract with Carlo and thereafter all the ice came from that firm.

But in 1857, four hundred tons represented one shipload of ice, so one can assume Carlo was beginning to import ice that year, or one or two years earlier, and that he built or expanded his ice well at New Wharf Road at the same time.

One of the great virtues of ice from America and Norway was its great purity. One can imagine how filthy ice off the canal must have been! And from the 1850s onwards the ice trade accelerated rapidly, with Norway becoming the principal and cheapest exporter to Britain. It could, however, be a very precarious trade as so many unknown factors were involved. Ice depended for both its quality and quantity on the Norwegian winter and the trade depended on the demand of a hot or cool British summer. Prices varied considerably as a result.

The ice came in sailing ships from Kragero to Regent's Canal Dock at Limehouse. It was unloaded, checked and weighed out. By the 1900s there were Gatti ice wells all along the canal, at Kensal Green, Haggerston Basin, Hackney, in Shoreditch, Islington and King's Cross. There were other separate wells like Caledonian Road which meant ice was delivered from the docks both by barge and by cart.

It is difficult to extrapolate the exact speed of development of the trade in Carlo's lifetime, but two obituaries confirm he began to import ice in 1857 and that in a short time he became the largest ice merchant in London with 60 vans and carts. It is also suggested that he himself had enlarged consumption and demand in ice, so one can assume he had an established trade in local ice before 1857.[35]

In 1857 there were ten ice merchants listed in London. Most of these started as fishmongers. Carlo was the first of the caterers. The trade grew rapidly from the 1860s. By the 1890s, competition was cutthroat and artificial ice was beginning to penetrate the market. It was in 1901 that the Carlo Gatti Company amalgamated with two other firms to become the United Carlo Gatti, Stevenson and Slaters Company, which was to run successfully until 1981. Slaters was a caterer too and went early into artificial ice. I have spoken to a number of ice roundsmen, then in their eighties, who delivered ice for the company all their working lives. Mr Dadomo could remember being personally searched by Rosa to see that he had not short-changed the company! Mr Rimoldi remembered a photograph, now lost, of Carlo and a younger Rosa selling ice from a cart in the street. This must have been a very early photograph, but its memory remains clear.

The old men remember the huge ice wells holding 2,000–3,000 tons of ice at a time, the company buildings, with carts garaged on the ground floors beside the offices, and stables overhead where the horses went up to regular grooms who cared for them. There were huge bins full of corn and beans, straw and hay, and wheelwright shops to service the vans. There were 73 rounds in London and it is Gatti's yellow and black carts which elderly people in London still remember.

In his funeral oration[36] in Bellinzona in 1878, it is suggested that it was Carlo who had the idea to import ice from Norway. This, of course, is completely untrue. The first shipment of ice from Norway was in 1822 by William Leftwich's father and Wenham Lake ice from America was introduced in the 1840s. What was original about Carlo was that, so early on, he foresaw the big possibilities of ice in the catering trade, particularly in the mass production of ice cream. From 1857 his fortunes took a sharp rise and his ice business became the cornerstone of his increasing wealth.

Figure 13 Delivering ice in London. The yellow and black carts were a familiar sight, right up to the 1950s.

12 The Norwegian ice industry

The Norwegian ice industry is a lost industry. It lasted for nearly a hundred years from the 1820s to the 1920s with Britain as its main customer and London as the principal port of entry. The first import of Norwegian ice was in 1822. Imports accelerated from the 1850s onwards and by the 1890s stood at 340,000 tons of natural ice a year. The success of the industry corresponds exactly to Carlo Gatti's expanding Ice Company. From the 1890s the trade declined as artificial ice came onto the market and ice merchants gradually turned over to that product.

It is interesting that the old icemen whom I interviewed always swore by natural ice. They praised its purity and the fact that nothing put on natural ice ever lost its flavour. Artificial ice made from the British water supply in the 1890s was less attractive and on its introduction great controversy raged on the respective virtues!

Norwegian ice export 1860–1915[37]

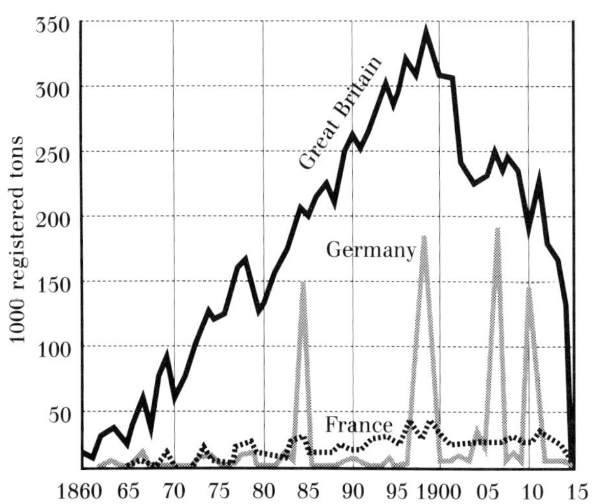

In the 1850s, when Carlo began importing, natural ice was cut in the spring from natural lakes and loaded directly onto the ships for the spring sailings, but as demand grew, dams were built and land flooded to increase the acreage. Ice proved an excellent crop. In hard winters, once the lake was cleared, a new crop would quickly form.

16

18

From then on ice was cut and stored in ice houses – wooden houses with double walls, filled with sawdust for insulation. This meant that ice could be exported all through the summer months and right into the autumn.

Many people are amazed to hear that ice can be

17

Figures 16, 17 First the ice, which by now was 1–2 feet thick, had to be cleaned, cleared of all leaves, twigs, grasses and snow. The ice ploughs, drawn by horses, traversed a section of the lake, cutting the ice in long strips about two feet wide.

19

Figures 18, 19 A gang of men with huge hand saws cut these strips into two-foot squares. It was a skilful job cutting the ice, so to speak, from under their feet, and hooking each block out of the water with a giant pair of tongs, or 'dogs'.

kept in this way for months on end. There is, of course, wastage – about a quarter of the whole – but ice in a mass and in insulated sheds or in the ship's hold melts very slowly. Cargoes of ice made the journey to India and were still viable. Initially ice was cut by local farmers on their own property but then larger ice producers leased land and lakes, cut the ice and shipped it direct to overseas markets. Johan Dahll of Kragero, Carlo's supplier, was one of these.

As the markets increased, so the technology improved. One does not know if ice ploughs were in operation when Carlo first began importing, but cer-

20

21

22

tainly they arrived soon afterwards. The routine is described in Figures 16–24.

Most of the workmen in ice production were sailors. Norwegian sailing ships transporting ice went home in the autumn. Their crews were signed off and the ships lay idle, locked into the ice of the fjord from October to March.

The sailors usually found casual work either in the timber trade or in ice and would spend the winter cutting, loading or storing until the ice began to melt in the fjord. Then they would sign on as crew again for the spring sailings.[38]

The crew of an ice ship had a particularly tough time. It was cold and wet – the only heat was the galley fire – and it was very hard work, for there was great competition between the various ships to make the fastest possible journey. Six to seven days was record time across the North Sea and sometimes the battle raged on a turn round and return journey. But it brought prestige and honour to the crews which made it all worth it. It also created rival sets of fans who laid wagers on their favourite ship and would come to blows in the local pubs.

23

Figures 20, 21, 22 The steep sides of the fjord made delivery to the ship difficult so a series of wooden slides or shoots was constructed, allowing the blocks of ice to slide down the hillside to the jetty, where they were loaded on to the ship or stored in ice houses alongside.

Figures 23, 24 Dahll's sailing ships came up the Thames and docked at Regent's Canal Dock, Limehouse. There the ice was unloaded and accounted for by a sworn weighmaster, seen here in a bowler hat. Then the ice was loaded on to barge or cart and carried up to one of Gatti's ice wells where it was stored block upon block, layer upon layer, ready for delivery to customers.

13 Of ships and men

Hearsay has it that Carlo Gatti had a fleet of sailing ships bringing ice from Norway to London. Numbers vary from 28 to 50 ships.

Goethe Goethesen, my Norwegian colleague, thinks such stories highly unlikely.[39] Anyone owning a fleet of ships would require a regular two-way trade and there is no suggestion that Carlo traded in any other commodity. Ships in ballast are not a long-term economic proposition. What is most likely is that a regular number of ships, owned or commissioned by Johan Dahll of Kragero, brought ice into Regent's Canal Dock each spring and summer, and these in the eyes of the family and workforce became Gatti's ships. Lloyd's Register only provides a list of manager owners from 1875, but at that date, Gatti's name does not appear. The only other possibility is that he had shares in the ships, or that he himself chartered them.

If Carlo imported ice from Norway, he also imported men from the Blenio, first from his own village and then further afield. It is difficult to estimate exact numbers during his lifetime. It is said that he brought over between 1,000 and 2,000 Bleniesi but I suspect this is something of an overestimate, or it refers to both 19th and early 20th century emigration.

The Unione Ticinese, a mutual aid society founded in 1874, had 101 founder members, described as a group of emigrants 'already resident and well established in the great metropolis'. Most of these men were employed or stemmed from the Gatti enterprises. They were obviously senior members of the workforce and included the Gattis themselves (see Appendix III).

If one reckons each member had at least part of his family with him – four or five persons – together with many younger single men in humbler positions, the total lies well within 1,000. If, however, one takes a longer term look at the developing business under Carlo's daughter in the 1880s and 1890s, the figures rise substantially.

In those years Bleniesi spread out to other areas, and within 50 years every major south coast town had a Ticinese establishment. Italians, too, were brought over by the Corazzas from around Piacenza and Salsomaggiore, so that by the turn of the century, the figure of 2,000 is more realistic. This corresponds to the overall numbers of Italians in London. In 1861 and 1871 the figures are 2,041 and 2,553. Big increases come from 1891 to 1911, where numbers rise from 5,000 to 11,000.[40]

In the early years, 1851–71, the census returns on Gatti's properties record men from Dongio, Torre, Aquila, Malvaglia, Corzoneso, Olivone, Semione, Marrogia and Stattino. Exactly how they were recruited is not certain, but it was probably entirely by word of mouth.

This recruitment coincided with a Ticinese Government scheme to increase emigration from certain valleys as a result of the further poverty incurred by the Austrian blockade. This blockade was imposed as a punishment on the Ticinesi for their support of the Italian Liberation movement and the harbouring of revolutionaries. A scheme of emigration to Australia was mounted and navigation companies advertised chartered voyages, sailing from Hamburg, Southampton and Liverpool.

Giorgio Cheda in his book *L'Emigrazione Ticinese in Australia* includes many letters from emigrants in transit who passed through London and received help and advice from Carlo, who, on occasion, took groups of men to his home, where they were treated very kindly, or, more often, negotiated better terms and conditions on the ships on which they were to travel. He is recorded at Liverpool getting the fare to Australia reduced to £20. Many navigation companies accepted money in the Ticino for second class accommodation which proved on embarkation to be steerage only![41]

It may be that Carlo acted as an agent for the Government, receiving some sort of commission. There were established couriers in the Ticino and in Paris to speed the emigrants on their way. All these emigrants to Australia came from the Maggia Valley. Whether the Bleniesi en route for London made use of this system is hard to tell. In the very early days some would have walked all the way – one must remember Carlo himself walked to Paris. They would set off in a small group from their valley, taking the Lucomagno or the Gotthard Pass. Once they had traversed those formidable mountain paths, they worked as they went, paying their way by cutting hay, harvesting, picking fruit, sleeping under haystacks or in outbuildings, singing, playing the *zambogna* or hurdy-gurdy. It would have taken them five or six weeks or more.

If there was money available they would take a train all or part of the way. Letters from Australian emigrants record they would start by walking to the nearest stop of the diligence and take the carriage through the Gotthard Pass – one, travelling in January, went by sledge – then on by steamer across Lake Lucerne, again by diligence to Basle, where they would get on the train, a hard wooden seat in an open carriage, open to wind and rain. In Paris they would find help and advice from compatriots who would set them on their way to the Channel ports.

In spite of the hardships of the journey, these letters show a sense of excitement and a deep sensitivity to all the new sights and sounds and experiences beyond their valley. One was overwhelmed by the High Alps, another, although he was very sick, was exhilarated by a storm on the Channel crossing, yet another was touched and amazed at the help and advice he received from Ticinesi throughout his journey.

Thus one can suppose that the Bleniesi coming to London would have received equal help on their way and would have been met on arrival and given lodgings over the shop or premises where they were to work – in communal dormitories, probably in the attics. At the ice well at New Wharf Road there were lodgings with a housekeeper and, later, two lodging houses in Albion Street.[42]

Most of them came as single young men, boys of 15 or 16, and they were expected to turn their hand to anything. Older men with special skills, such as confectioners or chocolate-makers, would have an assured place, but the rest would start in the kitchen or as a waiter and rise perhaps to run their own kiosk or café under Carlo's patronage. Or in winter they might cut ice and in the summer unload the ice ships, fill and stock the ice wells or sell ice on the streets. Or they might work as shopmen, bricklayers, carpenters or billiard markers. Presumably they gradually settled into a job which suited both employer and employee. Mr Rimoldi's father started as a commis waiter at Gatti's in Villiers Street, then became a weighmaster at Regent's Canal Dock, weighing ice cargoes, and eventually became the manager of Sutton Street Depot.

Although they came into an alien environment, one thing they could be sure of – they would live in a Bleniese ambience, speak their own patois, eat their traditional food. It was some compensation against homesickness and the loss of a rural life.

Much has been said about the Gattis as exploiters of men. Knowing the background to employment in Britain in the 19th century, I find this hard to support. Life for the ordinary working person in Britain was very hard indeed. Hours were often 12 hours or more a day. Living and working conditions were poor and cramped, food often inadequate, holidays, other than days off, unheard of and little concern or allowance made for an employee's personal problems. There were, of course, good employers and bad employers, but all exacted the utmost from their employees at very low wages. Carlo was, I believe, no different.

There is little evidence for the level of pay employees received in the restaurants, cafés and music-halls. Confectioners, cooks, senior staff would have received fixed wages, but waiters, although hired by the Gattis, would have been assigned a number of tables and lived entirely on tips. This was established practice in the 1890s.[43]

There is evidence, however, of payment to the icemen. Right up to the Second World War, the icemen were paid a basic £3 a week or £3 10s if they worked on Sunday. An iceman's cart carried two tons of ice. That was a load and the iceman might sell two or even three loads a day at the height of the season. Mr Rimoldi describes it this way:

> You went out with two tons of ice. If you were a good roundsman and looked after your customers, treat them well, give them the service, carry the ice in, take it upstairs, downstairs . . . all the butchers had boxes, clean his box out, put fresh ice in . . . You did all this service and then you charged him your price and he paid you. But when you got home at night, if you'd sold two tons of ice the Gov'nor wants you to account for two tons ice . . . Anything you made over and above that was yours. You only got a wage of £3 a week so it was up to you . . . You're not going to work from 3 o'clock in the morning until 10 o'clock at night for £3 a week.
>
> You were like your own Gov'nor. Although you didn't have to buy your horse or the van – that was given to you free – you go out get the trade, look after it and providing

you brought back what you took out, the money over and above was yours. You had to be strong, to want to work and put up with all the hardship. We used to work six days a week night and day and we earnt our money . . .

And there was real hardship involved – out on an open cart in all weather, or arriving back at the wells for your second load in sweltering heat only to be frozen in the wells as you prepared your ice, your shirt sticking rigid on your back. Many a time, the iceman slept by his horse to rise again at 3 or 4 in the morning.

This system of work certainly dates back to the 1890s so I have no reason to believe that it would not have held good in Carlo's time. It may be that rather the same system was applied to the men who ran the cafés and kiosks for Carlo. He provided or rented the premises, lent money for equipment and every Monday morning came round in his dog cart to collect the takings. Perhaps he exacted a standard charge and the men kept any money they made over and above that. Whatever the method, we know that these men, once they became independent, were proud to show in their windows that they had worked for Gatti.

14 Mid-career

Carlo Gatti gained naturalisation as a British citizen on 22 May 1858 at the age of 41.[44] He was a married man with a wife, Maria, and four daughters, Rosa, Clara, Katerina (Nina) and Agostina. The census records Rosa was born in the Ticino, Clara and Nina in Holborn. I have no record of Agostina but Mary Wynne Williams, Carlo's great grand-daughter, says she was born in London. None of Carlo's daughters was registered at birth.[45]

Mrs Wynne Williams says that Carlo set great store on his British citizenship and urged his daughters to bear their children in England. Accordingly Agostina, who had five children, always came to England in the last weeks of her pregnancies! I believe many of his diverse family in Switzerland and Italy still hold dual nationality and British passports.

Britain in 1858 was recognised as a great power and to be associated with the country and its great commercial expansion must have proved both an attraction and a business asset. But it is hard to imagine Carlo becoming anglicized. At one time he called himself Chas. Gatty, at another Charles Gatti, but ultimately he seems to have returned to his own name and that is the name his Ice Company held until its demise a few years ago in 1981. He never lost touch with the Blenio and seems to have visited regularly until he retired there.

In the Blenio, Carlo was known as 'Milord'. It was the recognition of an emigrant's success in London – 'the capital of the lords and the fabulous pound sterling.' One feels his huge impressive figure, his energy and his geniality merited some title but it is important to understand that in the highly stratified society of England of that time, Carlo, even at the height of his fortunes, would have been recognised only as a successful businessman. It is unlikely that he ever mingled among 'the lords' or even the professional classes except on a business footing. In England in the 19th century men in 'trade', however ingenious and successful, had their proper place.

It was his nephews, Agostino and Stefano, who in the 1880s and 1890s made a breakthrough into Society, particularly in the theatre and the arts, and his great nephew, John, was indeed knighted Sir John Gatti, Lord Mayor of Westminster.

In 1858, Milord was at a turning point in the family fortunes. His Norwegian ice business was accelerating, he and his brothers had a wide range of shops and cafés, a chocolate manufacturing business and a Steam Works, and the destruction of Hungerford Market was imminent with the possibility of substantial compensation. What was to be the next move? I suspect pressure from his more sophisticated brothers to go upmarket was a consideration. Certainly the 1860s were to see another sharp rise in their reputations and prosperity.

15 Branching out

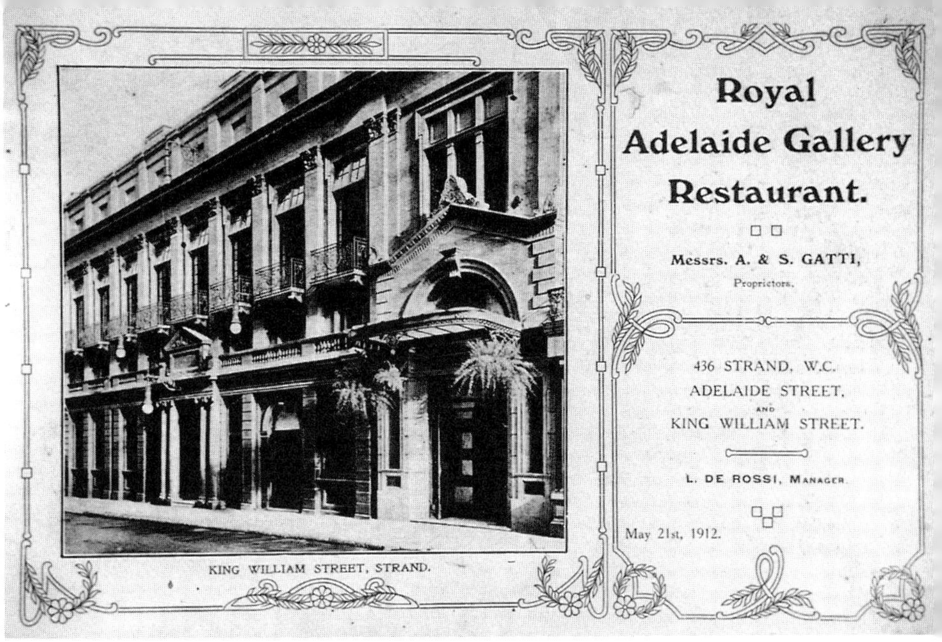

Figure 25 The Royal Adelaide Gallery Restaurant entrance in King William Street

As Hungerford Market was slowly demolished, the Gattis lost no time in setting up new businesses. In 1862, Carlo and Giovanni opened a café-restaurant in Westminster Bridge Road across the river in Lambeth, with a view to developing it as a music-hall. Some years later Gatti's Palace of Varieties was launched.

On May 24th 1862 Agostino Gatti and Giacomo Monico, describing themselves as ice manufacturers and confectioners, opened the Royal Adelaide Gallery, Adelaide Street, as Refreshment Rooms. The Royal Adelaide Gallery was part of a triangular complex facing on to the Strand, bounded by Adelaide Street on one side and King William Street on the other. It was part of Nash's West End Improvements and was finished in 1831. This elegant building with its peppercorn turrets included the glass-domed Lowther Arcade, famous for its toy shops.

The Adelaide Gallery of Practical Science was opened in 1832 for 'the exhibition of models, inventions, works of art and specimens of novel manufacture' but by the 1860s had fallen upon hard times and when the Gattis took over, it had lain empty for some years.[46] Nevertheless, it provided beautiful rooms and a striking ambience.

It must have been a big step forward for Agostino Gatti and Giacomo Monico, both 22, and Stefano Gatti at 18. Funding must have come from their fathers, Giovanni Gatti and Giuseppe Monico, and from Carlo. No doubt there was plenty of help from the older generation, but these three young men were to become famous restaurateurs in their own right, the Gattis at the Strand and the Monicos at the Café Monico in Piccadilly.

From the first Agostino and Stefano 'worked literally hand in hand and advanced in prosperity by leaps and bounds. From morn to night they might be seen at the receipt of custom, directing waiters and supervising everything. Holidays were unknown to them and their only distraction was business.'[47] It was all part of the Gatti supervision and attention to detail. And if they needed any advice, they had only to cross the road to Carlo's new house and confectioner's shop at 52 Strand which he bought in September 1864.[48]

Unlike many modern Italian restaurants today which serve their own country's specialities almost exclusively, the Gattis offered a primarily English menu – Roast Beef and Yorkshire Pudding, Boiled Fowl and Rice and a wide range of chops of every kind. Some fish and entrée dishes are couched in French, but there is no sign of different pastas or any well-known Italian dish. Macaroni Italienne or Macaroni au Gratin, at 9d and 1s respectively, are listed under Cheese and Sundries in 1905.[49] There was, however, continental music in the evenings, both before and after the theatre and on Sundays.

The Royal Adelaide Gallery formed the nucleus of the business, but as trade expanded, more rooms were taken over for formal and private occasions, the kitchens were enlarged and new entrances were opened in the Strand and King William Street. This famous restaurant ran long after the deaths of Agostino in 1897 and Stefano in 1906 and finally

Figure 26 The Royal Adelaide Gallery

closed in 1939. It is remembered by many elderly people in London, particularly theatre-goers.

But back in 1862 one can imagine the excitement of setting up the new Refreshment Rooms in such elegant surroundings. Great changes were coming to the Strand. The new railway crossing the river brought in a larger and more sophisticated clientele. A great new hotel, the Charing Cross Hotel, was rising out of the ruins of Hungerford Market. On April 11th 1864, thousands gathered in the Strand and Trafalgar Square to greet Garibaldi, the Italian patriot, and welcome him to London. Business must have been brisk that day!

In the 1870s not only did the Gattis run their restaurant, they organised prom concerts and pantomimes at Covent Garden, and in the 1880s they installed a generator in the basement of the Adelaide Gallery to provide the restaurant with electric light. In 1885 they had mains laid in the Strand to light the Adelphi Theatre which they had acquired. As it was forbidden to lay the mains in daylight hours, they laid them at night and on Sunday, thus circumventing the regulations. When the noise of the more powerful generator disturbed theatre-goers in the nearby Vaudeville Theatre, they solved the matter by buying the theatre.[50]

In fact their acquisition of theatres and the extension of their electricity system went hand in hand and by 1889 the Charing Cross and Strand Electric Supply Company was formed. This Company, under Agostino's son, Sir John Gatti, ultimately served a wide area from Buckingham Palace into the City and after some amalgamations was nationalised in 1948.

What early photographs survive of the Gattis'

restaurant are always those of the formal rooms, or the Gallery itself, set for some great occasion, but it was the café on the ground floor which played an equally important part in the life of the establishment. This account from the 1880s gives a vivid picture of the daily routine.

It is close upon five o'clock when we turn out of Adelaide Street, Charing Cross, into the Grand Café of Messrs A and S Gatti. The light is bright full and clear, and the large room looks gay and comfortable with its four long rows of small iron-legged marble topped tables . . . The place is thinly peopled yet. Here and there a table has one guest, but many tables are laying fallow, each with its box of Swedish matches that light only on the box. Here and there is a newspaper. Beside us is half the Standard for this day; it has already absorbed quite as much grease as is good for it . . . About nine-tenths of the men now eating are past the middle age . . . Most people are drinking tea and reading papers . . . In the remoter corner on our left they are playing chess . . . 'Bread, butter, chop, potatoes, and half of bitter.' . . . 'How much?' . . . 'One and two.' The capacities of the ordinary domestic saucer never struck us before. At Gatti's they do everything with saucers. Your bread comes in a saucer, your half-pint pewter comes on a saucer. If you have an ice, its glass rests in the centre of a saucer. Gatti's seem to look on plates as sacred, to be used only on occasions of great solemnity and importance . . . while we were at Gatti's the only thing we saw honoured by being set on a plate was our own chop . . . It is now past six o'clock. Age no longer predominates at Gatti's. There is youth now, and manhood and female loveliness . . . We look around cautiously and find no woman but one beyond middle age. Most are young, the majority under five and twenty. Many are pretty and prettily dressed. Each is in company with some young man. Between them is a teapot, bread and butter, the smiles of sweethearts, and the manners of a festival. The sixpenny tea alone does not make the festival. It is the situation which lends to the charm. The men have brought the girls to show them a little blameless 'life' and the girls are smiling and nodding in undefined gratitude, unformulated pleasure. For them Gatti's has a foreign flavour. There are the French rolls, the Italian waiters and the cosmopolitan crowd. To see men smoking and drinking coffee and wearing their hats and to be able to talk to a sweetheart and drink tea all at the one time is the nearest thing in the world to being on honeymoon in Paris.

It is now eight o'clock, and the clatter is prodigious. Hear the wild tumult of the saucers . . . Down the room, eight deep, what a heterogeneous gathering of people! Men from every country in Europe. Here are Germans, French, Russian, Greeks, Italians. Men who for pleasure, or for fear, or for profit have fled their native lands. Here are French Communists, and German Socialists and Spanish Intransigentes, and Russian Nihilists, and Italian Carbonari, smoking, chatting, drinking tea or coffee, playing chess or dominoes, side by side . . . None but the men gravitate towards the bottom of the right-hand half of the room. The majority here are British subjects . . . This 'chess corner' is a kind of little club where you may see almost the same faces every night.

Up those steps you walk and sit in that gallery and have your tea, while spread at your feet lies the great room and behind the gallery is a kind of sanctum sanctorum, where you can take your sweetheart and treat her to all the delicacies of the place, and where 'no pipes are allowed'. Down the staircase is the billiard room, containing about sixteen tables. You descend if you like; but we are off.[51]

Figure 27 Chefs at work in the kitchen

Figure 28 Cartoon of a Prom Concert from the *Penny Illustrated*, September 1878. Arthur Sullivan, of Gilbert and Sullivan fame, was the conductor, A. & S. Gatti were the promoters.[52]

16 The music-halls

After the destruction of Hungerford Market, the partnership between the Gattis and Guiseppe Monico seems to have been dissolved, Guiseppe going off to set up his own restaurant in the City and the Gattis crossing the river to Lambeth to embark on furthering their career in music-halls. Both Carlo and Giovanni were familiar with the French tradition of the 'Café Concert', where in a large café, refreshments were served and musical entertainment was provided by an orchestra with a number of singers or artistes.

The English music-hall grew out of the rather more robust tradition of the song clubs or saloons within taverns or inns where a Chairman – a popular local – presided over the proceedings, introducing various acts, rebuking interruptions from the floor, and encouraging the customers to drink up.

The Gattis clearly combined these two traditions over the years and their music-halls were formally recognised. Figure 29 – a programme cover of the 1890s – shows Gatti's Palace of Varieties, with the restaurant which was first established in 1862 on the left of the hall.

The Palace was at 212–4 in the newly renamed Westminster Bridge Road and stood almost opposite the shop where Agostino and Gaspero Gatti were Artificial Florists and Plumasiers in the 1850s. In fact Carlo must have been familiar with the Lambeth area and recognised it as the early heart of the amusement world. Vauxhall Gardens, Apollo Gardens and Astley's were all there in the 18th century, and in 1852 the father of the true music-hall, Charles Morton, set up the Canterbury in Lower Marsh, Lambeth and made the transition from tavern to Hall in a more theatrical manner. In 1854, he set up a larger hall to accommodate 1,500 people. It was expensively decorated, with large marble reliefs, a balcony which ran three sides of the building, large supper rooms and a picture gallery. It became known as the Royal Academy over the Water.

Gatti's Palace of Varieties – sometimes known as Gatti's over the Water – was certainly not as big as the Canterbury but the Gattis must have been willing to compete with it and with Astley's further down Westminster Bridge Road which mounted spectacular shows. Essentially the music-hall offered respectable entertainment to a working class and lower middle class audience. Later on the middle class were drawn in.

The programme cover stresses Gatti's Music Hall as a Family Resort in the continental tradition and a special notice on the programme states. 'All possible care is exercised to ensure perfect propriety in the Entertainment. The Manager will, however, be obliged to members of the audience who will report to him anything in the slightest degree objectionable.' This respectability was common to most music-halls. The artists were 'robust yet subtle, not vulgar or overemphasised'.[53]

It is difficult to know which of the Gattis played the most significant part in setting up the music-halls. Giovanni is supposed to have been the most talented and cultivated of the family and also something of an impresario, so it may have been he who set the standard for the hall, just as he may have influenced his sons in the setting up of the Adelaide Gallery Café-Restaurant and the Prom concerts they ran in Covent Garden. He may too have been responsible for bringing over continental artistes. Unfortunately I have no evidence to substantiate this. It is based on hearsay, but it seems likely.

Although the programme cover says the hall was established in 1864, the Gattis did not get a licence for music until 1865. Obtaining a licence for music from the Middlesex Justices could take several years or might be blocked in some areas entirely. Some Justices had friends who were in the brewing trade or were publicans who feared loss of custom.

But once the licence was obtained an advertisement appeared in the weekly *Era* as follows: 'The above elegant Hall is open every evening supported by the following unparalleled array of talent. The Great Lingard, Albert Steele, Charles Woodman (the celebrated Double Voice vocalist), Dashing Dunbar, Fred Wallingford, Smith and Williamson (Negro Delineators) Parelli and Costello (outstanding gymnasts) Miss Etty Gray . . .'[54]

From the start Gatti's over the Water seems to have been a success. By 1866 George Leybourne, the famous Lion-comique of Champagne Charlie fame,

Figure 29 Programme cover for Gatti's Palace of Varieties, known as Gatti's over the Water

had appeared there. In January 1868 the *Era* reports the Hall crowded, with improvised seating or standing only and on April 26th gives it this accolade:

Notwithstanding the extraordinary attractions which are being held at a neighbouring similar establishment, the patronage enjoyed by this place is, if possible, greater than ever. Here as there, success has been deserved and secured by liberal and judicious management. Messrs Carlo and Joseph Gatti have quite lately had their Hall richly decorated at considerable cost and the place now looks very bright and pretty. The status of the artistes who constitute the present Company also shows the Proprietors are not sparing in their regular working expenses . . .

It is clear that Joseph (Giuseppe) put money into the

Figure 30 Programme cover for Gatti's in the Arches, Villiers Street

Hall, and by 1871 Rosa, Carlo's daughter, was named as a Proprietor and was living there with her two children.[55] But by then the success of Gatti's over the Water had led to another new venture.

In 1867 Carlo, describing himself as a licensed victualler and giving his address as Wharf Road, Islington (this was the site of his first ice well), sent a petition to the Middlesex Justices. The petition stated that he had taken a lease on premises in Villiers Street, being two of the Arches under the South Eastern Railway, numbered 174 and 175, which consisted of two large rooms, one being used as a billiard room 250 feet long containing seventeen large billiard tables and the other being a coffee room 150 feet long . . . A large sum of money had been spent on decorations. He had been 'for a period of seven years the proprietor of extensive Coffee and Ice Rooms in Hungerford Market, where your petitioner held a licence for Music without any complaint ever being made against him'. His petition was accompanied by a testimonial of 39 inhabitants residing in the immediate neighbourhood – no doubt Carlo got some of his old regulars in the Market to support him.[56] The Justices of the Strand Division described the granting of such a licence 'not only unnecessary but highly objectionable,' but in spite of this, it was granted at the following Quarter Sessions, and Carlo returned to a familiar area where he was well known. I believe that the Arches are in fact the original arches of the Market onto which Charing Cross station was built, just as the original piers of Brunel's suspension bridge are still part of Hungerford Bridge to this day.

The programme cover in Figure 30, dated 1897, shows what was known as Gatti's in the Arches in its heyday. The buildings facing onto Villiers Street lay immediately below the station, whose canopy is visible. One imagines that this complex was developed over the years and the music-hall – which is today the Players Theatre – grew up together with Carlo's Grand Café-Restaurant de la Confédération Suisse and the Largest Billiard Saloon in the World with its thirty full-sized tables. Today only the Players Theatre remains, the whole complex having been rebuilt as Embankment Place, although the family house Carlo bought in Villiers Street in 1873 still stands and was retained by the family until 1988.

But in 1872 the Postal Directory for Villiers Street records 'Carlo Gatti (founder of the late Hungerford Hall) Grandest Café in the Kingdom'. Carlo was a great self-publicist and all his music-hall programmes carried advertisements for all other Gatti establishments including Gatti's High Class chocolates 'unrivalled for their purity and excellence and sold by the best and largest confectioners in the United Kingdom'.

There seemed no limit to Carlo's confidence and prosperity. But he never lost touch with each and every development. He was the presiding genius at the Villiers Street restaurant and could be seen there almost nightly. 'This Gatti remained and was proud to remain what he was at the start.'[57]

17 Family matters

Throughout his years in London, Carlo visited his family home in Marogno – a tiny hamlet adjoining the village of Dongio. At some time he extended and built onto the original family house. It now stands a large impressive house with pretty ironwork portico and balustrades with his initials C and G interlaced. Giuseppe and Giovanni shared another bigger house nearby.

How regularly the brothers returned to the Ticino I do not know, but one suspects that there was much toing and froing of families, though the journey was long and exacting. In later years they would have been able to take a train, probably via Paris as far as Lucerne in Switzerland. From there they would go by steamer across the lake to Flüelen and then on by stage-coach, through the Gotthard or Lucomagno Passes to the Blenio Valley.

In 1867 Carlo, recognised by now in the Ticino as a 'successful son', was elected to the Grand Council in Bellinzona. He served as a Councillor for the Malvaglia District, which included Dongio, until 1875 and must have been required to attend regular meetings as his brother Giuseppe had done before him.

Meanwhile his four daughters were growing up. In 1864 Rosa, just 19, married her cousin Giuseppe Gatti and in 1868 Clara, who seems to have spent much time in Dongio as a girl, married Luigi Gianella, a doctor, and settled in Dongio.[58]

In the same year Carlo's wife Maria died. Hearsay has been unkind to Maria, describing her as a girl who herded goats on the hillsides near Castro and as an illiterate – there is a famous story of her reading a newspaper upside down. Suffice it to say she was

Figure 31 Carlo Gatti's house at Marogno

Figure 32 Giuseppe and Giovanni, who both died before Carlo, shared the house in the foreground

also known for her kindness and good works. It must have been a demanding life for a country girl and difficult to cope with the success and prosperity of her husband and his more sophisticated relations. Two years after Maria's death, Rosa's husband died tragically leaving her with two small daughters, and in the same year Nina married Giuseppe Gianella, a confectioner working for Carlo at 52 Strand. This left the youngest daughter, Agostina, aged 15, at home.

I know little of Clara and Nina but it is clear that from an early age Rosa took an interest in her father's business and supported him in many ways. She was, too, his favourite daughter.[59] As a child she rode out with him in his horse and trap to collect the weekly takings from his subsidiary cafés or to sell ice; she worked as a cashier in the café and by 1871 she was co-proprietor of the music-hall, Gatti's over the Water. She was to become a very competent, tough businesswoman and after Carlo's death ran his multifarious concerns. In fact she appears to have inherited all her father's business acumen but little of his geniality.

She and her sister, Agostina, married two brothers, James and Luigi Corazza. The Corazza family originally came from Dongio but the brothers had land around Poviglio, near Parma, in Italy. The girls probably visited there on holiday and both, after marriage, chose to settle in the area, Rosa living at the Castello Tabiano, an ancient castle which she restored, and Agostina at the Villa Agostina, which she and her husband built near Salsomaggiore.

In 1870, Carlo had embarked on another venture. He had bought himself a small farm, not far from the Edgware Road in Hendon.[60] Renters Farm, now submerged under a motorway, is recorded in the census of 1871 as 60 acres in size with a farm bailiff and two men living at the farm.[61]

What the exact reason was for this purchase remains unknown. Certainly it provided country air and a respite from London, and many years later the Corazzas sold the farm but retained a farm cottage there. The Corazza children, living in some comfort in the Castello Tabiano near Parma, used to spend holidays at the cottage under the care of an old Cockney nanny. It is said that, as a result, Rosa's son Carlo, an elegant Italian gentleman, would welcome his English visitors on arrival at the castle in strong Cockney accents! But in 1870, I can only suppose that Carlo's intention to buy a farm provided a new outlet and interest for his innovative mind. He was to develop a number of farms in the Ticino some years later.

Another new development was his marriage in Dongio in 1871 to Marietta Andreazzi. She was 23. From that time on, Carlo seems to have spent more time in Dongio and Bellinzona, where he had another house, than he did in London.[62]

He was said to be a conscientious Councillor for the Malvaglia District. He sat 'on the left', holding liberal political opinions and not surprisingly 'having lived amid the very active English populace, he could not understand a republic which did not grasp impatiently after progress'.[63]

Although he spoke only twice in the Chamber – once to complain of a draught – he pursued various projects with great energy, particularly the building of the Lucomagno Road. This road across the Alps which was to bring economic benefits to the Blenio and mitigate its isolation, had been proposed in 1820, but had never been built because of lack of funds. Carlo provided the capital at low interest. There were other gifts too. *The Times* reported his death, describing him as a generous benefactor to his canton.[64]

Perhaps his experience at Renters Farm and his increasing knowledge of agricultural matters made him more aware of the very primitive methods of agriculture in the Valley and the need to improve and develop them. Setting an example he bought two wine-growing properties in Gudo and Sementina, near to Bellinzona, and a vast expanse of land in the plains of the Moleno, an almost deserted area, which he envisaged bringing under cultivation according to experimental methods 'used in England and the big estates in Italy'.[65] He also had plans for a large cheese factory.

No doubt he supervised all this work personally, 'dressed like a peasant, wearing clogs and his trousers tied up with bands of willow'. It was a fall from a loft which set off his decline. His family in London hurried to his death bed. He died in Dongio on September 6th 1878 at the age of 61.[66]

Figure 33 Carlo's new house was built onto the original home

Figure 34 The ironwork carries Carlo's initials C and G interlaced

18 The death of Carlo Gatti

Carlo Gatti did not receive as many obituaries in the national and local papers in London as one might expect of a well-known London businessman. This is perhaps because he had already retired to the Ticino and had disappeared from the public eye. Another reason was that on September 2nd, four days before he died, there was an appalling disaster on the Thames, a collision of a saloon steamer, bearing hundreds of trippers, with a larger ship. Hundreds of people were drowned. It was a major tragedy. As a result the papers devoted almost all their pages to the sinking of the *Princess Alice*, to the list of names of the dead or injured, to eye-witness accounts, reports of the inquest and the funeral services for nearly a fortnight. Other current news seems to have been blotted out.

However, within what had become a Gatti empire, all his establishments closed as a sign of respect. A

Requiem Mass was celebrated at 10 am on September 13th at Notre Dame de France, the French Church off Leicester Square. It attracted a large congregation and the bands of both the music-halls – the Arches and Over the Water – played at the Mass. There were many professional artistes present, together with the nephews, Agostino and Stefano Gatti.[67]

His English will dated August 27th 1873 with a codicil July 17th 1877 was proved on 27th December. The executrices were his second wife, Mrs Maria Gatti, and his daughter, Mrs Rosa Corazza, the personal estate being sworn under £60,000. To these two he gave all his estate and effects:

And I direct that my said wife and daughter shall stand and be possessed of all the property so given to them as trustees with the powers and the purposes following, that is to say, they and the survivors of them their heirs executors and administrators shall have the fullest and most absolute power of selling and leasing and otherwise disposing of the same as fully and as amply as I could done if acting on my own behalf in order that ? same may be dealt with as may be by them considered most advantageous to themselves and for my youngest daughter, Agostina, according to the shares and interests following . . .

The two daughters were each to receive the capital of one third part of all the business and property, while his wife received the life interest on the other third, until her death or remarriage, in which case the capital returned in equal parts to the daughters.

The two exemptions on his personal property were the bequest of his house, 52 Strand, which he left to his daughter, Nina, with all its fixtures and fittings and, in a codicil of 1877, a bequest to Elizabeth Osbourne of £2,000 when she became 21. She was to receive the interest at 4% half yearly until that time.

Elizabeth Osbourne is described as 'an infant of the age of some seventeen years or thereabouts who has been helping me and my family in my business'. Who she was must remain a minor mystery.

Interestingly he makes it clear that each of his gifts and bequests made in favour of a woman should 'be and continue to be for her sole and separate use, independent of her husband and not subject to his debts, control or engagements'. In the case of his wife, however, she did remarry and the third share returned in equal parts to Rosa and Agostina.

He refers in the will to his Swiss and Italian securities. I have no knowledge of the Italian monies. It may be that this was some sort of investment with his new sons-in-law. The Corazzas were the first to develop the thermal baths in Salsomaggiore, and very many years later put up capital for the tram system in the town and the railway from Salsomaggiore to Parma.

The Swiss codicil to his English will reveals some personal family difficulties. It was made on August 29th 1878, eight days before he died at Dongio, at his house 'on the second floor with the south-west facing windows'.

In it he makes further provision for Nina and her husband, Giuseppe Gianella. Each is to receive an annual income of 2,500 francs. To his servant Annunciata Radesino he leaves 1,000 francs and the same to a former servant, Giuseppe Marioni.

His daughter Clara is deprived of any inheritance because 'she has already wasted large sums and has brought much displeasure to her father and treated him badly'.

He did, however, leave 30,000 francs to each of her six children with an order that Clara's husband, Luigi Gianella, 'had no right to make use of or administer' his children's legacies. It was also made clear that the children would have no right to any other form of inheritance. Clara was later to have three more children.

What had happened to cause such a major breakdown between himself and his second daughter we may never know, but it is obvious that he was determined to safeguard his hard-won wealth and protect his daughters from unscrupulous husbands and even, in this case, from Clara herself!

So while it is clear why Clara did not inherit, the mystery remains as to why Nina was treated differently from the other two sisters. Why did she not inherit a third share of the estate? The present members of the family have never heard of her although they have links with Clara's descendants. I can find no trace of her in public records though I believe she died as a young woman.

My only assumption is that she might have been adopted or was an illegitimate child. We know that Carlo had at least two illegitimate children. One was a daughter, Signora Rattazzi, whom Mary Wynne Williams remembers going to visit with her grandmother, Agostina. They were on friendly terms. The other was a son, born some months after Carlo's death, of whom there is now no trace. The family has always believed that such a son would have inherited substantially, had Carlo lived, for he had long desired another son.

It is said that Carlo died a millionaire. Some say he left £4 million. Unfortunately there seems little chance of discovering what his overall estate was worth, and it is not certain that he paid any duty on it.

In 1878, duties on 'real estate' as opposed to personal estate were chargeable either under Legacy Duty or Succession Duty. If Carlo paid either one of these, there is no longer any record of the payment available, as the documentation has been destroyed by the Inland Revenue. However, it is possible that he did not have to pay at all as the rules of Legacy Duty stated that if a man was domiciled (born) in another country and died in that country, his assets were exempt from tax. Although Carlo was a naturalised British citizen, this rule could have applied to him.

His personal estate was valued at under £60,000. In modern terms, that is about £2,046,000, but we shall probably never know what he was worth overall.

19 Last rites

In the Ticino Carlo Gatti's death was greeted with considerable public grief and was reported in some detail. It appears Carlo had expressed a wish on his death bed to be buried in the cemetery at Bellinzona. Thus, although the funeral service was held in Dongio, the principal ceremony was in Bellinzona and it is said about 2,000 people attended.

This description comes from the newspaper *Il Gottardo* of 11th September.

From the early hours of the morning an unusual animation could be perceived in the streets of the city. Confraternities of every hue, especially those of the communes in which the deceased had possessions, invaded the square in numbers never seen before. At 8 o'clock the Lugano Philarmonic Orchestra Society, summoned specially by the heirs, arrived and went to the Cervo Inn to wait for the funeral service.

At 9 o'clock precisely the clergy arrived at the church of San Rocco, transformed into a garden and mortuary chapel. A long procession formed. The town Band preceded it, followed by numerous confraternities from all the communes of the district, and those of the City, the Chapter, the priests, the Lugano Philarmonic Orchestra and the majestic funeral carriage, with its four horses, harnessed in deep mourning. The family, relatives, guests and friends of the deceased surrounded it. Then came the flag of the Blenio Democratic Society, veiled in mourning, followed by a numerous troop of associates and kinsmen from the Valley.

On the outside of the Church of San Rocco the following inscription read:

This ancient mother, centre of the friends
of the Bellinzona valleys, receives and shelters
with affectionate memory the ashes of Carlo Gatti,
a citizen of the Blenio.

The rich sarcophagus was lifted from the carriage and carried on the arms of men from the town Fire Brigade. It was placed on a magnificent catafalque, the base of which carried the inscription

He bequeathed great wealth, acqured by erudite hard work.
A name respected in his fatherland and abroad and an example to those left behind of commercial acumen and honesty.
The gratitude of the many he has helped, hovers over his honoured tomb.

The requiem Mass was performed by the Song Society, La Melodia.

The procession reformed and proceeded to the cemetery at mid day. It was already crowded. Once the bier was in place, the lawyer, Signor Stefano Gabuzzi, read the funeral oration and Signor Arcioni, in the name of the Democratic Society of Blenio, saluted the dead and the city of Bellinzona welcomed the remains inside its hospitable walls . . .

It is enough to quote only some of the long funeral oration which Signor Gabuzzi read 'in an emotional voice'.

Today we have accompanied to their ultimate resting place the mortal remains of a man who, for many reasons, deserves to be remembered and held as an example. The universal grief, the unusual pomp of the funeral ceremony, the large number of people from all over the Canton, are all proof of how highly he was esteemed. He who lives in laziness passes unobserved as does he who crosses the earth leaving only the mark of vice, but the man of action, who consumes life with working, does not leave the world without leaving a void of which his relations and fellow citizens are acutely aware. And that man of action was Carlo Gatti, a man of humble birth, who created a vast business in the English capital, acquired for himself conspicuous wealth, and while acquiring riches, knew how to keep the frank and simple habits of a man of our valley, together with that tireless industry which is the miraculous key which opens the door of success.

He then went on to outline Carlo's career, in some ways rather inaccurately, for there were many contemporary myths about Carlo Gatti. Then he continued.

It was luck, some may say, but he who thinks that fortune is a goddess who abandons herself to the first comer, is mistaken. Only the strong man, who knows how to catch her and hold her tight by the hair, will enjoy her favours . . .

But we should not only admire Carlo Gatti for being the creator of his own splendid fate; we should remember the worthy citizen whose fortune, success and fame which he enjoyed in the English capital, did not make him forget for one instant the humble village from which he traced his birth and the little republic which numbered him amongst their sons. And he gave proof of this affection for his own village when he brought many of his compatriots to London, employed them in his own business and then afterwards, if they were hard working and clever, directed them with means and advice towards their own independent positions. Many who are now rich or well-established owe their fate to Signor Carlo Gatti . . .

Figure 35 The tomb of Carlo Gatti

Then followed more details of his current works in the Ticino and then long emotional farewells in the 19th century tradition, concluding:

You are no more, but we will remember you and coming here will pray to the angel of the sepulchres for eternal rest for your bones; and to the angel of memory we will draw the attention of our children to the words of the wise man on your tomb. The most cruel death may be considered a light ill if one has the comfort of a life usefully led, and it is great only in the case of one who has achieved the glorious privilege of handing down such a lesson and such an example to his successors.

Later a monument was erected to his memory. Carlo's bust is set on a high pillar, bearing family arms and guarded by two female figures.

The funeral oration seems to sum up many of the values and attitudes of the 19th century Ticino. Carlo Gatti was *figlio dello sue opere* – a self-made man – the most sought-after 'certificate of nobility for a republican citizen'.

To the people of the Blenio, condemned often to a life of poverty and isolation, Carlo, like others before him, had made the breakthrough to wealth and prosperity. His were the virtues of hard work and sacrifice – so familiar to all – his life had been crowned with success, but he had never deserted his roots and had returned to live amongst his own people.

Many Ticinesi followed his example all over the world with varying degrees of success. Many returned to proclaim their achievements. Those who failed, rarely returned. It was not until this century, with the development of the Ticino, that its people could hope to achieve fulfilment and prosperity in their own country.

20 Who was Carlo Gatti?

Figure 36 Carlo Gatti

In the light of his huge success in London and his impact on the people of the Blenio, one might suppose the name of Carlo Gatti would still be well-known in the Ticino. In fact this is not so. There are stories, a few articles and Pino Peduzzi's book *Pionieri Ticinesi in Inghilterra* which gives a perspective on the Gatti family. No one has troubled to record his achievements in detail, those of the restaurateurs, Monico and Pagani, being stronger in public memory. But it was Carlo who came first and encouraged the others to follow.

I have no personal details of the man. No letters – he was said to be near-illiterate – no documents except his wills, one photograph showing a rather corpulent, dull-looking person and one or two stories from his great-grandchildren who never knew him. Only recently did I see a delightful family portrait. Yet in spite of this, his personality comes through strongly in all my researches. For me, he is personified in the drawing above. A man of energy and dynamism, a rough, burly, rather untidy man who got on with people. He was genial, likeable, a great gossip, a man who 'overcame all difficulties and prejudices' in spite of the British dislike and suspicion of foreigners at that time.[68] Surprisingly he became an astute businessman who caught the tide of economic expansion flowing strongly in the 1850s and 1860s in Britain.

He was something of a rebel from the first. He ran away from school, losing out on an education. He found little to attract him in the family business in Paris and spent years as a seasonal chestnut-seller, building up debts with Belgeri, the baker in Dongio, in the summer, and leaving in the autumn for Paris, to evade the worst consequences! To family eyes, he married beneath him. It seems he felt more at home in rougher, less cultivated circles.

So what was it that turned him from a ne'er-do-well in his brothers' eyes to the businessman of acumen who advised and guided them in their own first commercial enterprises in London some years later?

Was it the death of his only son and little daughter within a month of each other that induced a stronger sense of responsibility to his family? Did he finally feel a need to prove himself to those back home?

Or from his coffee stall or his first café in Holborn Hill, did he perceive that gap in the market which all true entrepreneurs seek to fill? London in the 1850s was booming. G. M. Young, the historian, wrote 'of all the decades in our history, a wise man would choose the eighteen-fifties to be young in'.

Was it the London atmosphere of confidence and expansion which finally galvanised him to action or simply that he found the English ambience more congenial?

Perhaps it was a mixture of a number of these factors, but from 1851 onwards his rise and spread of business was astonishingly swift. He was an innovator – first the small café-restaurant, which he propagated many times over, continental chocolate manufacture, then the penny ice cream which became a craze. He collaborated with his brothers in a Steam Works, brought the first water lift to London, was a pioneer in large scale grills in restaurants and introduced music into many establishments. This led to the music-halls with continental artistes.

Another major contribution was in the conservation of food. His Norwegian ice business, together with other ice importers, laid the foundations of better conditions for foodstuffs, both commercially and domestically.

All these enterprises remained under his watchful eye – a routine weekly visit to all his small cafés, a position of control from a high stool at the cash desk of his principal café. There was a willingness to take off his jacket in time of crisis, an interest in the advancement of an able man to run his own business, or to help a worker with personal problems. In this he was joined by his brother, Giuseppe, who we know made a number of small loans.[69]

This concern may have been one of the underlying reasons for the formation in 1874 of the Unione Ticinese, a benevolent society, whose first president was their nephew, Stefano Gatti. The Unione Ticinese still exists today as a rallying point for Ticinesi in Britain, a society designed to keep members in touch and support kinsmen and their families (see Appendix III).

Finally there was Carlo's interest in new experimental agricultural methods in the Ticino itself which he followed at first hand. It was this attention to detail in all his managements, which he must have taught to his nephews, Agostino and Stefano, whose fame in London finally eclipsed his own.

I have been intrigued by the fact that although Carlo's name is remembered by both the English and Italian branches of his family – a portrait and a bust adorn the Castello Tabiano – nevertheless very little is actually known about his career in London and his climb from a coffee and waffle stall to successful entrepreneur has never been understood and documented.

I suspect a certain snobbery here which might have arisen shortly after his death. His wealth set the family on a rapid upwardly-mobile path. Rosa and her husband ran the business and were to develop it substantially. Before long both Rosa and Agostina moved to Salsomaggiore, where Rosa was established in the Castello Tabiano and Agostina in the Villa Agostina close by. Most of their children married Italians, members of the aristocracy, and their lives became centred in Italy. In such a situation Carlo was, perhaps, too rough a diamond to be worthy of memory except in terms of his millions. Our modern preoccupation with 'roots', particularly the rougher ones, was not fashionable in the 1880s and 90s!

In London, Agostino and Stefano Gatti were also moving up into higher society through music and the arts, the sons going to Oxford and Cambridge. I am told that the Gattis of the Strand disassociated themselves from Gatti's, the ice merchants.[70]

It was Agostina Corazza's son, Joe, who ran the business after Rosa retired. Brought up and educated in Italy, he was probably less familiar with his grandfather's career. He settled in London and all his children, Agostino, Mary and Louis, married and live here, though they have close links with their Italian family in Salsomaggiore or Parma (see Appendix I).

One by one the Gatti enterprises closed. Gatti's in the Arches in Villiers Street was taken over just before the First World War. Gatti's in the Strand closed in 1939 and Gatti's over the Water was turned into a cinema and destroyed by a bomb in the Second World War.

The United Carlo Gatti, Stevenson and Slaters Company, however, developed and diversified highly successfully until it was bought out in 1981.

All these changes over the years explain why the founder of the family, Carlo Gatti, and his remarkable career, have been lost to view.

That Carlo was a tough businessman who struck a hard bargain and exacted long hours and toil from his employees, there is no doubt, but he was also a man of vision, 'a man with a great heart, with much natural intelligence, matured in the school of life',[71] and he deserves to be better remembered.

Notes

1 Frederico Bruni, *I cioccolateri, dall'artigianato all'industria*, Edizioni Grassi, Bellinzona 1946

2 *Kelly's Post Office London Directory*, Bridge St. Lambeth, Coppice Row Holborn. Postal Directories cannot be relied upon as an exact source of yearly dating. In 1841 Kelly took over the existing London Directories and by 1847 was employing 'selected whole time paid agents' who took the name only of those who wished to be included in the Directory. Officially the Directories were updated every year but accuracy depended upon the efficiency of the individual agents. Therefore there could be delays of a year or sometimes more from the date a shop opened to its inclusion in the Directory. As Carlo was an excellent self-publicist, however, we can assume that he would have seen to it that his shops were included as soon as possible.

3 Jacques Hillairet, *Dictionnaire Historique des Rues de Paris*, Les Editions de Minuit, 1979

4 Pino Peduzzi, *Pionieri Ticinesi in Inghilterra*, Edizioni Casagrande, Bellinzona 1985

5 Obituary of Carlo Gatti, *Penny Pictorial News*, September 21st 1878

6 Riccardo Saglini, *Il Blenio*, 1971

7 *Kelly's Post Office London Directory*, Fish Hill, Lambeth

8 Obituary of Mrs Agostino Gatti, *Daily Telegraph*, September 10th 1925

9 Home Office Papers HO 5, Certificate 1673, July 2nd 1847

10 Registra della Popolazione del Commune di Dongio, Archivo Historico, Bellinzona

11 Obituary of Carlo Gatti, *Penny Pictorial News*, September 21st 1878

12 Registra della Popolazione del Commune di Dongio, Archivo Historico, Bellinzona

13 *Kelly's Post Office London Directory*, Holborn Hill

14 Obituary of Carlo Gatti, *Penny Pictorial News*, September 21st 1878

15 Henry Mayhew, *London Labour and London Poor*, vol. 1, *Of street sellers of ice and ice creams*, 1851

16 Great Exhibition, 1851, *Official Descriptive and Illustrated Catalogue*, vol. 1

17 The Queen's Exhibition Journal. Royal Archives, Windsor Castle

18 Registra della Popolazione del Commune di Dongio, Archivo Historico, Bellinzona

19 *Kelly's Post Office London Directory*, Farringdon Road and Vine Yard Walk

20 *Kelly's Post Office London Directory*, Hungerford Market, Strand

21 Henry Mayhew, *The Morning Chronicle Survey*, vol. 6, December 5th 1850

22 Henry Mayhew, *London Labour and London Poor*, vol. 1, *Of street sellers of ice and ice creams*, 1851

23 Ralph Pomeroy, *The Ice Cream Connection*, 1975

24 *Ice cream Topics*: Summer 1969.
Remembering what used to be said about the famous cream ices in London's hotels, restaurants and the best known ice cream shops, such as Gatti's, Veglio's etc., and perusing recipe books, one finds the traditional recipe was:
1 gal cream (25% fat was usual in those days of hand-skimming), 1 gal milk, 4lbs of sugar, 80 egg yolks and 2 or 3 sticks of vanilla
Later small ice cream shops appeared in large numbers and their average recipe was:
1 gal milk, 1¾ lbs sugar, 8 eggs, 6oz cornflour and half stick vanilla

25 Gustave Doré, *London: a Pilgrimage – Humble Industries*, 1872

26 Marcus Fall (Richard Dowling), *London Town – At Gatti's* , 1880

27 Obituary of Stefano Gatti, *Caterer's and Hotel Keeper's Gazette*, November 15th 1906

28 A. Bruneton-Governator, 'La Chataigne en France', *Annales*, November/December 1984
'Marron', *La Grande Encyclopédie Larousse*, 1975

29 Pino Peduzzi, *Pionieri Ticinesi in Inghilterra*, Edizioni Casagrande, Bellinzona 1985

30 *Illustrated London News*, April 8th 1854

31 *Kelly's Post Office London Directory*, Knightsbridge

32 Rate Book, Hungerford Market, Parish of St Martin's, 1861

33 *Illustrated London News*, December 27th 1862

34 Dahll Archive, Kragero Museum, Norway

35 Obituary of Carlo Gatti, *Penny Pictorial News*, September 21st 1878

36 *Il Gottardo*, September 11th 1878

37 Official Statistics, Norway. Norwegian ice export to Great Britain 1860–1915

38 Goethe Goethesen, *Under Seil*, Grondahl 1982

39 Goethe Goethesen, *Med is og plank i Nordsjofart*, Grondahl 1986

40 Lucio Sponza, unpublished thesis, 1973

41 Giorgio Cheda, *L'Emigrazione Ticinese in Australia*, Armando Dado' Editore, 1976

42 National Census, New Wharf Road, 1871

43 Interview with Peter Jacomelli

44 'Naturalisation and Denization', Home Office Papers HO 1, Certificate 2665, May 22nd 1858

45 The National Register of Births and Deaths was established in 1837, but registration was not made compulsory until 1874
46 Rate Book, 7/8 Adelaide Street, Parish of St Martin's, 1861/2
47 Obituary of Stefano Gatti, *Caterer's and Hotel Keeper's Gazette*, November 15th 1906
48 Rate Book, Strand, Parish of St Martin's, 1864
49 Menu, March 5th 1905
50 J. W. O'Connor, *Regional Power*, vol. 4, 1961
51 Marcus Fall (Richard Dowling), *London Town – At Gatti's*, 1880
52 *The Playgoer* (Penny Illustrated Paper), September 7th 1878
53 Colin MacInnes, *Sweet Saturday Night*, 1967
54 *The Era*, November 19th 1865
55 National Census, 214 Westminster Bridge Road, 1871
56 Middlesex County Record Office, M and D 25/30, 25/47a, 16/1
57 Obituary of Mrs Agostino Gatti, *Daily Telegraph*, September 10th 1925
58 Registra della Popolazione del Commune di Dongio, Archivo Historico, Bellinzona
59 Interview with Signor Giancarlo Corazza
60 Rate Book, South Hendon, 1870
61 National Census, South Hendon, 1871
62 Archivo Historico, Bellinzona
63 *Il Gottardo*, September 11th 1878
64 *The Times*, September 24th 1878
65 *Il Gottardo*, September 9th 1878
66 'Emigration – Carlo Gatti', *Voce di Blenio*, February 1971
67 *The Era*, September 15th 1878
68 Obituary of Carlo Gatti, *The Graphic*, October 5th 1878
69 Pino Peduzzi, *Pionieri Ticinesi in Inghilterra*, Edizioni Casagrande, Bellinzona 1985
70 Interview with Mrs Stephen Gatti
71 *Il Gottardo*, September 11th 1878

Appendix I: The Gatti family

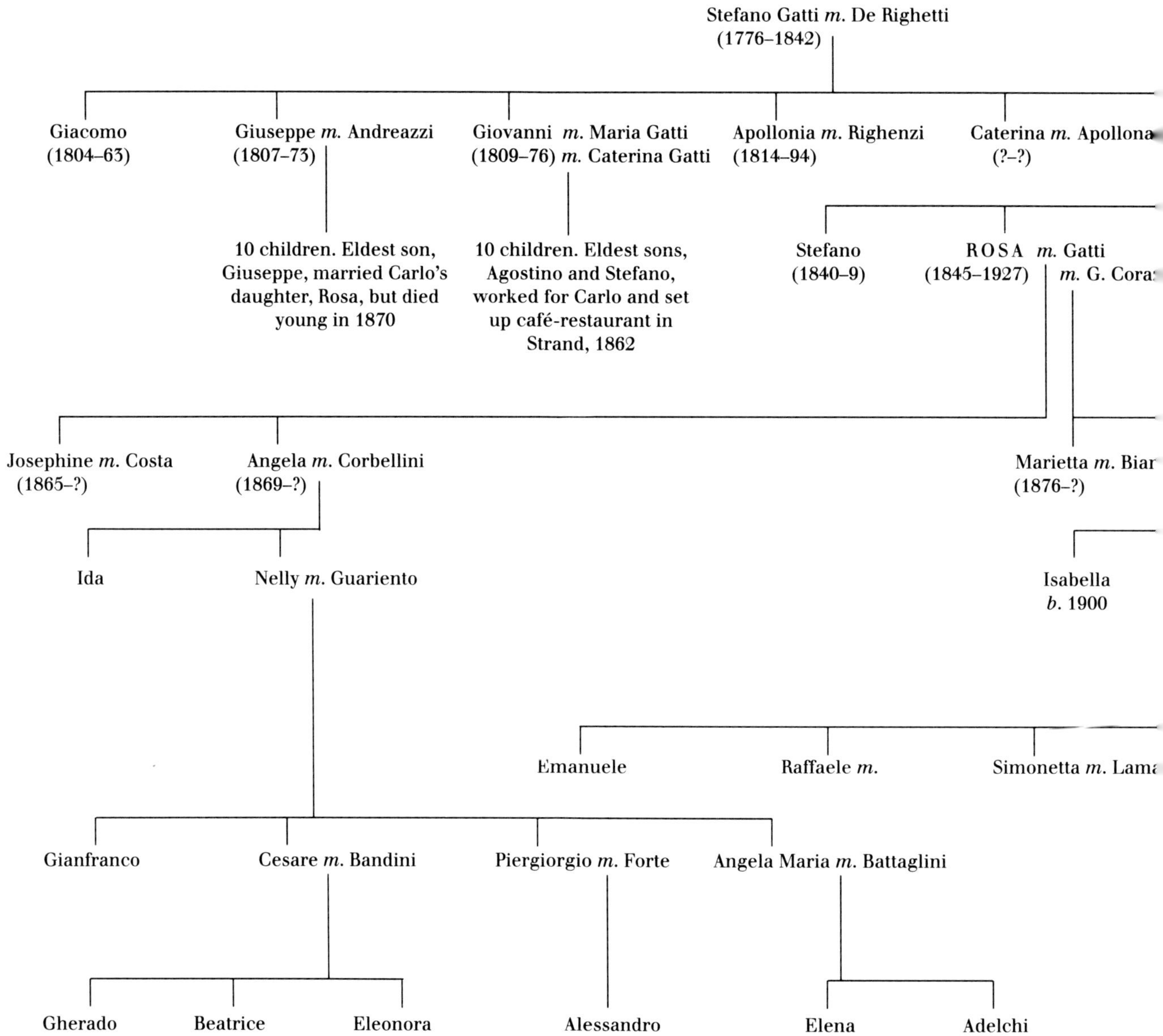

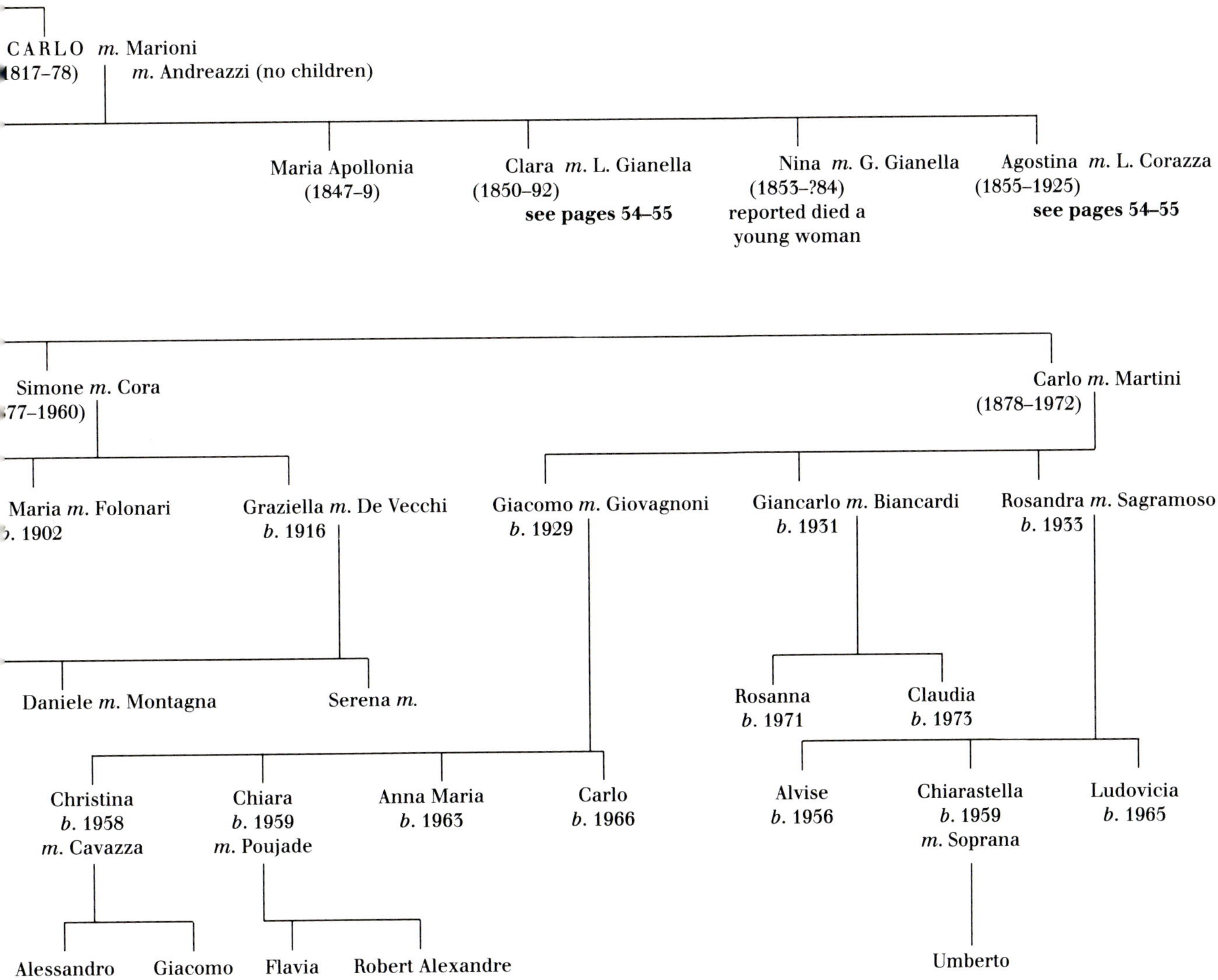
CARLO m. Marioni
(1817–78) m. Andreazzi (no children)
Maria Apollonia
(1847–9)
Clara m. L. Gianella
(1850–92)
see pages 54–55
Nina m. G. Gianella
(1853–?84)
reported died a
young woman
Agostina m. L. Corazza
(1855–1925)
see pages 54–55
Simone m. Cora
77–1960)
Carlo m. Martini
(1878–1972)
Maria m. Folonari
. 1902
Graziella m. De Vecchi
b. 1916
Giacomo m. Giovagnoni
b. 1929
Giancarlo m. Biancardi
b. 1931
Rosandra m. Sagramoso
b. 1933
Daniele m. Montagna
Serena m.
Rosanna
b. 1971
Claudia
b. 1973
Christina
b. 1958
m. Cavazza
Chiara
b. 1959
m. Poujade
Anna Maria
b. 1963
Carlo
b. 1966
Alvise
b. 1956
Chiarastella
b. 1959
m. Soprana
Ludovicia
b. 1965
Alessandro
Giacomo
Flavia
Robert Alexandre
Umberto

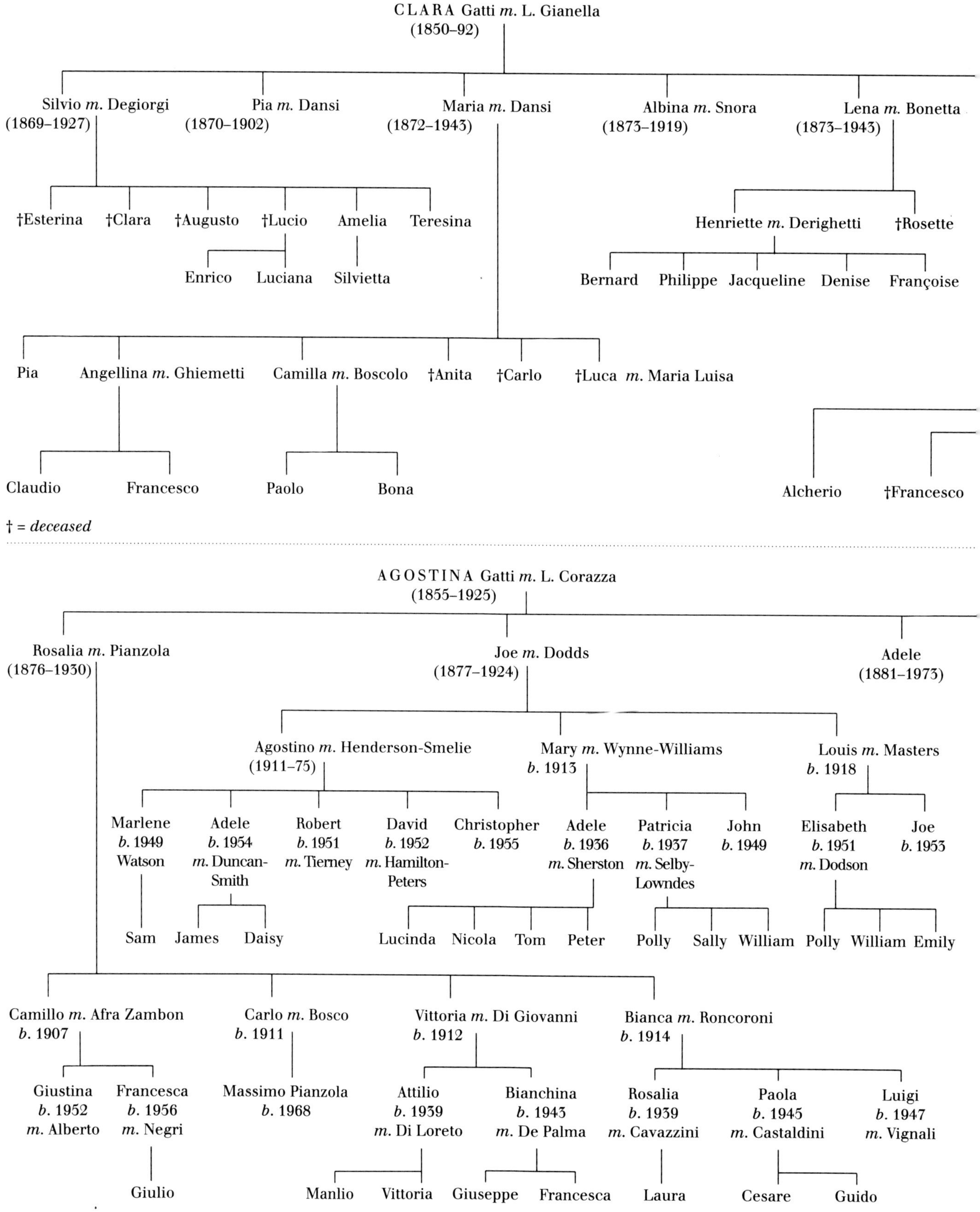
CLARA Gatti m. L. Gianella
(1850–92)
Silvio m. Degiorgi
(1869–1927)
Pia m. Dansi
(1870–1902)
Maria m. Dansi
(1872–1943)
Albina m. Snora
(1873–1919)
Lena m. Bonetta
(1873–1943)
†Esterina
†Clara
†Augusto
†Lucio
Amelia
Teresina
Enrico
Luciana
Silvietta
Henriette m. Derighetti
†Rosette
Bernard
Philippe
Jacqueline
Denise
Françoise
Pia
Angellina m. Ghiemetti
Camilla m. Boscolo
†Anita
†Carlo
†Luca m. Maria Luisa
Claudio
Francesco
Paolo
Bona
Alcherio
†Francesco
† = deceased
AGOSTINA Gatti m. L. Corazza
(1855–1925)
Rosalia m. Pianzola
(1876–1930)
Joe m. Dodds
(1877–1924)
Adele
(1881–1973)
Agostino m. Henderson-Smelie
(1911–75)
Mary m. Wynne-Williams
b. 1913
Louis m. Masters
b. 1918
Marlene
b. 1949
Watson
Adele
b. 1954
m. Duncan-Smith
Robert
b. 1951
m. Tierney
David
b. 1952
m. Hamilton-Peters
Christopher
b. 1955
Adele
b. 1936
m. Sherston
Patricia
b. 1937
m. Selby-Lowndes
John
b. 1949
Elisabeth
b. 1951
m. Dodson
Joe
b. 1953
Sam
James
Daisy
Lucinda
Nicola
Tom
Peter
Polly
Sally
William
Polly
William
Emily
Camillo m. Afra Zambon
b. 1907
Carlo m. Bosco
b. 1911
Vittoria m. Di Giovanni
b. 1912
Bianca m. Roncoroni
b. 1914
Giustina
b. 1952
m. Alberto
Francesca
b. 1956
m. Negri
Massimo Pianzola
b. 1968
Attilio
b. 1939
m. Di Loreto
Bianchina
b. 1943
m. De Palma
Rosalia
b. 1939
m. Cavazzini
Paola
b. 1945
m. Castaldini
Luigi
b. 1947
m. Vignali
Giulio
Manlio
Vittoria
Giuseppe
Francesca
Laura
Cesare
Guido

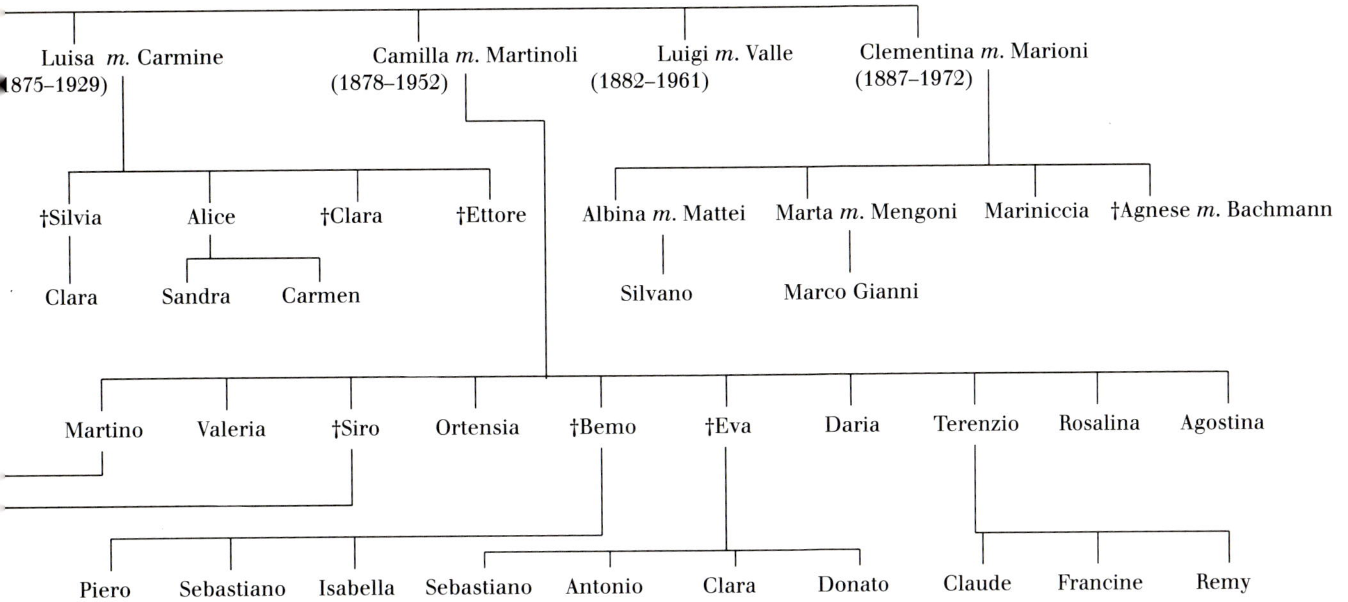
Luisa *m.* Carmine
(1875–1929)
Camilla *m.* Martinoli
(1878–1952)
Luigi *m.* Valle
(1882–1961)
Clementina *m.* Marioni
(1887–1972)
†Silvia
Alice
†Clara
†Ettore
Clara
Sandra
Carmen
Albina *m.* Mattei
Marta *m.* Mengoni
Mariniccia
†Agnese *m.* Bachmann
Silvano
Marco Gianni
Martino
Valeria
†Siro
Ortensia
†Bemo
†Eva
Daria
Terenzio
Rosalina
Agostina
Piero
Sebastiano
Isabella
Sebastiano
Antonio
Clara
Donato
Claude
Francine
Remy

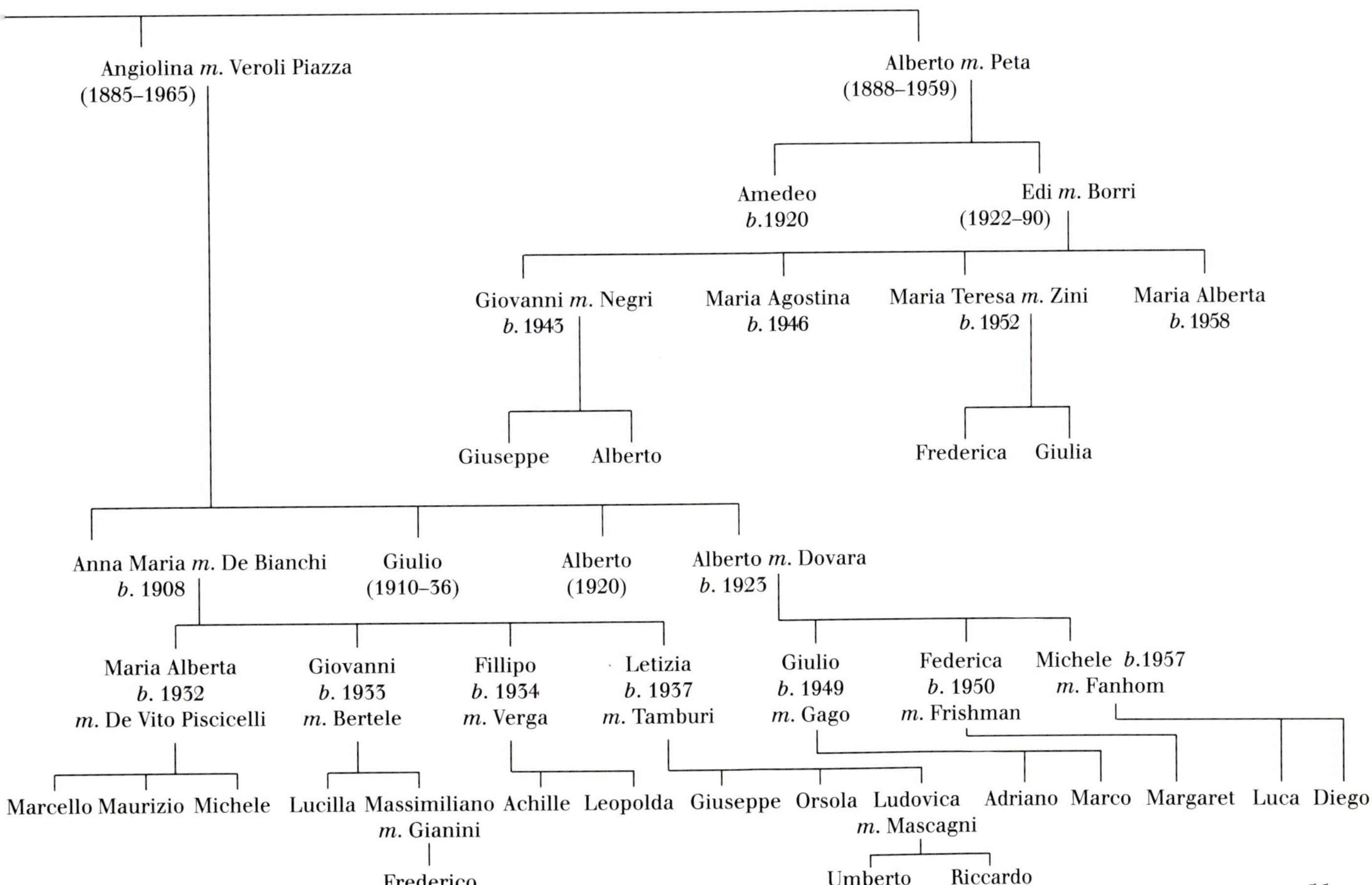
Angiolina *m.* Veroli Piazza
(1885–1965)
Alberto *m.* Peta
(1888–1959)
Amedeo
*b.*1920
Edi *m.* Borri
(1922–90)
Giovanni *m.* Negri
b. 1943
Maria Agostina
b. 1946
Maria Teresa *m.* Zini
b. 1952
Maria Alberta
b. 1958
Giuseppe
Alberto
Frederica
Giulia
Anna Maria *m.* De Bianchi
b. 1908
Giulio
(1910–36)
Alberto
(1920)
Alberto *m.* Dovara
b. 1923
Maria Alberta
b. 1932
m. De Vito Piscicelli
Giovanni
b. 1933
m. Bertele
Fillipo
b. 1934
m. Verga
Letizia
b. 1937
m. Tamburi
Giulio
b. 1949
m. Gago
Federica
b. 1950
m. Frishman
Michele *b.*1957
m. Fanhom
Marcello
Maurizio
Michele
Lucilla
Massimiliano
m. Gianini
Frederico
Achille
Leopolda
Giuseppe
Orsola
Ludovica
m. Mascagni
Umberto
Riccardo
Adriano
Marco
Margaret
Luca
Diego

Appendix II: National Census 1851–1881

The following are the lists taken from the National Census 1851–1881 which record those persons living at Gatti premises at the time of the census. The enumerators clearly had some difficulty in recording Italian names and the author has had difficulty in reading their hand-writing! Hence there may be a number of mistakes.

1851, City of London/Holborn, Parish of St Andrew

129 Holborn Hill

Charles Gatti	33	Chocolate Manufacturer	Switzerland
Mariale Gatti	35	Wife	"
Rosemarli	5	Daughter	"
Clara	10m	Daughter	Holborn Hill
Battista Bolla	31	Partner	Switzerland
Mary Sherwood	24	Shopwoman	Holborn
Charles Langrom	48	Workman	Switzerland
Barthes Borsa	20	"	"
Barthes Garrone	21	"	"
Luke Corazza	34	"	"
Aubron Dyt	21	"	"
Alexander Buchi	21	"	"
Lutine	15	"	"
Burgonino	33	"	Italy
Julian Bolla	14	Son in law?	Switzerland

1861, City of London/Holborn, Parish of St Andrew

129 Holborn Hill

This number is marked as an uninhabited building. The numbers seem to be confused and the census papers are badly torn. However we know that the shop was functioning during those years, and in 1871 the shop is listed as number 130.

1871, City of London/Holborn, Parish of St Andrew

130 Holborn Hill

Battista Bolla	48	Chocolate Manufacturer	Ticino
Louisa Bolla	26	Wife	Middlesex
Peter Bolla	45	Chocolate Manufacturer Brother	Ticino
Abbondio Carraugli	17	Assistant Brother in law	Middlesex
Giacomo Macilvani	38	Cook	Ticino
George Allen	23	Shopman	Middlesex
Mary Gilkam	47	General Servant	"

Although Carlo had shops in Hungerford Market in 1851, there was no evidence of any living accommodation.

1861, Strand area, Parish of St Martin's

12 Upper Area, West Side, Hungerford Market

Carlo Gatti	43	Ice Merchant	Switzerland (Naturalised)	
Maria Gatti	45	Wife	"	
Giaftian Gatti	5	Daughter Scholar	"	Ticino

Giovin Brugali	29	Servant	"	"
Girvia Bubi	24	Servant/Labourer	"	"
Vinexfo Valexman	23	"	"	"
Battista Balone	44	"	"	"
Domenico Angellino	31	"	"	"
Angelino Rodefino	17f	Servant	"	"
Taflati Torvian	42	Confectioner urovitte	"	"
Rosa Torvian	29	malie	"	"
Richo Torvian	34	son?	"	"
Felix Spizzi	29	Surgeon's Instrument maker	"	"

Hungerford Market, Upper Hall

Agostino Gatti	20	Head, Refreshment Room Keeper	Switzerland
Giacomo Monico	20	Assistant	"
Stefano Gatti	16	"	"
Battista Monico	16	"	"
Lucca Gatti	19	Waiter	"
Giuseppe Menagatti	24	"	"
Luigi Ferrioli	23	"	"
Panifico Buratti	24	"	Italy
Domenico Cozaa	35	Cook	Switzerland
Giuseppe Marione	39	"	"
Pasquale Fialli	19	"	"
Lorenzo Branca	20	Shopman	"
Mary Sauvage	23	Servant	London
Mary Coffier	24	"	"

Hungerford Market was destroyed in 1862.

In 1862, Agostino and Stefano moved to Adelaide Street. In 1864, Carlo bought a house at 52 Strand and at the same time the Gattis acquired 212–4 Westminster Road as restaurant and music-hall. About 1867 Carlo acquired premises in Villiers Street for a restaurant and music-hall.

1871 Strand area, Parish of St Martin's

7/8 Adelaide Street

Luigi Pagani	43m	Cook	Forre, Switzerland
Roberto Mentasti	18	Undercook	Abriola, Italy
Giacomo Tini	31	Chocolate manufacturer	Aquila, Switzerland
Giovanni Frongi	24	Billiard Marker	Malvaglia, Switzerland
Mattino Cizzio	24	"	Corzoneso, Switzerland
Vincenze Piazza	23	"	Olivone, Switzerland
Carlo Ferrari	35m	Waiter	Semione, Switzerland
P— Mentasti	19	"	Abiolo, Italy
Cristofero Fasola	22	"	Marroggia, Switzerland
Isodore Pagani	20	"	Corre, Switzerland
Paulo Andezzi	21	"	Dongio, Switzerland
Frederico Fontani	20	"	Stattino, Switzerland
Catherine Leeny	40	Servant	Ireland
Mary Sullivan	41	"	Ireland

52 Strand

Joseph Gianella	28m	Confectioner	Switzerland
Nina Gianella	18	Wife/ "	Holborn

Augustino	21	Brother/Waiter	Switzerland
Marian Cutmore	21	Barmaid	Soho
Sahia Robinson	26	General Servant	Beds
Giavannia Boldrini	27	Cook	Milan
Pistio Pregonze	20	Waiter	Italy
Pietro Brentini	21	Apprentice Pastry Cook	Switzerland
Camillo Gianella	26	Brother/Billiard Marker	"
Carlo Manoro	46m	Carpenter	

The Arches, Gatti's Music Hall and Billiard Saloon

Jean Brusali	38m	Restaurant Manager	Switzerland
Giandelli Vinienzo	28	Asst Manager/Barman	Italy
Luigi Marioni	30	Waiter	Switzerland
Pertro Pagani	23	"	"
Jean Orlandini	28	"	"
Giuseppe Taragnole	21	"	"
Jean Cuzzia	19	"	"
Faustina Kiber	18	Servant	"
Luigi Derighetti	22	Cook (Cousin)	"
Daniel Togni	25	Asst Cook	"
Antonio Maddabna	22	Servant	"
Louis Osborne	16	"	Islington
Sarah Jane Pye	15	Barmaid	Islington
Mary Ann Pye	17	"	Surrey
Esther Bond	19	Servant	Middx Westminster
Elizabeth Smith	17	Barmaid	"

1881, Strand area, Parish of St Martins

By 1881, Agostino Gatti together with his family and his brother, Stefano, were living at 10 Bedford Square.

8/9 Adelaide Street

Carlo Bruschi	22	Assistant Manager	Switzerland
Giacomo —	37	Refreshment Dept	Switzerland
Luigi Darant	25	"	"
Giuseppe Gusi	25	Waiter	Italy
Enrico Mentatti	34	"	Switzerland
Pacifico Demazia	20	"	"
Luigi Figlio	33	"	"
Gationero Jamolli	32	"	"
Davide Jamolli	24	"	"
Macnozio Togni	33	"	"
Giuseppa Bassi	23	Box Keeper	"
Luigi Biucchi	19	"	"
Luigi Brusela	19	"	"
Luigi Vogni	30	Billiard Marker	"
Pietro Peduzzi	25	Waiter	"
Giacinto Benedotte	26	Hall Porter	"
Vani Giacomo	20	Cook	"
Giulio Strazzini	27	Cook	"
Leandro Giuliani	20	Waiter	"
Giovanni Lazzaari	64	Sculleryman	"
Albino Blotta	17	"	"
Antonio Guardi	23	"	"

Angelo Tegrussa	40	Chocolate Maker	"
Gullisa Agostino	16	Barman	"
Angelo Ferrari	21	Waiter	"
Ettore Galeazzi	23	Billiard Marker	Italy
Crozzi Giovanni	40	General Servant	Italy
Eurlio Vassi	21	Sculleryman	Italy
Oncelli Carlo	32	General Servant	Italy
Gactano Vorlasco	22	Barman	Italy
Aristide Munghetti	31	Ices Maker	Italy
Carlo Massella	40	General Servant	Switzerland
Fortunato Peroni	21	Ices Maker	Italy
Carmelio Derighi	25	Cook	Switzerland
Giulo Gauitira	37	Carman	Italy
Lizzie Keen	38	Housekeeper	Westminster

1881, Strand area, Parish of St Martin's

10 Villiers St

James Corazza	37	Restaurant Keeper	Switzerland
Rosa Corazza	35	Restaurant Keeper	Switzerland
Marietta Corazza	5	Daughter	Surrey, Westminster
Simone Corazza	4	Daughter	"
Carlo Corazza	2	Son	"
Lurignoli Eugene	25f	Wardrobe Keeper	Italy
Carrie Pye	56	Nursemaid?	Surrey, Brixton Rd
Isabella de Carthur	21	Barmaid	Surrey, Stockwell
Harriet Lake	26	Barmaid	Middx, Holloway
Louise Hart	17	Barmaid	Surrey, Stockwell
Ceci Maryann	18	General Servant	Italy
Mary Burchnell	16	Undernursemaid	Surrey

20 Villiers Street

Phillip Inaltrin	20	Manager, Restaurant	Switzerland
Attillio Biffo	18	Servant	Italy
William Magnolfi	18	Waiter	Italy
Joseph Andercaff	17	Servant	Switzerland
John Ferr	19	Shopman	Italy
John Rota	44m	Shopman	Italy
Jervell Nodiroti	18	Servant	Switzerland
Raphael Ferr	20	Servant	Italy
Ferdinand Cima	19	Barman	Italy
Antony Ferrioli	22	Cook	Switzerland
Charles Plangy	22	Liftman	"
Giacomo Dionella	31	Iceman	"
Second Iccardi	48	Cook	"
Dominick Runcia	21	Assistant Cook	Italy
Henry Stickle	23	Attendant	Kent, Hythe
Masari Lawrence	26	Cook	Italy
Charles Melloni	23	Attendant	Italy
Joseph Bicheli	30	Cook	Italy
Joseph Catalini	29	Bricklayer	Italy
Antony Cecil	30	Carpenter	Italy?
Henrique Scorticate	48	Bricklayer	Italy

Joseph Cortelli	30m	Coachman	Italy
James Villa	42	Cook's Attendant	Switzerland
Charles —	40	Cook's Attendant	"
Charles Ulrich	19	Scullery Boy	"

26/27 Villiers Street

Giovanni Metali	34	Restaurant Keeper	Switzerland
Luigi Metali	21	Assistant Restaurant	"
Battista Pezzoti	21	Waiter	"
Farcisco Maletti	22	Cook	"
Jolinda Metali	24f	General Servant	"

1871, Lambeth

214 Westminster Bridge Road – previously 76 Bridge Road

Rosa Gatti	25m	Music hall Proprietor	Switzerland
Josephine Gatti	5	Daughter	Lambeth, Surrey
Angelina Gatti	1	Daughter	Lambeth, Surrey
Rudolph Vanina	21	Waiter at Music hall	Switzerland
John Vanina	24	"	"
Peter Golda	21	"	"
Joseph Mentata	19	"	Italy
Joseph Andrazzi (cousin)	2	"	Switzerland
Joseph Marruvi	19	"	"
— Forni	16	"	"
Peter Bolla	19	"	"
Kelly Morris	18f	Housemaid	Middlesex
Rose Crass	13	Barmaid	Lambeth

1881, Lambeth

214 Westminster Bridge Road

Molro Achille	25	Refreshment Manager	Switzerland
Arnold Ferrari	16	Waiter	"
Gabuzzi Gactano	16	Barman	"
Ortali Italo	19	Barman	Italy
Ortali Gactano	16	Waiter	Italy

Living accommodation is not recorded at the Ice Wells in New Wharf Road in 1851 and 1861 but it appears in 1871.

1871, Islington

New Wharf Road Ice Wells

Julia Osbourne	30wid	Housekeeper	Lambeth
Veranzia Monighetti	31	Ice Man	Biasca, Switzerland
Giovanni Offridi	41	"	Pegheria, Italy
Desicero Guidotti	27	"	Simone, Switzerland
Faustino Guidotti	19	"	"
Joseph Ferrario	39	"	"
Alfonso Ferrario	23	"	"
Antonio Monico	28	"	"
August Lazzari	30	"	"
Louis de Giorgio	26	"	"

Appendix III: The foundation of the Unione Ticinese

(From the centennial brochure celebrating the Society's 100 years in 1974)

On the 8th of February 1874 there was constituted in London the UNIONE TICINESE – a Society for Mutual Aid – by a group of well meaning immigrants already resident and well established in the great metropolis.

The Minutes of the first Meeting read as follows: Today 8th February 1874, the founder members of the Unione Ticinese met in the Electric Hall, Denmark Street, W.C.1. Of the 101 enrolled members, 98 were present and unanimously approved the report and accounts for the last Dance and Social organised by the Committee, composed of V. Piazza, S. Bruni, F. Gallizia, D. Togni, R. Vanina, M. Pagani and G. Archioni. This Committee, as commissioned at a prior Meeting, presented the proposed rules of the Society. The rules were approved by all those present and the first Committee was elected as follows:

President: Stefano Gatti, Vice President: Mario Pagani, Secretary: Vincenzo Piazza, Treasurer: Stefano Dell'Oro, Members: Giovanni Veglio, Franco Brentini, Dazio Trongi, Roberto Vanina, Francesco Gallizia, and Giacomo Monico.

On the 12th February 1874 there took place the first meeting of the new Committee at the house of the Brentini family, 100 The Strand, and among the many decisions taken was the following: 'To deposit the Society's funds with the Institute of Credit, Birkbeck Bank, Chancery Lane, provided the bank was found to be sound; to register the Society with the London Legation; to inform the Council of State in Ticino of the formation of Unione Ticinese; to send a copy of the rules of the Society to the Swiss Consul'.

The broad aims of the Society have not changed over the years and were laid down as follows:

(a) to assist all members during illness or in grave necessity.
(b) To maintain and develop among the members the spirit and success of the Ticinese character and to strengthen the bonds of friendship and brotherhood.
(c) To promote and encourage activities of a benevolent and patriotic nature.

UNIONE TICINESE LONDRA

Founder members 8.2.1874
Gatti, Stefano – Pres.
Pagani, Mario – V. Pres.
Piazza, Vicenzo – Sec.
Dell'Oro, Stefano – Treas.
Brentini, Francesco – Comm.
Trongi, Dazio – "
Gallizia, Francesco – "
Monico, Giacomo – "
Simona, Giuseppe – "
Vanini, Rodolfo – "
Andreazzi, Domenico
Andreazzi, Giuseppe
Andreazzi, Paolo
Arcioni, Gregorio
Bernasconi, Batta
Bernasconi, Giacobbe
Berti, Agostino
Biucchi, Abramo
Brentini, Emanuele
Brentini, Francesco
Bruschi, Carlo
Bruschi, Giovanne
Bottani, Giuseppe
Bozzini, Agostino
Bozzini, Antonio
Carrocciero, Ambrogio
Chiapuzzi, Giuseppe
Cima, Giovanne
Cima, Vicenzo
Cittadini, Battista
Cizzio, Carlo
Cizzio, Giovanne
Cizzio, Massimo
Cizzio, Salvatore
Conceprio, Giacomo
Conceprio, Luigi
Cortesi, Giuseppe
D'Alesandri, Alessio
De Bolla, Battista
De Giorgi, Giacomo
De Grussa, Angelo
Depeli, Giovanne
Dirighetti, Geo. Francesco
Fasola, Cristoforo
Ferrari, Carlo
Ferrari, Celeste
Ferriroli, Paolo
Ferriroli, Pietro
Fondini, Federico
Forni, Achille
Forni, Salvatore
Gatti, Agostino
Gatti, Carlo
Gatti, Giacomo
Genoni, Carlo
Gianella, Francesco
Gianella, Vincenzo
Giuliani, Domenico
Guglielmazzi, Ferdinando
Guidotti, Desiderio
Gemini, Giacomo
Kiber, Danieli
Lompa, Mansueto
Lussi, Basilico
Marioni, Domenico
Marioni, Giovanne
Marioni, Luigi
Martinotti, Cassinare Gio.

Metalli, Antonio
Monico, Costante
Monighetti, Andrea
Monighetti, Venanzio
Milli, Giacomo
Odoni, Francesco
Pagani, Isidoro
Pagani, Luigi
Pagani, Pietro
Pagani, Tebaldo
Pelandra, Giuseppe
Protti, Stefano
Peggiori, Luigi
Peggiori, Pietro

Rigozzi, Carlo
Rodesino, Giuseppe
Rodesino, Luca
Scerri, Camillo
Scheggia, Giulio
Scossa, Luigi
Tognacca, Giacomo
Tamanti, Giacomo
Togni, Battista
Togni, Daniele
Trongi, Gio. Antonio
Veglio, Carlo
Zeglio, Carlo
Zeglio, Luigi

Joined later in 1874
Sargenti, Gioachino
Pazzi, Pietro
Gianella, Giuseppe
Simona, Pietro
Ferrari, Alfonzo
Sorgesa, Carlo
Bolla, Domenico
Bolla, Battista
Gorla, Romualdo
Branca, Achille
Taragnoli, Attilio
Job, Carlo
Sorgesa, Giuseppe

Bibliography

General

Barron, C., *Parish of St. Andrew, Holborn* 1979
Cruikshank, R. J., *Dickens and Early Victorian England*, 1949
Clunn, H. P., *The Face of London*, 1932
Dickens, C., *Oliver Twist* and *Hard Times*
Doré, G. A., *London Pilgrimage*, 1872
Fall, M. (Richard Dowling), *London Town*, 1880
Green, D. R., 'The Stability of Immigrant Communities: Little Italy in the 19th Century', unpublished thesis, 1976
Jackson, A. A., *London Termini*, 1969
Kitson Clark, G., *The Making of Victorian England*, 1965
Knight, C., *Pictorial Half Hours of London Topography*, 1851
Marin, U., *Italiani in Gran Bretagna*, 1975
Mayhew, H., *London Labour and the London Poor*, 2 vols., 1851
Schama, S., *Citizens*, 1989
Sims, G. R. ed., *Living London*, 1902
Smiles, S., *Report on the proposed extension of the railways to the West End*
Survey of London, vol. 18 *Strand, St Martin's in the Field*
Tallis, J., *Streets of London*, 1838–46, revised 1847
Tannahill, R., *Food in History*, 1988
Thomson, J. and Smith, A., *Street Life in London*, 1877
Young, G. M., *Victorian England*, 1936

The Great Exhibition

Fay, C. R., *Palace of Industry*, 1851, pub. 1951
Gibbs-Smith, C., *The Great Exhibition of 1851*, V & A, HMSO, 1981
Great Exhibition Official Descriptive Catalogue, 1851
Great Exhibition Report by Juries, 1852

The *Illustrated Cyclopedia*, 1851, has a variety of articles related to the art, design and inventions presented at the Exhibition. It includes a long article on the making of artificial flowers.

Regent's Park Canal

Through the canal 1885, British Waterways, 1977
Dickens, C., *Household Words*, August 16th 1851
Hadfield, E. C. R., *British Canals*, 1969
Saunders, A., *Regent's Park*, 1969
Spencer, H., *London's Canal*, 1976

Chocolate and ice cream

Blegny, M. de., *Le bon usage du thé, du café et du chocolat*, Lyon 1687
Bruno, F., *I cioccolatieri dall'artigianato all'industria*, Bellinzona 1946
Cox, J. S., *Ice Cream in Queen Victoria's Reign*, 1970
Dickson, P., *The Great American Ice Cream Book*, 1972
Francatelli, C., *The Modern Cook*, 1846
  The Royal English and Foreign Confectioner, 1862
Hocquart, E., *La Cuisinière Modèle*, 1860
Jarrin, G. A., *Italian Confectioner*, 1827
Jeanes, W., *Gunter's Modern Confectioner*, 1861

Lacam, P. and Charabot, A., *Le Glacier classique et artistique en France et Italie*, 1893
Masters, T., *The Ice Book*, 1844
Michael, P., *Ices and Soda Fountain Drinks*, 1923
Pomeroy, R., *The Ice Cream Connection*, 1975
Tomlinson, C., *Cyclopedia of Arts and Trades*, 1854
Williams, I. A., *The firm of Cadbury*, 1831–1931

Ice Cream Topics – a trade magazine no longer in existence – offers many short articles on the history of ice cream, particularly those by A. Pompa. Some of these must be treated with discretion, but are a fund of information from 1945 to 1974.

The March 1950 issue of *Il Gelato* – an Italian trade magazine – carried a long historical article by Professor Rossano Zeggos.

Dr Harmer's *Report on the Preparation and Sale of Food in London*, LCC 1899
'The Halfpenny Wafer', *Lloyds Log*, April 1968

Music-halls
Ewing, R., *The Nightside of London*, 1857
Hollingshead, J., *Footlights*, 1883
Howard, D., *London's Theatres and Music Halls 1850–1950*, 1970
Journal of a London Playgoer 1851–86, 1886
MacInnes, C., *Sweet Saturday Night*, 1967
Mander, J. and Mitchenson, R., *Lost Theatres of London*, 1968

Era – the theatrical weekly – is a vast source of information on shows, artistes and includes reviews. (1838-1939)

The ice industry
Alward, G. A., *The Sea Fishers of Great Britain and Ireland*, 1932
Cummings, R. O., *The American Ice Harvest 1800–1918*, 1949
Ellis, M., *Ice and Ice Houses through the Ages*, 1982
Gillett ed., *A History of Grimsby*, 1970
Goethesen, G., *Under Seil*, Grondahl 1982
Med is og plank i Nordsjofart, Grondahl 1986
Knight's Cyclopedia of the Industry of all Nations ('Ice'), 1851
Master, T., *The Ice Book*, 1844
Stevens, R. W., *The Stowage of Ships and their Cargoes*

Cold Storage – a trade magazine – has contemporary articles from 1878 to 1899 and includes
Fussell, G. E., 'Nineteenth Century Ice Importation – Notes and Queries', March 1956

Harmsworth Magazine, May 1897
'The introduction of Wenham Lake Ice', *Illustrated London News*, May 17th 1845
'London's First Ice Men', *Lloyds Log*, July 1968
Maritime Monograph No. 49, 'Ice Carrying Trade at Sea', National Maritime Museum, 1981
Sondeled Historielag Arsskrift, 'Issjau', 1981, 'Kjodvik Isforretning', 1982